Breaking Up With Jesus

Why I Left a Faith I Loved

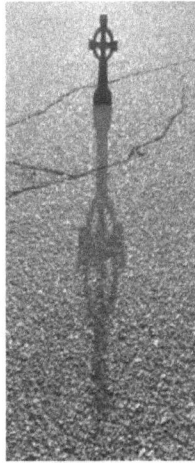

Steve Dow

Dedication

To Evan and Alec:

Never fear the truth.

Seek it with honesty.

Accept it with gratefulness.

Use it with fervor.

I love you.

**

And to my dear nephew Andrew:

You were a bridge-builder.

You are loved and missed.

Your memory is cherished.

Preface

This book was written over approximately seven years (2015-2021), with the majority of it written during limited free time, and the rest during a period of more focus amid the Covid-19 pandemic in 2020.

There are several places in the book where I reference specific moments in history, but these may not flow chronologically, as I have not necessarily written each section in its current order. Nonetheless, I have kept these references to events in the text as I feel they help anchor the book to the time written and hopefully add a more journal-like feel for the reader.

I refer in the text to differences in tone used throughout this book, but I feel it may be helpful for the reader if I say it here at the very outset as well. Parts of this book include deep analysis of religious texts and technical details of the atheist vs. theist debate. Other parts are more personal in nature — stories that help explain my thinking and my emotions as I began to recognize my atheism.

For readers who might not be interested in the technical analysis, by all means feel free to skip ahead. I suspect that different readers will have varying degrees of interest in those types of details. Either way, it was important to me that I go through that analysis in an effort to provide a comprehensive look at this important topic. I believe it may be helpful to many.

Thank you for your interest in this writing. It was one of the larger projects I have taken on, and it is one that I am happy to have finished.

Contents

Introduction

I am an atheist.

For some, those four words are enough to close this book, put it back on the shelf, and walk away.

For others, those words will fill them with sadness. Their compassionate hearts burst with love for God and it saddens them that I am somehow not experiencing it — that perhaps I am not open to it. To them, I am missing out on the best thing possible. Some of them might also fear for my eternal soul and view those words as evidence that I am leaning my eternity in the wrong direction.

For others, those words may push them even further. They may incite an anger that lies just under the surface. They are a line drawn in the sand, representing an arrogant defiance and a battle cry, a gauntlet thrown down before the feet of their God. As soldiers of God, they may sense a need to respond to this attack, this provocation, this willing slight to their King. And even if those words are not quite considered a full attack, they at least ready the army for countermeasures.

But for some, those four words are intriguing. They might be surprised at how blatantly I'm admitting this — that there are people like me who so openly question, and even reject, the predominate viewpoint. If they knew I was once a believer, their intrigue might increase. They might think, "How can he be so certain of his beliefs that he is willing to label himself a term with such baggage?"

For others, those words might seem very freeing (as they do to me). Saying that sentence might release a heavy burden they might not have even known they were carrying.

Truth be told, I now also expect that there are many people who would read those words and think, *"OK, so what? Who cares?"* I would not have expected this even a few years ago, but I have noticed a shift in beliefs about religion (especially in the United States among younger people). I believe the number of people like me is increasing — and quickly.

My experience is that most people do not fit perfectly in any given category. Any person may react in one or more of the ways listed above or may react in some other way entirely. When I decided to write this book, though, I decided that I did not want to write it for one specific group of people. I am writing it — truly — for myself, as there are many thoughts I consider important and I simply feel compelled to get them out of my head and into the public sphere. My hope is that every reader will be able to take something positive away from this effort.

I am also writing this book because although I know of many writings that make very convincing arguments for the reasonableness of an atheistic worldview, I am not aware of many books that also dive into the nuances of a person's worldview changing from religious to non-religious. Having had a religious upbringing, I understand the difficulty of letting go of what you grew up with, especially when it can provide such support at difficult times in life.

I am reminded of a famous picture of a line of penguins preparing to jump into cold water. None of them knows for sure if there is a predator waiting just below the surface. Some may prefer to simply stick their heads in the snow and wait indefinitely, but it's the first penguin who reminds the others that it can be done — that, in fact, it must be done. Their entire survival as a species depends on their collective ability to face reality and recognize the need to jump into that water to hunt. I certainly do not see myself as the first penguin by any stretch, but I am one of the penguins in line. I have recognized that I am hungry (for truth) and pretending it away doesn't do it for me anymore. Writing this book is, in some ways, my metaphorical jumping into the water, my separation from myth and superstition, and my attempt to educate others about the importance of doing the same. Ultimately, I believe our survival depends on it.

**

This is the part where I tell you that I don't really want to talk about me — yet I am writing a book about my experiences, so I guess I at least partially do. As a means of introduction, it first makes sense to discuss my background to some extent, especially as it relates to my feelings on, and ties to, a religious worldview.

I was born in 1973, my parents' fifth and last child, under circumstances that were apparently noteworthy from a medical standpoint. My brothers and sisters were all born in a hospital near our home in Tinton Falls, New Jersey, but my mother had serious medical issues when she was pregnant with me, so I was born under the watchful eye of a more specialized medical team in Philadelphia. According to my father, there were real concerns about both my mother's and my ability to survive the birth — so much so that medical staff recommended that the pregnancy be terminated (the Roe v. Wade decision had been made a few months earlier). Fortunately for me, my mother disagreed with this recommendation and decided to continue the pregnancy. I was born healthy, my mother survived, and we were both released from the hospital soon after my birth.

Once I was old enough to understand, my mother would tell me that they gave me the middle name Jude because she would frequently pray to St. Jude (the supposed brother of Jesus and the patron saint of hopeless causes) during her pregnancy. St. Jude has been special to me ever since. My wife and I gave our oldest son the middle name Jude and we still have a St. Jude statue in our house to this day.

**

Given that I am writing a book about atheism, I can understand why many religious people would think that they would not be able to relate to my life experiences. But I did not always subscribe to this worldview, and I very much believe that many would have taken me for quite a religious person for a majority of my life. That said, it may be helpful to start with a list of some "I was truly a religious person" street-cred facts. (Please forgive my list-oriented way of thinking, but I am trained as an engineer and this is often how I think.)

1. I grew up going to church every Sunday, usually at St. James Roman Catholic Church in Red Bank, New Jersey, or St. Leo's Roman Catholic Church in Lincroft.

2. I was a star student in my weekly Catholic catechism class.

3. I was thankful for the gift boxes of canned and boxed food from the local church community when our family went through hard economic times. I was too young to understand anything about economics, but I remained thankful to the church for that assistance as I grew.

4. I was a member of both a local CYO (Catholic Youth Organization) and also actively involved with my two best friends' Protestant youth group, going so far as to lip-sync "To Hell with the Devil" (a song by Christian metal band, Stryper) during a youth group talent show.

5. I went on a summer-long Protestant missionary trip with one of these best childhood friends (and about 20 others) to the jungle village of Serbananti, Indonesia, in 1990. Aside from helping to build a water distribution system, the "greater mission" of my group was to convert as many of the local people to Christianity as possible. (The predominant religions in this village were Islam and a local religion based in animalism.)

6. I wrote, "I can do all things through Christ who strengthens me. (Philippians 4:13)" in pen on my track shoes in high school.

7. I believed that there was a real chance that I might one day become a priest. For a portion of my youth, the priesthood was indeed an aspiration.

8. I was the youngest team member on a service trip during Villanova University's 1991-1992 winter break to a Catholic Mission in Wacuco, Panama (in the Darien jungle).

9. I was actively involved in Villanova's campus ministry group, often serving as a lector at mass and even as a Eucharistic minister during my sister's wedding mass.

10. Despite many opportunities (please note the sarcasm), I maintained my virginity throughout college, due in no small part to my religious beliefs about sex and my stereotypical Catholic guilt.

11. I received all of the Catholic sacraments that applied to me, up through marriage.

12. My wife and I had both of our sons baptized in the Catholic Church.

For those readers who might say that the facts above don't really mean anything — as many people give lip-service to God but don't truly "live in the Spirit" — I will tell you that I believed I felt God very strongly at several points in my life, even writing poems and songs about these feelings. My point in listing all this religious-street-cred stuff is so readers can understand that I truly was a believer (or at least I was thoroughly convinced that I was). Some people assume that once you've been *that* religious, there's no changing. I'm exhibit A that this is not true. If you are a theist reading this, I may not square with what you consider to be a typical atheist. If you knew me 20 years ago, I suspect you would have found my beliefs to be similar to your own.

**

I am already feeling different sides of my personality pull on me as I write. I've provided evidence of my early religious leanings, an approach that clearly comes from my left-brain/engineering side. But there is much more to me than this. I feel that swell, that rush, that awe of life that fills the lungs of the poets. As I've aged, I've recognized that this makes me feel simultaneously connected and separated from others — connected because I can feel that awe, that oneness with life, but separated because I don't get the sense that many people I know have these same impulses.

My mom was paralyzed when I was seven and died when I was 14. Because of this, I tended to be more ponderous than the majority of my peers growing up. I was alone with my grandmother when she nearly died not long after my mother had passed. I was a kid who thought about things deeply. I don't know that I showed it, but under the surface, I had a nagging fear of losing people I loved. I was keenly aware of my mortality in a way that it seemed my peers were not.

General life stuff and the responsibilities of being a father and husband may often suppress this side of me, as I'm frequently focused on more immediate issues. But I remain very much that same person. I truly am amazed by my life, life in general, and existence in general. One of my favorite quotations is from the researcher and poet Lewis Thomas:

> *"Statistically, the probability of any one of us being here is so small that you'd think the mere fact of existing would keep us all in a contented dazzlement of surprise."*

My head may be an engineer, but my heart is a poet and philosopher.

**

I moved to San Diego from the East Coast in 1997, and although the beauty of the area and the differences from where I grew up were numerous, it wasn't long before I began to take these differences for granted as I settled into my new West Coast life. I had the typical grinds of a day job and felt like I was floating a bit when it came to finding a greater purpose for my life.

One Saturday morning, I decided to shake things up to hopefully snap myself out of the rut I had found myself in. I got up at around 3 a.m., drove down to Torrey Pines park, and went walking throughout the park and on the beach. For anyone who has not been there, Torrey Pines is a beautiful cliff-canyon area next to a world-famous golf course and steps away from the Pacific. I found it to be a drastically different landscape than what I had been used to for most of my life. It was still dark when I started walking and I had never walked the area before.

Other than knowing I was generally walking north (with the Pacific to my left), I didn't know where the paths led — which ones doubled back, or which ones led to a dead end. As the sunlight eventually filtered in from the east, I periodically saw things that the dark would not have allowed when I started — a surfboard stored in a gap in the cliff, squirrel holes dotting the sandy ground, and even the famous Torrey pine trees themselves. It was a wonderful opportunity to clear my head and I needed it. A seal mirrored my curiosity, periodically popping her head up to look at me as she swam alongside for quite some time as I walked.

As I walked over the bumpy terrain, I occasionally came across small wooden bridges over a trench or stairs built into the hillside. As I climbed one of the larger sets of stairs, a thought hit me. Someone labored to build these stairs for others to use, to show others a way forward. To me, it represented what might be built by a life guided by truth-seeking. My path that morning was humanity's path. Those stairs were left for others to use to push forward on their own quests for self-discovery and discovery of truths. People walking these stairs would continue on to find new paths and construct their own bridges and stairs for those after them to follow. I found the thought beautiful and inspirational. I still do.

It is my hope that this book (and, to a greater extent, my life) become part of this path — perhaps a small bridge or stair — for others to follow on their own pursuit of knowledge and self-discovery. I hope that the path I create is clear and easy to follow.

**

There are four main sections to this book:

In Part 1, I dig into the meanings and connotations of some key words (most notably, "atheism") and how and why these connotations are difficult to change today.

In Part 2, I lay out what I feel need to be the general rules for the "atheism vs. theism" debate and I discuss the arguments for atheism that basically tipped the scales for me.

Part 3 aims to capture the process by which I came to accept that my beliefs had evolved from being grounded in a religious worldview to being based on a non-religious one. I specifically wanted to capture many of the fears and emotions that came with that process.

Lastly, Part 4 looks forward and lays out my vision for what a world that is not overwhelmingly impacted by religious dogma might look like. It's my attempt to flesh out John Lennon's song, "Imagine." It is my hope for the future.

Note to the Reader:

Looking back over this book before publishing it, I recognized that these four separate parts could almost be four separate books, as they've each struck me as having a significantly different tone. In general, I feel Parts 1 and 2 are more detailed and rely heavily on research to present an argument, while Parts 3 and 4 focus more on personal stories.

Some sections dive deep into details that might not be of much interest to the average reader. The detailed analysis of specific wording used in Catholic teachings seems like a good example of this. Although I found it important to go into these details, and I expect that some Catholic readers may also be interested in them, I recognize that many readers (especially those who are not Catholic) may simply want to skip — or at least gloss over — that section.

Rest assured, I understand this, and I encourage you to skip around as you see fit. I am grateful that you've selected this book, and I certainly will not presume to dictate the best way to read it.

Part 1: Misunderstanding Atheism

The Word

"And the Word became flesh and dwelt among us." (John 1:14)

I remember sitting in catechism class as a boy trying to wrap my young mind around the confounding idea that God had spoken a "word" and that this *word* was a promise of redemption to mankind — and that God's very breathing of this *word* had mysteriously materialized into human form (his son, Jesus). I didn't understand how, exactly, but I somehow intrinsically knew that this idea flowed seamlessly between metaphor and non-metaphor while simultaneously touching both. It existed in that space between hope and what is hoped for. It was, in short, a *mystery*, but it was even more than that — it was a *beautiful mystery*.

The Almighty God cared enough about us to humble himself to walk among us because he loved us. My focus was on the power inherent in the idea that the Almighty could also be all-humble, all-loving, and willing to sacrifice himself for us. I focused on the beauty of this idea. The mystery part just came with it. I accepted it, I presume, because the beauty overshadowed all else. The emotional response to such a touching concept simply overpowered my ability to understand that this simply made no sense whatsoever outside the realms of mythology or storytelling.

It's hard to think of another concept besides this "word-made-flesh" that has been so confounding, so perplexing and open to interpretation — or misunderstanding — while at the same time connoting such a strong idea to so many. There is one word, however, that does come to mind — albeit a word with a more negative connotation for most people. That word is "atheism."

Atheism: Definition and Connotations

Atheism is defined as the "lack of belief in the existence of God or gods." No more, no less. It really is that straightforward and simple. Perhaps we can call it a day and move on to Part 2?

If only it were that easy. Although a single line probably should be enough, it clearly is not. Realistically, the words "atheism" and "atheist" come with *so much* connotative baggage that it would be a disservice to the reader — neglectful, even — to pretend otherwise.

To what connotative baggage am I referring? Here are some words and phrases used to describe atheists that I have either read or have heard personally. A handful of these have been launched at me directly. According to many, atheists are: evil, arrogant, immoral, amoral, angry, ignorant, pushy, militant, anti-family-values, nihilistic, scary, foundationless, and God-haters.

I'm sure I could come up with some others if I thought more about it, but this list is enough to make my point. Atheists have quite the image problem. One might argue that a public-relations campaign is in order. In fact, such campaigns do exist. Some in the secular community even believe that the word "atheist" has become too distracting, too weighed down by centuries of negative connotations, to be useful in a practical sense. Many use other words in an attempt to shed these undesirable associations. "Skeptics," "unbelievers," "secularist," "nonbelievers," "humanists," and "freethinkers" are just some words that have been used to express this general idea.

In deciding to write this book, I wracked my brain trying to come up with a catchy substitute for "atheist" that would be palatable to all and take the world by storm. Since I come from a religious background, the phrase *"Fool me once, shame on you; fool me twice, shame on me"* came to mind. I spent a good few minutes messing around with derivatives of this phrase, ending on "folmencer" (from "fool-me-once-er"). Something tells me there's no need to call the trademark office just yet, but if you ever see a *folmencer* t-shirt, please let me know so I can get a cut of the profits. Jokes aside, it's interesting and telling that the simple idea of "not a theist" must seemingly be put through mental gymnastics just to come out in a form that is acceptable to the greater public.

I believe that many theists have become so hung up on the negative connotations of the word "atheist" that they are indeed incapable of seeing beyond them. The simple definition of the word has been conflated with something monstrous. Richard Dawkins, the Oxford scientist and renowned atheist, often repeats comedian Julia Sweeney's story of when she told her mother she had become an atheist. With a response that I could imagine from some in my own family, her mother retorted with horror, "It's one thing to not believe in God, but an *atheist*!?!?!?" For Sweeney's mother and many others, the A-word has an unmistakable bogeyman feel to it.

**

The power of words should not be understated. I am reminded of a "scare dare" when I was a child. I can't claim to remember exactly who told me this or how I learned of it, but the story went that if you ran up the basement stairs in my childhood house at the stroke of midnight while saying the three syllables of the word "Lu-ci-fer" as you stepped on each of the three middle stairs, the devil himself would come out, grab you, and take you with him back to hell.

(Presumably, this would also be the case if one ran *down* the basement stairs at midnight, but who in their right mind would ever do this while running *into* the dark abyss of our basement? That would be *pure lunacy*. I recall that this portal to hell was apparently in *our* basement, but in hindsight I suppose the devil was an equal-opportunity grabber and would allow portals into anyone's home with the prerequisite three middle basement stairs.)

I was too scared to ever try this as a child, but my imagination went wild wondering what would happen if I did. I do recall that years later, when I was in high school, I happened to be climbing the same basement stairs at 11:50 p.m. and it popped into my mind. I made a point not to say the word, but I thought it. I remember being scared that *maybe* that was sufficient — thinking the word instead of voicing it. *And what was 10 minutes anyway? Maybe it was close enough?* I recognized that it was an irrational fear, but I was nonetheless quick to shut the door behind me as I got to the top of the steps.

For some religious people, the word "atheism" falls under the same terror umbrella as "Lucifer" did for me back then. There is a hidden fear that the word is more than the word itself. It's as if the mere thought of atheism might indeed open a small gateway into hell.

Atheism's Difficult History

So when did atheism get such a bad rep? Eastern philosophies tend to have a more complicated relationship with the idea of no "prime causer," but evidence of potential anti-atheism in western culture goes back at least to the "first atheist," Diagoras of Melos, who, like Socrates, was condemned for his nonbelief. Although Socrates' atheism may be up for debate, it is clear that he was executed in 399 BC in part because of his failure to honor the Athenian gods.

But I suspect anti-atheism existed long before Diagoras of Melos. It makes sense to me that atheism started getting a bad reputation the moment any society became convinced that theism was the most logical lens through which to view existence. Ancient cultures that believed in a "prime-causer" rain god didn't want to do anything to draw that god's wrath.

It's understandable that early humans would ascribe human characteristics, such as anger and jealousy, to powers in nature that they did not understand. A flood meant that the rain god was angry. If there was a drought, it also meant the rain god was angry with, or at least inattentive to, the worshipers below. Offerings were needed to ensure that this god was not offended and that his or her ego was properly stroked.

Open declarations of doubt about such a divine entity would be understandably seen as a slight to the deity. Not only would such a declaration be viewed as wholly countercultural, it would likely be considered dangerous. Insulting the rain god could bring a flood on the whole community. For this reason, an atheist might be viewed as a direct threat to the community. One could see why refusing to believe in a powerful deity would be forbidden.

As I write this, my wife and I are preparing to take our boys to visit Mayan ruins in the Yucatan Peninsula in Mexico. In Chichen Itza, gory human murders occurred as a sacrifice to the deities. I find it interesting that we now recoil at the idea of human sacrifice to a deity, yet this same underlying impulse of ensuring that a deity isn't offended remains a big part of the negative knee-jerk reaction many believers have towards atheism. In Bill Maher's movie *Religulous*, a Christian man becomes visibly upset when Maher, simply by asking questions, apparently offends the man's god. The man would have none of it and walks away.

Political Power and Demonization of Atheists

I can understand why nonbelievers may have been shunned and feared as human societies developed. When Western culture traded in multiple gods for one, little changed.

In 313, Constantine's Edict of Milan helped curb the persecution of Christians; and in 800, Charlemagne was crowned Holy Roman Emperor by Pope Leo III. In less than 500 years, western civilization saw a drastic shift in power. In this period, Christians went from people being who could be persecuted to people with the political power to persecute.

The powerful beauty of Christianity's teachings and narratives no doubt had an enormous impact on its growth over the centuries, but we cannot underestimate the importance of Christianity joining forces with the political powers of the day to spread the religion worldwide. In 2010, more than 2 billion people considered themselves members of the Christian faith, 500 million more than

Islam, the next most popular religion. If not for the alliance between government and religion, Christianity may have stayed a local faith with a number of followers closer to Judaism (roughly 10 million in 2010), from which Christianity originated.

So now the complexities of being anti-atheist grow. Is the fear of, and vitriol against, atheists over the last millennium and a half still rooted in concerns about offending the Almighty? Or did this fear become more terrestrial in nature? Did early leaders of the church believe atheists were a threat to its political power (and the political power of those countries that had aligned themselves with the Vatican)?

The reasons for one person's fear are psychologically complex. The reasons for a group of people's fears are even more so. When you muddy the waters by mixing political motivations with religious motivations of a large group of people, you've created a situation where it may indeed be impossible to argue one specific motivation over any other. My point, however, is that for longer than a millennium, there have been many reasons for religious and religiously-tied political structures to fear atheists, and these reasons often blur into each other and overlap, indeed supporting each other.

All the above is said in acknowledgement of the reality that religious beliefs were central to the political and social structures of many pre-Christian societies. I am simply saying that the explosion of Christianity (and now Islam) throughout the world had the power to create and strengthen the negative perception of the word "atheist" that exists today.

Atheism was a clear threat to the legitimacy of the powerful Catholic Church and, by extension, to the political status quo. It makes sense that, over time, the public-relations spin doctors would demonize freethinkers at every chance. Groups such as the Freemasons, most of whom did likely believe in a creator God (just not a personal God who listens to the prayers of a Pope) were still condemned as groups that might guide people towards atheism. Many Freemasons were politically influential and driven by fact.

The ability of such people to provide evidence that the Church may be wrong was too great of a risk. Such people needed to be discredited, if not directly attacked or killed. Under these conditions, one can see how continued vilification of atheists would result in average people thinking that atheists were villains.

Facing the Abyss

Putting aside the historical record, one can understand why people may fear — even hate — atheists. Atheists (at least the ones who are not closeted) openly admit that they do not believe in God (or gods). They do not believe there is someone watching over them, looking to protect them. Although one need not believe in a god to believe in an afterlife, many atheists do not believe in an afterlife. The whole notion of living forever in paradise with a loving god (and with loved ones who've died) is basically the cornerstone of many theists' hopes.

The very existence of people who say, "Yeah, I don't believe that," makes some people who do believe uncomfortable. The atheist is not going along for the ride. She is not shaking her head in agreement. There is potential discord here, someone who is not part of the tribe. That can be disconcerting. I hope theists reading this will forgive the analogy, but if you have a group of students preparing for a test by finding the best way to cheat, and then one person in the group says, "No, I'm not going to cheat," that defiance pushes back against the peer pressure of the group. Openly admitting that you do not believe something that others may believe without question is a similar pushback.

It may force them to rethink and to really question why they believe what they do. The very thought that their protector may not be there — that life after death may not be what they hoped for (or even exist at all) — can be a terrifying thought. They had found a way around the "death problem" and this defiant refusal to go along with the groupthink can do real damage. It may lead to the exposure of significant cracks in the armor of their whole way of thinking. Death once again is staring them in the face and this time there may be no shield or mirror to deflect its gaze.

For many, facing our mortality can indeed be supremely horrifying. For this reason alone, a portion of believers may have a personal aversion to atheists. For some believers, atheists are gleefully standing there with a big needle, ready to pop their belief bubble. They are happy with what they believe, and that needle is a threat. I've heard many believers say they have no problem with atheists as long as they are not actively looking to push their atheism onto others. In other words, keep that needle far, far away.

**

After eventually realizing and accepting my atheism, I was struck by just how different my concept of the word "atheist" was compared to the negative associations. Previously, the word scared the hell out of me. I think, subconsciously, I was not allowing myself to pull that thread. For me now, though, the word means something completely different. It now connotes "courage," "individualism," "honesty," "truth-seeking," and "freedom." Whereas the "word-made-flesh" discussed in the Bible was a promise to mankind for salvation, atheism for me is the breaking of that promise. Or, more accurately, it's the recognition that there likely is no promise, no promiser, and no need for divine redemption in the first place.

Agnostic, Atheist, Anti-theist

In Part 1, my main goal is to strip the word atheism of its negative connotations and highlight its true meaning. There are other words that are often associated with atheism that I should cover as well: "agnosticism" and the newer kid on the block, "anti-theism." I've noticed that these words are often used interchangeably, but like many things in life, nuance matters. An agnostic is defined as "a person who believes that nothing is known or can be known of the existence or nature of God." An anti-theist is someone who not only doesn't believe in a God or gods but is actively *against* such a belief.

**

One important point of clarification about atheism is needed before continuing. Atheism is a lack of belief in a God or gods. It is *not* a declarative statement that there definitively is no God. One might ask, *"Well if you aren't saying that there definitely isn't a God, doesn't that mean that you're an agnostic and not an atheist because you're open to the idea?"* Well, no, not in my book — at least not practically speaking.

A man named Bobby Henderson wrote an open letter to the Kansas School Board in January 2005 that's as highly regarded by some atheists as the gospels are by some Christians. It's an absolutely brilliant piece that argues his "belief" that the Flying Spaghetti Monster (FSM) is the creative force behind intelligent design. The letter satirically lobbies for the inclusion of the FSM theory in the school curriculum alongside evolution and the biblical teaching of creation (for which many religious members in the community had lobbied).

This letter is effective for many reasons, but one thing it does well is highlight just how difficult it is to prove a negative. How can you *prove* that there is *not* a Flying Spaghetti Monster floating around in space right now? In nearly every way it seems inconceivable, absurd, and ridiculous, but how can we *know* that no such creature exists? Space, after all, is a big place. Maybe we haven't found it yet because we're not looking in the right place. In truth, we can't *disprove* FSM's existence just as we can't disprove God's existence. But we *can* absorb the evidence. We know that we've not located FSM to date and that the existence of such a creature would conflict with everything we've learned in biochemistry and physics — not to mention the culinary arts. We can let this data inform our belief system.

Am I, in the most literal sense, agnostic about the FSM? Perhaps, but I'm more accurately an "aFSMist" because I do not believe that the FSM exists. Am I, in the most literal sense, agnostic about

God or gods? Perhaps, but I'm more accurately an atheist because I don't believe that a God or gods exist.

Below is part of a written response I gave during a back-and-forth with a Christian friend about this topic in late 2016. I made minor edits to the text, but the heart of what I said remains unchanged. I'm including it as I think it sheds additional light on the points I'm trying to make:

> *Atheists — by definition — simply do not believe there is a supreme being/creator/ruler. They are not convinced that the evidence is there to support such a belief.*
>
> *Agnostics — by definition — are people that think nothing "can be known of the existence or nature of God." I see this — in a practical sense — as indistinguishable from atheism.*
>
> *In this manner, I am agnostic about lots of things — about God... but also fairies and leprechauns. They all COULD exist. Given that I cannot inspect every cave or be under every piece of rocky moss in Ireland at one single instance, for example, I can't declaratively state that there DEFINETELY are no leprechauns — and if they are magic anyway, maybe they'd just be invisible. But since I do not believe there is sufficient evidence for them, I do not believe in leprechauns.*
>
> *As Richard Dawkins has previously said, I am an atheist in the same manner I am an aleprechaunist and an afairyist. God COULD exist, but I simply do not think there is enough evidence to support such a belief. The amazing and beautiful things in life/the universe that you see as evidence supporting a God, I see simply as amazing and beautiful things.*
>
> *Last point — agnosticism also doesn't come with all of the negative-connotation baggage (which I'd argue is completely unfair) associated with atheism, so I understand why a theist would find agnosticism less offensive. It is certainly more "politically correct" to be an agnostic than an atheist in many parts of the world.*

This last point about agnosticism being more politically acceptable to religious folks is important. Many will interpret agnosticism as a *"Well, who knows? Let's call it a 50/50 chance"* belief. Religious people may tolerate this idea because it implies that the agnostic is right down the middle. If they are right in the middle, they are not perceived as really calling out religious belief as unwarranted. After all, if it's 50/50, religious belief is just as justifiable as non-religious belief.

The Greek etymology of the word "agnosticism," however, essentially translates as "not known" and "not knowing." This doesn't inherently imply a 50 percent chance of "yes" and a 50 percent chance of "no." When the chances go 49 percent for religious belief and 51 percent against religious belief, this starts to look more and more like an attack on religion and the religious defenses, in my experience, start to increase.

To further illustrate my point: If my favorite basketball team is losing 100 to 0 with less than three minutes left in the game, I do not believe that my team will win the game. Is there a chance they could win? Well, I suppose if a truly amazing set of circumstances were to unfold. Perhaps the very second the opposing team inbounds the ball, my team immediately steals it, then immediately gets fouled, stops the clock, and makes two free throws. Perhaps this exact same set of unlikely events repeats for the next 50 inbound passes. In this case, I'd be right back in the game. So you could say that although I don't believe my team will win, I can't officially rule it out. After all, *it ain't over till it's over.* But to imply that my not knowing the outcome of the game is equivalent to me thinking that my team has a 50 percent chance of winning the game is wholly inaccurate.

This is also the case in relation to God. I do not believe in God, so therefore I am an atheist. Will I admit a possibility that I could be wrong and that God may exist? Sure, so call me an agnostic if you must, but know that I consider myself agnostic only in this most technical sense. It's most certainly not a 50/50 proposition in my view. Ultimately, I see the whole framework of the agnostic vs. atheist debate largely as a word game and, thus, a distraction.

**

So now we're on to what may be the most offensive word of all in the atheistic realm: "anti-theism." Anti-theism is more than just saying you don't believe in a supreme ruler. You are saying that you are actively *against* the idea of such a being.

It's one thing not to believe in God — but to be ANTI-God? What gall! Well, obviously not everyone thinks the same thing when they hear the term "God." If God is meant as compassion or love, that is one thing. If God is meant as an all-powerful ruler (and punisher), that is quite another.

I've often heard certain religious people say things like, "Well, atheists just hate God. That's their problem." My response is always a touch of bewilderment. How can I hate something if I don't believe it exists? This is the case, as well, for anti-theists. They don't believe that God exists, but some of them might indeed loathe the idea of a divine dictator. They actively dislike the idea of skirting responsibility by putting it — in their view — on the back of a fictitious character. They find the idea of a supreme ruler to be harmful and/or morally bankrupt.

There was no more celebrated anti-theist than author Christopher Hitchens. He was unapologetically passionate in his anti-theism until his death in 2011. He cut to the core in highlighting the plan of a creator god whereby "we are created sick and then commanded to be well," a plan in which this god is then "swift to punish the original sins with which it so tenderly gifted us in the very first place." His argument for anti-theism is succinct and effective.

The Sacrament of Perpetuation

In the last chapter, we touched on some likely reasons why atheism developed such a bad reputation. Fear of the unknown (if a god was to be offended), fear of death (without a promised re-birth), and backlash from real-world power structures all likely resulted in atheism becoming something to avoid. But what about today? Some people will argue that with all the atheist scientists and the college institutions that seem to "favor" atheism, the power of those old connotations has simply been tossed out the window.

If only this were the case. There are indeed more people coming out of the atheist's closet and I do think this is having a positive impact. When folks learn that their friends and neighbors are atheists and yet don't hold animal sacrifice rituals in their basements, the fear of atheism should fade over time — for some. But many don't have atheist friends or neighbors, at least not ones who are open about it. At the very least, being an atheist is still a weird thing in many parts of the world and, for the foreseeable future, there remains a headwind to confront.

Anti-Atheism Infrastructure

In 2015, race relations in the U.S. were put in focus after several shootings of unarmed Black people by law enforcement. There were also race-driven murders, most notably the massacre of Black churchgoers in South Carolina during a prayer service. I did not have any close Black friends at the time, so I reached out to a Black acquaintance whom I saw every few years. We talked for a few hours about what was going on in the country and I put more effort than I had before in trying to imagine myself in someone else's shoes. I did not — and do not — consider myself a naïve person, but I was reminded that day of the nuanced, yet vital, difference between knowledge and understanding. Absorbing all that made my brain hurt.

I am a Caucasian man born in the United States. My family was certainly not rich growing up, but we had no reason to fear starvation and we all received a good education. Compared to the upbringing of many, mine can justifiably be considered privileged. From this perspective, I simply didn't understand what so many Black folks were concerned about. After all, there was a Black president and the Civil Rights Act had been signed decades ago. With a handful of exceptions, I rarely exposed myself to the plight of others in less-privileged positions. I certainly did not hate others, but I was preoccupied with my own world — my own perspectives. My conversation with this man made this painfully obvious.

After absorbing the fire hose of information that came with trying to see things through his eyes, I felt exhausted, but I also felt it was important to capture my thoughts. I immediately started writing and ended up posting an article a few weeks later on the topic. I tried to poetically sum up one of the biggest takeaways from this experience: "*History is not some dead thing. It is very much alive, spreading its fingers throughout today and tomorrow.*" Clearly, the history of race relations in the United States has resulted in an infrastructure that still supports certain kinds of racism today. Period. Full stop.

Historical treatment of atheists has constructed an anti-atheism infrastructure over time that we experience today. As many White people are starting to recognize that institutional racism is not just some empty politically correct phrase, it is my hope that religious people also start to become more aware that atheism is very likely not as described by their places of worship. The idea that bigoted beliefs can and do attach themselves to institutions and social systems is clear.

Components of the Anti-Atheist Infrastructure

A claim that there is a social and cultural infrastructure built up against atheism will seem obvious to some and crazy to others. Geographic location, cultural background, and educational level all likely impact whether one accepts or denies such a claim. Again, I want to point out that I am in no way trying to portray a "woe is me, poor atheist" victimhood. I am not lobbying for anyone to feel bad for atheists. I bring it up because I want people to be aware of it, not just because it exists, but because it is continually maintained and nurtured — and in ways that many people might not even be aware.

So, what are the pipelines of this anti-atheism infrastructure? What valves exist and who turns them? Where are the potholes in the road and where are roads continually paved over with a thin sealcoat without truly addressing weaknesses below the surface? Let's take a look at some of the things that support this anti-atheism infrastructure.

**

I recently watched the 2015 movie *Concussion*. Actor Will Smith portrays Dr. Bennet Omalu, the forensic pathologist who discovered CTE (chronic traumatic encephalopathy), a disease that he showed had a significant connection to head trauma (such as what occurs on a daily basis on the football field). When he made his findings public, he met expected pushback from NFL leadership. They have a vested interest in contesting any inference that the sport they sell is inherently unsafe.

In one powerful scene, Dr. Omalu sits across from his lawyer who is trying to make sure the doctor understands the power structure he is confronting. By continuing to shine a light on the connection between CTE and football, Dr. Omalu was making enemies with the NFL. As he rationally pleads his case, his lawyer's frustration builds until he finally blurts out something to the effect of, "*Jesus, Ben, they OWN a whole day of the week!*" (a reference to the millions of football fans who essentially put the majority of their day on hold so they can go through their Sunday, or Monday night, football-watching rituals). Some take it even further and delve into "fantasy football," focusing on the stats of individual players across every team to monitor the points they have achieved that day. For many, football is indeed an all-consuming sport.

Given the enormous popularity of American football, it has been inferred at times that it is gradually replacing "church" as *the* Sunday event in some parts of the United States. Even with clear evidence that actual church attendance in the U.S. is declining, I find such a "church (mosque/temple) replacement" claim to be absurd.

A 2015 Pew Research Center study found that in 2014, half of American adults attended religious services at least monthly. With more than 240 million adults in the U.S., that equates to approximately 120 million people. That is more than the estimated 111 million people who watched the 2017 Super Bowl. Keep in mind, though, that the Super Bowl is viewed worldwide while Pew's church attendance estimate is only for the United States. When you understand that the U.S. represents only around 4 percent of the world's population, and you research religious service attendance worldwide, you can see that it's unlikely religion will disappear anytime soon.

With at least a Super Bowl's worth of people attending religious services each month in the U.S., the opportunities for churches to perpetuate stereotypes about non-religious people remain plenty. Millions of Americans come together weekly to listen to a worldview espoused by preachers, rabbis, or imams that is often quite unkind to those who think differently.

Supporting Soil

Religion's hold on a whole day of the week is indeed a key component of the anti-atheist infrastructure. The demonization of atheism in many a sermon often comes hand-in-hand with it. The religious documents and dogma themselves — often preached to a captive audience — can act as the soil supporting much of this anti-atheism.

There are many examples of religious texts that are used to perpetuate the distancing from — if not outright vilification of — nonbelievers. The examples below are by no means an exhaustive list, but let's take a look. After each verse, I have included a quick note capturing my gut-level response. I was going to call these "inferred takeaways," but in several cases, there's not much left to infer. Some of the verses are quite direct.

This section focuses on Abrahamic religions. Regarding these religious texts, please recall that:

- The Old Testament applies to Judaism and Christianity (and Islam, in some cases).

- The New Testament applies to Christianity (and Islam, in some cases).

- The Quran (Koran) applies to Islam.

Old Testament

Numbers 14:11: "And the LORD said to Moses, 'How long will this people despise me? And how long will they not believe in me, in spite of all the signs that I have done among them?'"

Aside from painting nonbelievers as cruel and foolish, this verse is logically circular and misleading. How can one despise an entity that she doesn't believe exists? An atheist (or anti-theist) might despise the *idea* of God, but despising a fictional character has never been a problem before. Are theists to be vilified for hating Darth Vader?

**

Deuteronomy 13: 6-11: "If your very own brother, or your son or daughter, or the wife you love, or your closest friend secretly entices you, saying, 'Let us go and worship other gods' (gods that neither you nor your ancestors have known, gods of the peoples around you, whether near or far, from one end of the land to the other), do not yield to them or listen to them. Show them no pity. Do not spare them or shield them. You must certainly put them to death. Your hand must be the first in putting them to death, and then the hands of all the people. Stone them to death, because they tried to turn you away from the Lord your God, who brought you out of Egypt, out of the land of slavery. Then all Israel will hear and be afraid, and no one among you will do such an evil thing again."

The call to murder here is disturbing. On a technical level, this text doesn't apply to atheism, as it refers to the worship of "other gods." Many theists, however, believe atheists do worship other gods — the "god" of science or the "god" of logic. I find arguments that atheism is somehow its own religion to be extremely weak; I'll address this later in the book.

**

Psalm 14:1: "The fool says in his heart, 'There is no God.' They are corrupt, they do abominable deeds, there is none who does good."

Psalm 53:1: "The fool says in his heart, 'There is no God.' They are corrupt, doing abominable iniquity; there is none who does good.

These lines, repeated within pages of each other, are a reminder of the Bible's evolution as a single document. If the Bible is truly to have been divinely inspired, God may need to take some basic editing classes. (Note to the reader: If you find any typos in this book, understand that I claim neither infallibility nor omniscience.)

New Testament

Matthew 5:8: "Blessed are the pure in heart, for they shall see God."

If you have not seen God — and especially if you do not believe in God — it's probably because you are *not* pure in heart.

**

Matthew 12:39: "But he answered them, 'An evil and adulterous generation seeks for a sign, but no sign will be given to it except the sign of the prophet Jonah.'"

Anyone who is skeptical of God's existence and asks for evidence is evil and adulterous. Either that or these people will be swallowed whole by a whale. (For those who don't know the Bible story, the prophet Jonah was temporarily swallowed by a "great fish.")

**

John 3:18: "Whoever believes in him (Jesus) is not condemned, but whoever does not believe is condemned already, because he has not believed in the name of the only Son of God...."

Those who don't believe are "condemned already" and likely to be a lost cause. In other words, don't waste too much time with them.

**

2 Corinthians 6:14-18: "Do not be unequally yoked with unbelievers. For what partnership has righteousness with lawlessness? Or what fellowship has light with darkness? What accord has Christ with Belial? Or what portion does a believer share with an unbeliever?... Therefore go out from their midst, and be separate from them, says the Lord, and touch no unclean thing; then I will welcome you, and I will be a father to you, and you shall be sons and daughters to me, says the Lord Almighty."

Nonbelievers are not on equal footing with believers. They will only hold believers back and it is therefore necessary to separate from them.

I remember this text being drilled into my brain when I was on a Protestant missionary trip in Indonesia as a teenager, and I also remember it from readings from mass during my Catholic upbringing. It is by no means obscure scripture among Christians. I see it as particularly dangerous because it urges Christians to reject other points of view.

**

Ephesians 4:18-19: "They are darkened in their understanding, alienated from the life of God because of the ignorance that is in them, due to their hardness of heart. They have become callous and have given themselves up to sensuality, greedy to practice every kind of impurity."

Atheists are ignorant, greedy, impure, and they have hard hearts.

**

Colossians 2:8: "See to it that no one takes you captive by philosophy and empty deceit, according to human tradition, according to the elemental spirits of the world, and not according to Christ."

Philosophy is "the study of the fundamental nature of knowledge, reality, and existence." While researching for this book, I came across several internet resources designed to assist Christians in their discussions with atheists. This Bible quote was deemed particularly helpful to an evangelistically minded audience. I can't help but interpret this as, "Hey, if they start coming at you with heavy philosophical stuff and you don't know how to respond, just throw this quote out there."

**

2 Thessalonians 2:9-12: "The coming of the lawless one is by the activity of Satan with all power and false signs and wonders, and with all wicked deception for those who are perishing, because they refused to love the truth and so be saved. Therefore God sends them a strong delusion, so that they may believe what is false, in order that all may be condemned who did not believe the truth but had pleasure in unrighteousness."

God in his infinite kindness has purposely deceived some people so they would specifically not believe in him, thereby ensuring that they will be condemned and perish. I repeat: God *purposefully deceived* some people specifically so they would not believe in God, *thereby ensuring that they will be condemned and perish.* This is both terrible and remarkable. I'd argue that a god who purposefully deceives people into believing things that will get them punished (for all eternity, no less) would be a god unworthy of worship.

**

Titus 1:15: "To the pure, all things are pure, but to the defiled and unbelieving, nothing is pure; but both their minds and their consciences are defiled."

Nonbelievers are not pure, and they are defiled.

**

James 5:19-20: "My brothers, if anyone among you wanders from the truth and someone brings him back, let him know that whoever brings back a sinner from his wandering will save his soul from death and will cover a multitude of sins."

Although much softer in tone compared to many other verses, this does still infer that if you are not in line with the Bible's "truth," you are a condemned sinner.

I specifically included this verse to point out that not *all* biblical quotations about nonbelievers are distancing and harsh. This one suggests Christians feel concern for nonbelievers. This verse, in many ways, is a fair juxtaposition with 2 Corinthians 6 regarding being unequally yoked with nonbelievers. Although it is kinder than many of these other verses, it still perpetuates negative connotations about atheists (as distracted and wandering away from the truth).

I'd argue that the very fact that it is softer and kinder is a bit of a double-edged sword. It provides a safe path for Christians who are not eager to see atheists burned at the stake, while still keeping negative connotations of atheists intact.

**

2 Peter 2:21-22: "For it would have been better for them never to have known the way of righteousness than after knowing it to turn back from the holy commandment delivered to them. What the true proverb says has happened to them: 'The dog returns to its own vomit, and the sow, after washing herself, returns to wallow in the mire.'"

This passage refers to followers of Jesus who turn away from him and his teachings. These people are like mindless animals who cannot understand a good thing. Though this passage doesn't specifically mention atheists, it is quite clear that nonbelievers are the dog and sow of the proverb.

**

1 John 4:8: "Anyone who does not love does not know God, because God is love."

If you do not "know God," you likely do not know love. "God is love," after all, so if you do not know one, how could you know the other?

I find this text to be particularly loaded; I'll discuss it in more detail later.

**

1 John 4:2-5: "By this you know the Spirit of God: every spirit that confesses that Jesus Christ has come in the flesh is from God, and every spirit that does not confess Jesus is not from God. This is the spirit of the antichrist, which you heard was coming and now is in the world already... They are from the world; therefore they speak from the world, and the world listens to them...."

It is noteworthy to see the "of this world" vs. "not of this world" dichotomy here. If someone does not agree with Christian beliefs, she is deemed "of this world." This is not a compliment. That person is mired in the non-transcendental. She is a drone in this world only. She is a species of animal that is not capable of understanding the majesty of an invisible friend that demands worship. This is clearly condescending, yet in the mind of many a believer, such condescension apparently seems justifiable.

**

Revelation 21:8: "But as for the cowardly, the faithless, the detestable, as for murderers, the sexually immoral, sorcerers, idolaters, and all liars, their portion will be in the lake that burns with fire and sulfur, which is the second death."

If you honestly don't believe (i.e., you don't have faith in God), you deserve a punishment similar to that of a murderer.

Quran (Koran)

2:6-7: "As for those who disbelieve, it makes no difference whether you warn them or not: they will not believe. God has sealed their hearts and their ears, and their eyes are covered. They will have great torment."

Don't waste your time on nonbelievers. God has made them that way, and he will torture them because of it.

Recognize the similarities between this verse and 2 Thessalonians 2:9-12? I find it astonishing that some people seem to find it acceptable for God to purposefully create people who cannot believe in him, only to then torture them for eternity because of their divinely provided disbelief. How is this not the very definition of sadism? Yet, we are continually reminded by some of how merciful God is. This makes no sense to me.

**

2:171: "Calling to disbelievers is like a herdsman calling to things that hear nothing but a shout and a cry: they are deaf, dumb, and blind, and they understand nothing."

Nonbelievers are too stupid to believe, so don't waste your time with them.

**

2:217: "...And whoever of you reverts from his religion [to disbelief] and dies while he is a disbeliever — for those, their deeds have become worthless in this world and the Hereafter, and those are the companions of the Fire, they will abide therein eternally."

Familiar theme: to the fire forever with the nonbelievers.

**

3:85: "And whoever desires other than Islam as religion — never will it be accepted from him, and he, in the Hereafter, will be among the losers."

Anyone who does not believe the tenets of Islam is a loser.

It is 2017 as I write this, the first year of Donald Trump's presidency, so I wanted to throw this one in here. Trump absolutely relishes every possible opportunity to refer to people he does not like as "losers." If only he had known that his own vernacular shares similarities with this Koranic text, perhaps he would have been softer in his push for a ban on people coming from predominately Muslim countries.

**

8:55-56: "The worst creatures in the sight of God are those who reject Him and will not believe; who, whenever you [Prophet] make a treaty with them, break it, for they have no fear of God."

Not much left for interpretation on this one. God has contempt for those who do not believe in him. Have no qualms about breaking your word with anyone who does not believe as you do. Atheists are not "worth" your word in the first place.

**

29:49: "But no, [this Qur'an] is a revelation that is clear to the hearts of those endowed with knowledge. No one refuses to acknowledge Our revelations but the evildoers."

If the "revelations" of the Koran are not clear to you, you are stupid and an evildoer.

45:7-8: "Woe to every lying sinful person who hears God's revelations being recited to him, yet persists in his arrogance as if he had never heard them — [Prophet] bring him news of a painful torment!"

Nonbelievers are arrogant and will be tortured because of it.

47:12: "God will admit those who believe and do good deeds to Gardens graced with flowing streams; the disbelievers may take their fill of pleasure in this world, and eat as cattle do, but the Fire will be their home."

Nonbelievers are akin to mindless beasts and they will go to the fire.

98:6: "Indeed, they who disbelieved among the People of the Scripture and the polytheists will be in the fire of Hell, abiding eternally therein. Those are the worst of creatures."

Nonbelievers are the worst creatures who will — once again — go to the fire forever.

Catholic Soil

But are Catholics Different?

Having considered myself part of the Catholic "family" for much of my life, I have a personal interest in a deeper dive into this specific class of soil. Roman Catholicism is a subset of Christianity, so the Bible verses that would apply as "Christian soil" would also apply to the Catholic subset. As a boy, I recall some of these verses being used as a basis for teaching in mass, in my Sunday catechism class afterward, or in my Catholic high school. The Catholic claim, however, goes beyond the generic Christian claims.

Catholicism's authority claim is unique in that its interpretation of scripture (most notably, Matthew 16:19) not only opens the door to assert "official" authority for the "correct interpretation" of all scripture, but to also create offshoot teachings that it can claim to be divinely sanctioned. The Bible is still important, but the final say on Jesus' teachings ultimately rests with the Pope and the political hierarchy within the Vatican.

Because the Catholic Church is a political entity, it's not surprising that it's adapted with the times, though a segment of Catholics (typically more conservative ones) will vehemently argue that the teachings of the Church are "capital T, True" and therefore unwavering. But the very fact that there have been Vatican Councils addressing Catholic teaching is evidence of a perceived need for adaptation. (These conservative Catholics will argue "clarification" over "adaptation," but these are nuances I have little interest in arguing here.)

There is another branch of the Catholic tree, however, that applauds the reforms and adaptions made via the Second Vatican Council (1962-1965), also known as Vatican II. These Catholics tend to see the Church as reasonable and open to change. In my experience, there is no shortage of Catholics who consider Catholicism to be the most reasonable and, by extension, the most educated group on the Christian tree. They will highlight scientific discoveries made by priests such as Gregor Mendel, as if this somehow gives credibility to all other claims upon the nature of reality made by the Church. It's not difficult to argue that logical fallacies abound in such thinking.

That said, Catholics' claim of being the most reasonable Christians might hold water in some regard (turning a blind eye momentarily to beliefs related to bread-to-body, wine-to-blood rituals). Catholics tend to generally accept evolution, after all, and Pope Francis' push for the acceptance of global warming as a reality is admirable and probably helpful. Compared to certain fundamentalist groups that spend their time building "replicas" of Noah's Ark next to a museum that houses an exhibit featuring a dinosaur wearing a saddle (i.e., the Creation Museum in

Petersburg, Kentucky), it's understandable that some Catholics believe they're the more rational Christians.

So if Catholics tend to at least partially accept science and are also open to adapting some of their teachings to the modern world, does it make sense to think that perhaps they have a more reasonable view of atheists? Are there softer, more liberal readings of Catholic teaching that avoid demonizing those who don't share their beliefs?

Old Catholicism and Atheism

The Church's ties to the violent killings of non-Catholics over the centuries is a huge and inescapable part of its history. From the Crusades to the colonization of the Americas, there are numerous examples of a propensity towards violence and murder. The Spanish Inquisition (1478-1834) is a well-documented example of this violence. Several years ago, I visited a traveling Spanish Inquisition exhibit and the horrific and diabolical nature of the torture devices cannot be understated. Although the Spanish Inquisition focused in large part on Jews, Muslims, and even Protestants, atheists were also targets for torture and murder. Freemasons, many of whom may not even have been atheists, were considered people who might *lead* someone to atheism. That alone could do them in.

In researching for this book, I remembered my Catholic upbringing and recalled the use of the Baltimore Catechism in my Confraternity of Christian Doctrine (CCD) classes in preparation for the sacraments of First Communion, Reconciliation, and Confirmation. I learned that this version of Catholic catechism was intended for American Catholics. One might understandably think that, after being properly translated into the target language, the teachings of God need not be refined any further before crossing national borders, but apparently the American bishops thought differently.

It turns out that my memory was not fully accurate. I did not learn from the Baltimore Catechism. I learned from the *New St. Joseph Baltimore Catechism,* a document that resulted from post-Vatican II thinking that many old-school, conservative Catholics see as a huge mistake. No doubt, some of them would argue that the organizer of Vatican II (Pope John XXIII) was not a real Pope, but perhaps an "anti-Pope." The term "anti-Pope" may seem comical to anyone who's not heard this language before, but this is indeed a term that some people take very seriously. There are some who consider the current Pope Francis to be an "anti-Pope." Perhaps unsurprisingly, there seems to be a correlation, in my experience, between Catholics who are politically right-leaning and Catholics who question whether or not a more progressive Pope (such as Francis) is legitimate.

The friction between pre- and post-Vatican II Catholics can get heated. Like any large group of people who subscribe to certain beliefs, there are Catholics who push the edges of these beliefs on all sides — and some who even bend them. My focus for this section, however, remains: *What is the official Catholic teaching about atheism?*

For those who still focus on the older Baltimore Catechism, I have highlighted some key portions of Section 169 below regarding sins against the "Mystical Body of Christ" (aka, the Catholic Church).

> *"The Catholic Church is called the Mystical Body of Christ because its members are united by supernatural bonds with one another and with Christ, their Head....*
>
> *...In order that a person be a member of the Mystical Body in the full sense, it is necessary that he be baptized, that he profess the Catholic faith, and that he neither separate himself from the Mystical Body nor be excluded by lawful authority. 'And if he refuses to hear them, appeal to the Church, but if he refuses to hear even the Church, let him be to thee as the heathen and the publican. (Matthew 18:17).'*

...A baptized person separates himself from full incorporation in the Mystical Body by open and deliberate heresy, apostasy or schism....

...by heresy when he openly rejects or doubts some doctrine proposed by the Catholic Church as a truth of divine-Catholic faith, though still professing himself a Christian....

...by apostasy when he openly rejects the entire Christian faith....

...by schism when he openly refuses obedience to the lawful authorities of the Church, particularly to the Pope."

The key takeaway here is that if you're not feeling the "supernatural bonds" of the Catholic Church, you are to be treated as a heathen (or a "publican," aka, tax-collector, which may have had even worse connotations than heathen in Matthew's day).

You are a heretic if you *openly express* doubt about "some doctrine proposed by the Catholic Church." Doubt itself may be considered permissible — just don't talk about it. As I'll discuss later, some religions' acceptance of doubt is intricate and nuanced, providing doubting followers who have fallen from the Church's window with a small ledge to cling to so they're still connected with the Church in some way.

So, the passages above are based on the older version of Catholic catechism. What about today? I went to the Vatican's website for the up-to-date Catholic take on things. Although Pope Francis truly does seem to be pushing a softer approach toward nonbelievers (focusing on good deeds that all of us can do in the world), the Catholic documents themselves (even beyond biblical text) still provide a clear path for separation from and distrust of nonbelievers.

Current Catholicism and Atheism

When my wife and I were preparing to have our first child baptized a few months after his birth, we attended a pre-baptismal class required by our local church. As some parents in the class did not attend church regularly and were likely there only to meet the requirement, there were several conversations that stemmed from questions like, "So what does the Catholic Church officially believe about x, y, or z?" I particularly remember purgatory being discussed.

Purgatory, for those who don't know, is the waiting room at heaven's gate. You were good enough to avoid hell, but not quite good enough for immediate entry through the pearly gates. It is an area of final "purification." Church history is ripe with priests selling "indulgences" to the faithful, essentially providing a spiritual guarantee that their dead loved ones would be released from their purification cell (for the fee, of course). That fee would bump them to the front of the line, offering a fast pass into heaven. Among other promises made, fighters for the Church in the Crusades also came with a similar "get out of jail" card for dead loved ones — not to mention a guaranteed heavenly reward for a martyr's death.

Wanting my child to be baptized at that time, I didn't push back too hard about the many things I was doubting, but I did engage in the purgatory discussion. I was immediately assuaged by the Catholic "cool" couple leading the course that, no, *of course the Church does not believe in purgatory anymore*. That was a bygone era; purgatory was *so* pre-Vatican II.

Well, it turns out that this is not the case. In his November 30, 2007, encyclical, "Spe Salvi (Saved in Hope)," Pope Benedict did some word- gymnastics around the topic of purgatory, but he essentially supported the idea that prayers can help purify those in the waiting room. *"No one sins alone. No one is saved alone.... In the interconnectedness of Being, my gratitude to the other — my prayer for him — can play a small part in his purification.... It is never too late to touch the heart of another, nor is it ever in vain....*" Purgatory is the place for this "purification."

There are various diverging points in response to the "Spe Salvi" encyclical, but despite what spin may be happening to make the Church appear more reasonable and attractive to followers and non-followers alike, the actual teachings do not always support the spin. And despite the perceived openness, strict catechism is indeed taught and reinforced in many churches worldwide. Purgatory is just one example.

Even with the progressive Pope Francis now using conciliatory language regarding nonbelievers, teachings from the catechism on the Church's website (at the time of this writing in 2017) clearly suggest that Catholics should be wary of nonbelievers. Let's follow the logic below, which comes directly from current Catholic teaching about atheism.

Atheism is a Sin

First, Catholicism says atheism is a sin. I expect that there are some Catholics who might say this is not the case, but it is bluntly stated on the vatican.va website.

> "*Since it rejects or denies the existence of God, atheism is a sin against the first commandment.*" (Part 3, Sect 2, Chap 1, Art 1: 2140)

Other relevant teachings go into more detail.

> "*St. Paul shows that 'ignorance of God' is the principle and explanation of all moral deviations. Our duty toward God is to believe in him and to bear witness to him.*'" (Part 3, Sect 2, Chap 1, Art 1: 2087)

> "*...There are various ways of sinning against faith: Voluntary doubt about the faith disregards or refuses to hold as true what God has revealed and the Church proposes for belief. Involuntary doubt refers to hesitation*

in believing, difficulty in overcoming objections connected with the faith, or also anxiety aroused by its obscurity. If deliberately cultivated doubt can lead to spiritual blindness." (Part 3, Sect 2, Chap 1, Art 1: 2088)

I've highlighted some of the lines that I feel reflect the key takeaways from this section of the catechism. The inferences clearly are that atheists are ignorant and prone to deviation from good morals. Also notice that *"voluntary doubt about the faith"* is a sin against the faith. I must say here that someone needs to clearly explain for me the difference between "voluntary" and "involuntary" doubt. Doubt is either something you have or don't have. I assume that "voluntary doubt" means doubt to which you actually pay attention, while "involuntary doubt" is that stubborn doubt that somehow lingers after years and years of active attempts to repress it (perhaps via alcohol or some other coping mechanism).

It almost seems as if "involuntary doubt" is used as a stand-in for "denial," without the Church having to actually say that word. No need to give the flock any ideas. No need to highlight that denial is even an option.

Atheism is a Mortal Sin

Second, Catholicism says atheism is a mortal sin. Aside from "ignorance of God" being the "explanation of all moral deviations," there is more within current Catholic catechism that further clarifies the Church's position. (I am aware some readers may see my interchange of the terms "atheism" and "ignorance of God" as conflating two separate things, notably atheism with agnosticism. As I've already noted, however, I view such an argument as an unnecessary exercise in semantics.)

Growing up Catholic, I became well-versed in the difference between "mortal sin" and "venial sin." Venial sins were things like telling a white lie to your sister or eating your brother's cookie when he wasn't looking. These sins might land you in a time-out in purgatory. Mortal sins, on the other hand, were those really serious sins, like rape, murder — or masturbation. These types of sins could get you kicked directly to hell.

(I suspect a few eyebrows were raised after reading that masturbation is considered a mortal sin. To these raised eyebrows, I offer the following evidence:

> *"For a sin to be mortal, three conditions must together be met: 'Mortal sin is sin whose object is grave matter and which is also committed with full knowledge and deliberate consent." (Part 3, Sect 1, Chap 1, Art 8: 1857)*

Regarding masturbation being *grave*, Part 3, Sect 2, Chap 2, Art 6: 2396 of the catechism explicitly lists it as such. Regarding masturbation requiring *full knowledge*, I've never heard of someone accidentally masturbating. Regarding masturbation requiring *deliberate consent*, it involves consent, by definition. In most cases, I'd argue an *eager consent* may better describe it.)

There is enough in a reasoned reading of the catechism to conclude that atheism is indeed considered a mortal sin. Disbelief in God is certainly a grave matter. Acknowledging this disbelief shows knowledge. Accepting this disbelief shows consent.

> *"To choose deliberately — that is, both knowing it and willing it — something gravely contrary to the divine law and to the ultimate end of man is to commit a mortal sin. This destroys in us the charity without which eternal beatitude is impossible. Unrepented, it brings eternal death." (Part 3, Sect 1, Chap 1, Art 8: 1874)*

Catholic teaching even invokes the loving, self-sacrificing, and compassionate Jesus of the New Testament to further condemn nonbelievers:

> *"Jesus often speaks of 'Gehenna' of 'the unquenchable fire' reserved for those who to the end of their lives refuse to believe and be converted, where both soul and body can be lost. Jesus solemnly proclaims that he 'will send his angels, and they will gather ... all evil doers, and throw*

them into the furnace of fire,' and that he will pronounce the condemnation: 'Depart from me, you cursed, into the eternal fire!'" (Part 1, Sect 2, Chap 3, Art 12: 1034)

The Perceived Arrogance of Atheists

Third, former Catholics who have become atheists have committed especially grievous sins (see: heresy, apostacy, and schism), but the implications that atheists who were never members of a church can also be blamed for their atheism is clear as well. If you are a Catholic reading a book called *Breaking Up With Jesus*, an educated guess might be that you lean towards the progressive side of Catholicism. If that's the case, you might be aware of the various church documents stemming from Vatican II that use a softer tone towards those who have "not yet arrived at an explicit knowledge of God," but even those documents perpetuate inferences that I see as unfair (and largely inaccurate) about atheism.

The November 21, 1964, Vatican document "Lumen Gentium" includes the following:

> *"Those also can attain to salvation who through no fault of their own do not know the Gospel of Christ or His Church, yet sincerely seek God and moved by grace strive by their deeds to do His will as it is known to them through the dictates of conscience. Nor does Divine Providence deny the helps necessary for salvation to those who, without blame on their part, have not yet arrived at an explicit knowledge of God and with His grace strive to live a good life. Whatever good or truth is found amongst them is looked upon by the Church as a preparation for the Gospel. She knows that it is given by Him who enlightens all men so that they may finally have life"* (emphasis added).

So, there is hope for atheists after all. All that is needed is for them to *seek God with sincerity*. I will assume that you recognize the obvious problem with this thinking. Atheists, by definition, do not believe in God, so why would they seek an entity that they do not believe exists? Presumably, then, within a single paragraph, hope for salvation is back off the table.

Furthermore, if a person hasn't yet received the required "explicit knowledge of God" before their death, it is implied that they must have some "blame on their part" that prevented them from becoming a believer. After all, surely God would provide everyone with an opportunity to be properly "prepared" for the Gospel, so the blame *must* fall at their feet, not God's. Otherwise, that wouldn't be fair. An all-just God by definition has to be fair.

I want to dig deeper here. For many believers, it's inconceivable that some folks would not seek God. These people see it as obvious, fully logical, and even self-evident that God must exist. So not actively seeking God must reflect some error or fault on the part of the nonbeliever. The go-to default to explain this, of course, is that atheists must therefore be arrogant — the same sin that caused Lucifer/Satan's fall from grace.

The following is also from "Lumen Gentium":

> *"But often men, deceived by the Evil One, <u>have become</u> <u>vain</u> in their reasonings and have exchanged the truth of God for a lie, serving the creature rather than the Creator"* (emphasis added).

So even in some of the most progressive writings concerning nonbelievers, we are again back to the familiar starting point — *atheists are arrogant.* The perpetuation is perpetuated.

I will frequently bend over backwards in order to give someone the benefit of the doubt, often seeking to play devil's advocate against my own arguments in order to test the strength of my beliefs. I will attempt to do this now.

Perhaps what is meant by this is that a "good" atheist can still be saved even if she dies before being "properly prepared" for the Gospel because she will still have a chance for refinement — for purification — after death.

Here comes purgatory once again to save the day. In other words, if a person admits that she does not share the conviction that God exists (not to mention that Jesus is God), she has likely been duped by "the evil one" into losing her humility before God — hence, the reference to vanity.

After all, if she doesn't think God created her, is she not taking credit for her own creation? The answer is clearly no, but as I have come across this line of reasoning several times before, I will continue.

Hence, look at that vanity! She is placing humanity, she is placing herself, in God's seat. Where is the humility?

But for faithful Catholics who fear for the soul of a recently departed atheist friend, rest assured that there is still that chance for salvation. Perhaps St. Peter (aka, "Heaven's Bouncer") can still be convinced by your prayers. While your atheist friend is at the gate, Peter might hear your voice: *"Don't worry Peter, she's a good soul — perhaps a bit arrogant, but good overall. I can vouch for her."*

My college friends telling the bouncer at a club in Los Angeles that one of us was the nephew of the owner comes to mind. You've got to pull on the connections you have, right?

From a marketing perspective, purgatory truly is the gift that keeps on giving. If a dead atheist was generally a good and loving person, purgatory allows a Catholic a means to keep the faith without having to throw away their love of that person. It is the perfect negotiation — your faith need not be challenged by the thought that God has condemned your loved one to eternal torture — and that person *still* has a chance to enter heaven if only you pray just a little bit harder.

Sticking with the "atheists are arrogant" theme, also consider the Church's *Pastoral Constitution on the Church in the Modern World/Gaudium et Spes/Promulgated by his Holiness, Pope Paul VI on December 7, 1965,* a true gem that includes the following:

"...Thus atheism must be accounted among the most serious problems of this age... Undeniably, those who willfully shut out God from their hearts and try to dodge religious questions <u>are not following the dictates of their consciences, and hence are not free of blame</u>" (emphasis added).

For an institution that teaches about the arrogance of atheists, it apparently sees no arrogance whatsoever in claiming to *undeniably* understand the very personal *dictates of conscience* for billions of nonbelievers. It makes these claims having already presupposed a God, but I nonetheless find the hypocrisy here to be thick.

**

I've dug deeper into the Catholic soil primarily because that is the soil with which I am most familiar, but this isn't the only reason. As I mentioned, I believe Catholicism in general can be rather good at convincing people that it bridges the gap between a reasoned worldview and a worldview based on beliefs in the supernatural and magic. Some more progressive Catholics could argue that in listing the many harsh Bible verses that I have (such as Deuteronomy 13: 6-11, which demands that a man must immediately kill his brother if the brother asks him to reconsider his belief in the God of Abraham), I am providing only a snippet of their very deep and nuanced beliefs. Arguing that the verses have merit, they would say, would be arguing a position that is not their own. To avoid allegations that I'm making a strawman argument, I've researched the current interpretations and the current teachings of the Church via source documents.

Is the Catholic Church's teaching about atheism softer in post-Vatican II documents than in Deuteronomy? Of course, but I don't see that as anything to be proud of. Would you reward your son if he was caught bullying another child? I certainly hope not. What if his response was, "Well, come on dad, isn't it great that I didn't mutilate, rape, and murder him?" I don't doubt that you'd be horrified by such a response.

In summary, Catholicism may or may not be eager to throw nonbelievers into the everlasting fire (depending on which parts of which documents you focus on), but it clearly is wary of atheists and sees people thinking, and *especially speaking*, for themselves outside the guidelines of Catholic teaching as dangerous. The following section of Church canon law is current and included on the Vatican's website:

> *A person who in a public show or speech, in published writing, or in other uses of the instruments of social communication utters blasphemy, gravely injures good morals, expresses insults, or excites hatred or contempt against religion or the Church is to be punished with a just penalty. (Code of Canon Law, Book IV, Part III, Title I: 1369)*

Although "just penalty" is not clearly defined, I gather it isn't a mint chocolate chip cone at the corner ice cream shop. While I'm not aware of a current Catholic equivalent of the terrorist group ISIS, I can easily imagine how such a teaching could be interpreted by an unstable Catholic with a propensity for violence in defense of the faith.

Soil Summary

To recap, current documents and teachings of the Abrahamic religions act as fertile soil for the perpetuation of many of the negative connotations associated with people who simply do not believe in God. These documents, which are still used as a basis for teaching in churches, mosques, and temples, perpetuate the idea that atheists are foolish, corrupt, impure, arrogant, and/or greedy losers.

Allegations of foolishness strike me as insecure and a way to dismiss those who think differently. Although demeaning (and often purposefully so), these allegations are different than some of the harsher ones that imply atheists are evil. If someone truly believes that religious teachings are obvious or logical, it is understandable that he sees those who do not believe such obvious and logical things as foolish.

I can work with this "foolishness" allegation because it at least implies there is a level playing field on which to respond — the playing field of reason. In theory, at least, someone should be able to dismiss allegations of foolishness by making a reasoned argument explaining how and why she thinks as she does. I aim to do this later in the book.

It seems to be a different thing altogether to dismiss allegations that you are evil, but I am hopeful that the same hammer that destroys allegations of foolishness can at least dent allegations of evil. After all, if one is shown to be following a reasonable way of thinking, this means that others can understand that reasoning. It would follow that we are less inclined to describe someone's way of thinking as evil if we indeed can follow every step of their logic; otherwise, we run the risk of naming ourselves evil as well.

This Way to Avoid Hell

Now that we've discussed the road that leads to an anti-atheistic worldview and the soil that supports that road, let's talk about what one might see while peering out of the window while on the road.

One summer in the mid-1980s, when I was around 10 years old, some of my family took the long drive on the I-95 corridor from New Jersey down to visit my dad's parents in Fort Meyers, Florida. I don't remember too much from that trip: vague memories of being on a boat at Disneyworld, seeing the big Epcot Center "golf ball" building, seeing my grandfather actually play golf (the golf club scene was a foreign world to me), and being amazed by the gecko lizards that could walk on the ceiling in the motel cafeteria where we were staying. On the road, I remember that we played the alphabet game ("I see an 'A' on the *Welcome to Florida* sign" to "I see a 'Z' on the license plate of that tan station wagon"), that I played a cool football video game where the players were essentially red blinking dots, and I remember the South of the Border billboards.

Anyone who has taken this drive along the East Coast knows about the South of the Border rest stop/amusement park just south of the North Carolina/South Carolina border. The Mexican-themed site includes places to eat, relieve oneself, climb to see the highway from the "Sombrero-Tower," and, of course, ample opportunities to shop for a highly sought-after plastic mug with your name on it next to an image of maracas and the South of the Border logo. The draw of the park, though, is less the park itself and more the hundreds of billboards one sees along the road towards it. The signs can be entertaining (although some are quite bigoted), but they are effective. They make it clear that you are on the right path. For those who are actively opposed to atheism, there are similar (albeit metaphorical) signs that reaffirm your path as well.

Religious Spectacle: Under the Big Top

As a child of Roman Catholic parents, I attended and partook in all required Catholic functions and sacraments. My best friends growing up, however, were the sons of a wonderful man who happened to be a Protestant minister. This being the case, I attended both Catholic and Protestant youth groups for several formative years.

As a young teen, I felt at home with my friends in the Protestant youth group. My mother had been ill for nearly my entire childhood and she died when I was a young teen, so our weekly youth group meetings were a chance for me to explore some of the deeper issues that piqued my interest as a result of that experience. Questions about life, death, and meaning were certainly on my mind, more so than for most of my 14-year-old adolescent-boy peers.

It's one thing for a youth group to preach Christian love of self and others. It is another for it to teach that being "unequally yoked" with nonbelievers is a ticket to "h-e-double-hockey-sticks." While

I don't recall there being blatant fearmongering during the youth group meetings, I do recall sensing that the fear of hell was a not-so-subtle undercurrent for several of the teen members.

All this said, I enjoyed the group. We attended things like Christian Family Day at Six Flags Great Adventure theme park in New Jersey and I had a wonderful time. (My first concert ever was the Christian singer Amy Grant that night.) In hindsight, however, I now see how I allowed the comradery and friendships I experienced to blend with the dogma the group followed. This would not be the first or last time that I conflated good feelings with rules for spiritual salvation.

Several people in the youth group, including my two closest friends, had taken part in a program called Teen Missions International (TMI). TMI was founded in the 1970s and is headquartered near Cape Canaveral in Florida. Each year, hundreds of Christian teens descend on TMI's Lord's Boot Camp to learn how to become effective Christian missionaries while roughing it for two weeks in tents in the Florida heat and humidity. After two weeks of intensive Bible study, team bonding activities, and Christian rallies under a big top circus tent (literally), groups of kids are sent out into the world to preach to those who presumably had not yet heard the good news that Jesus had risen from the dead.

Within a year of my mother's passing in the late 1980s, I was signed up for a missionary trip to the village of Serbananti on the island of Sumatra in Indonesia. The trip would be life-changing for me on several fronts, but my prep time at the Lord's Boot Camp was also quite an experience for a 15-year-old.

The 2006 documentary *Jesus Camp* follows several young children at an evangelical Christian Bible camp in North Dakota where they learn to be "soldiers in the army of God." Although some Christians might argue that the movie purposefully portrayed evangelicals unfavorably, based on my experience at the Lord's Boot Camp, I suspect it was an accurate portrayal. Days at the camp were filled with manual tasks, individual Bible study, group

Bible study, and team-building activities, including an obstacle course complete with tire climbs, rope swings, and walls. Nights were saved for rallies under the big top. Here, we sang Christian hymns (sometimes holding candles) and listened to speakers from all over the world testify about their relationship with Jesus.

As the only Catholic teen in the group of approximately a thousand kids, I was particularly struck by a speaker from Northern Ireland who was happy to point out that *he* had the *right* Bible and that the Catholics did not. I recall that he took some nasty digs at Catholics, as did a Black preacher from the south who seemed to enjoy demeaning Catholics during his speech. I can't say that I felt particularly offended. I just found the speakers objectively interesting.

With Catholics (who are, after all, still Christians) being so openly and unapologetically maligned, it doesn't take much imagination to extrapolate how nonbelievers were viewed. We were required to memorize many Bible verses — and the *"do not be unequally yoked with nonbelievers"* verse was apparently a Lord's Boot Camp favorite. Anything that was not deemed "fully Christian" (such as non-Christian rock music, for example) was immediately suspect. One example perfectly captures this paranoid mindset.

Any teenager, religious or not, will look for ways to differentiate herself from others. As you might expect, a religious camp is not exactly conducive to fostering individuality, as its function is precisely the opposite. Religious youth camps exist to train, teach the value of teamwork, and install rules, not to foster individuality. That said, the teenage urge to stand out compelled us to find creative ways to express ourselves. One way was by threading string through the bottle tops of emptied milk jugs and wearing them as one would a necklace charm. The orange plastic bottle tops each had a white circular sticker on them prominently displaying sketches of the presumed owners of the milk supplier, an older couple.

Soon, many of the kids were proudly displaying Ned and Grace (I don't really recall their names) just above their heart. This only lasted a few days, though. I was not aware of any kid preventing any other kid from wearing a necklace, but it was nonetheless viewed by some as divisive. The Ned and Grace pendant meant you were in the cool club and there were not to be any cliques in the boot camp. That was one argument. The other argument, however, was stressed more heavily. Ned and Grace, as wonderful as they might be, were *not* our Lord and Savior Jesus Christ. Wearing their image was technically "idol worship" and that — as you'd expect — was a clear no-no in the Lord's Boot Camp.

The lesson was that even the image of poor old Ned and Grace, as innocent as it was, could be manipulated and used for evil. This is just how sneaky the devil could be. Be on watch. Put on the "armor of God" and always be prepared for a sneak attack from anyone or anything that wasn't fully in line with Christian teaching. The little orange bottle cap had morphed into a bright orange sign, reading "Warning: Slippery Slope to Hell."

Like traffic signs and billboards on the road, camps like this (and "religious revival events" in general) are geared towards grabbing your attention and pulling you in. And like Las Vegas casinos, some of these camps and religious events come with all the bright lights and pointing arrows. These religious events act as signposts, showing a pathway to the virtuous life, and they often seek to attract the attention of young children, like commercials during Saturday morning cartoons. It's true that compassion can be taught at these places, but at the events that I experienced, there is an unmistakable undertone that we are in the midst of a spiritual war with the devil, and atheists (if not an outright agent for evil) are fully compromised. Atheists must be treated as an absolute threat, so ready the "shield of faith."

Teen Missions International (and similar organizations) will argue that they are all about seeking out and engaging nonbelievers. It is, after all, an evangelical organization and its missionaries seek to fulfill what they feel is commanded of them by God: to spread the "good news" and to "save" as many souls as possible. But this engagement is never on equal footing (recall the "do not be *unequally yoked* with nonbelievers" verse). The nonbeliever is not approached as someone who may have worthwhile ideas about life and death. But for the efforts of these missionaries, she is (at best) a fool who is on a fast-track to eternal damnation. The engagement is purely to save her from hell because without the missionary's intervention, that is exactly where they believe she is headed.

Other Religious Spectacles

It may seem a bit much to say that theists are actively engaged in propagating an *anti*-atheistic worldview, but given that many theists see atheism as a direct attack on their beliefs, such statements are fully warranted. Demeaning atheists is often part and parcel of propping up the theistic worldview.

Evangelical Christian Bible camps are not the only religious spectacles to do this. As a former Catholic, I can attest that the Roman Catholic Church has much more than its periodic "Jubilee" festivals. In fact, there is no shortage of Catholic religious events and spectacles. Do a web search for a calendar of feast days for Catholic saints if you don't believe me. There is a patron saint for nearly everything and celebrations by the saint's homeland are common on the saint's birthday.

Whether it be Eid al-Fitr, Yom Kippur, or Easter, religious holidays serve as advertising billboards for their respective faiths. I believe that most people celebrating these and other religious holidays are sincere in their beliefs and are not necessarily looking to be vindictive against atheists as they celebrate their theism. Anti-atheistic infrastructure is simply a byproduct of building a theistic infrastructure. Propagating a faith often inherently comes with propagating a wariness of those who would challenge it. I don't know that this *must* be true, but I can attest that it *is* true given my experience.

I must touch on the darker side of religious spectacle. I would not intend to purposely focus on Islam as opposed to any other religion, but for the obvious and terrible violent spectacles performed by Muslim extremists in recent years. I expect that present in some readers' minds is a knee-jerk reaction: "*So what about the Christian-American pilot bombers who threaten areas of the Middle East and Afghanistan?*" This, in my view, is a valid perspective, but only partly so. I am open to having my mind changed, but I do not intend to go deep into the political rabbit hole here. Perhaps that could be a separate book.

I only want to point out that Al Qaeda and ISIS make it clear that religion is the justification for their acts. If the Spanish Inquisition was occurring now instead of hundreds of years ago, my focus on the darker side of religious spectacle would be Catholicism. Given a seemingly dark undercurrent of conspiracy theories espoused by some Christian Trump supporters recently, these groups likely deserve more focus as well. Some billboards on the road can be as dark as night. They keep riders on a theistic path, but it veers them to a place where murder is celebrated in the name of their God.

The Designated Driver

Public infrastructure doesn't always have to be something made of asphalt or steel. It often includes services. If a hotel has a pick-up service from the airport, that service and the vehicles and drivers that provide it might be considered part of the hotel's infrastructure costs. Likewise, one clear part of an anti-atheistic infrastructure is the parent or guardian who coaches her children into that worldview. She is the designated driver, the provider of a free ride to the nearest place of worship.

In September 2017, I was challenged by someone close to me when my wife and I took our two boys to a rally protesting action taken by President Trump to repeal the DACA ("Deferred Action for Childhood Arrivals") program. In this person's view, I was being a "radical" and I was indoctrinating our children with my radical beliefs. My response was, "Well of course I am. I don't agree with the word 'indoctrinate' in this case, but am I supposed to teach them based on someone else's beliefs?" A main goal as a parent is to teach my children the lessons in life that I have learned.

I let them know what I think is important in life and why I feel that way. I believe this to be at the heart of good parenting.

In my case, I purposely and frequently tell our boys that they are free to form their own beliefs regardless of what their mom or dad might believe on a given topic. More than anything, I want them to be able to make up their own minds. This is why I do not believe the term "indoctrinate" applies, as it implies teaching one to think uncritically. Since what I believe makes sense to me, I think it is likely that the same things may make sense to them as they become adults, but if they don't, they don't.

I believe most parents are like me in that we want to pass on to our children what we consider to be wisdom, but I don't expect that all parents are as willing to be so open-minded with their children, especially when religion is the topic. Because they may truly consider atheism to be a dangerous concept, many theistic parents may have no interest whatsoever in their children even being aware that it's an option. This seems much closer to indoctrination to me.

Frequently children look to what their parents believe about other people and they follow suit. Duke University fraternity kids sang racist songs on a bus in 2015 and a video of it went viral online. Some people might have been shocked by this (probably few minorities, though). Some might argue it was an old song from a previous time, but racism still exists today because it's passed on from generation to generation, as is hate in general. Many White supremacy groups exist in the former Confederate states for this reason. If young people are exposed to only one perspective on an issue, why would someone expect that they would grow up with any other perspective? Designated drivers raise future designated drivers and thoughts about things like race and religious belief are frequently preserved across generations in a self-perpetuating cycle.

Staying with the topic of race, I believe most Americans would agree that the United States has become a less racist society compared to the time of slavery. Granted, starting at slavery essentially puts the bar on the ground, but given ongoing societal issues as I write this in 2017, I don't want to assume too much. Whatever reduction in collective racist thought that has occurred since the time of slavery can likely be credited to people of different backgrounds being exposed to each other on a more personal level — on a human level. Police crackdowns on peaceful civil rights protestors in the 1960s horrified many. They saw people, including children and the elderly, acting with solemnity and dignity as they were subjected to terror and the risk of their bodies being ripped apart by police dogs. Many viewers empathized with those Black protestors and eventually, more and more people understood that it was morally reprehensible to treat other people like this.

My hope is that more theists over time might come to understand and focus on the many ways in which atheists and theists are similar. Just as openness to a human connection with "the other" has improved race relations for many, I hope a similar openness may start to bridge gaps between theists and atheists.

In a June 8, 2016, article in *Psychology Today*, titled "Killing Atheists: The persecution of secular people, explained," Phil Zuckerman, a professor of sociology and secular studies at Pitzer College, points out that atheists are being targeted and killed in several Muslim-majority countries today. It is *illegal* to be openly atheist in several countries, including current United States ally, Saudi Arabia, where atheists can be tortured and executed for openly discussing their disbelief. My hope is that the suffering of these atheists can trigger a response of outrage similar to the police attacks on peaceful protestors in Selma. Specifically, I hope that non-atheists might consider the fear atheists live with in many countries.

Will the drivers of anti-atheistic worldviews change in a vacuum? I think not. I believe it will take exposure to the plight of atheists worldwide and, most importantly, it will take more exposure to atheists, period. I believe theists' exposure to people who happen to be atheists can eventually have a noticeably positive effect. But as long as parents perpetuate the idea that atheists are evil and to be avoided, that divide will not be bridged easily, and if atheists continue to stay closeted, the divide runs the risk of growing wider.

The impact of a parent's beliefs on a child goes beyond just the continued exposure to those beliefs. Emotional ties to that parent or guardian are often woven together with the beliefs. If the parent is a generally loving person (most theists that I know are), this love might seemingly glue the belief to the person, making each undiscernible as separate entities or ideas. The emotional nuances in these situations are complicated. I will discuss these and their impact later in the book.

Ride Sharing with Nationalism

Regarding anti-atheistic infrastructure, so far we've discussed the following:

- The "roadway" of dedicated times and places for worship,

- The "soil" of sacred text that supports this roadway,

- The "traffic signs" and "billboards" of religious events that excite and direct believers to a continued theistic worldview, and

- The reality of "designated driver" parents who will pass on their theistic lifestyle to the next generation.

It is understandable that some might view what we've discussed so far as components of an infrastructure that supports a theistic worldview, not necessarily an infrastructure that specifically looks to undermine an atheistic worldview. I disagree.

In my personal experience, most theists find theism and anti-atheism as inherently inseparable, even though opinions of atheism might vary on a spectrum from "foolishness" on one side to "evil" on the other. The reality is that continued maintenance of a theistic infrastructure typically serves to torpedo anyone with an atheistic perspective. Ultimately, free thinkers will have to help build an infrastructure that is not entwined so tightly with religion — a topic I discuss later in this book.

Multiple waves of the religious "Great Awakening" movement have washed upon the shores of the U.S. since our inception as a nation. This religious water has saturated our land in such a way that it is often difficult for some people to recognize that religion and state are indeed separable. Strong soil that might support construction of a flourishing secular state is muddied by the influx of religious belief, but many simply do not see it this way. They see the water as giving life to the nation, perhaps allowing crops to grow. But while water typically does bring life, this water is laced with a toxin that can and often does go unnoticed.

One of the more recent iterations of the U.S.'s religious "Great Awakening" came with Pat Robertson, Ralph Reed, and the Christian Coalition of America in the 1980s and 1990s. This group sharpened religious teachings like arrowheads and shot them directly into the voting booth, often toeing (or crossing) the line established by 501(c)3 of the IRS code regarding influence on elections. To be a *true Christian* in the U.S. was to be a *true American* and to be a *true American* was to be a *true Christian*. The message the Christian Coalition sold was incredibly effective for many, as it played on tribalistic fears and desires that stemmed directly from our evolutionary nature (although most in that group would of course not admit this).

This "immaculate conflation" of theistic belief (i.e., Christianity in the U.S.) and nationalism (i.e., national exceptionalism in the U.S.) is obvious to anyone who objectively looks for it. "God Bless America" assumes there is a God to perform the blessing on our country *specifically*. Pledging allegiance to the flag "under God" assumes there is a God overseeing our country *specifically*. "In God We Trust" silently passes between hands in our everyday financial transactions. There really is no reasonable argument I can imagine that God and Country have not been conflated on a deep level. It dates back to the idea of the new world being a "promised land" for Puritan settlers. It includes the whole concept of manifest destiny. It's been around for a while. Folks like Robertson and Reed simply shot a steroid into that vein.

Just as our country is quick to side with God in our Pledge of Allegiance and on our money, churches are often quick to side with our country. Congregational prayers during Catholic masses I've attended throughout my life were often for the success of our military, with little question as to whether or not our leadership was morally right to activate the military in the first place. Cardinal Francis Spellman was famously quoted during the Vietnam era as saying, "My country, may it always be right, *but right or wrong, my country.*" For those words of moral ambivalence to come from the mouth of someone who claimed to hold moral authority strains belief, but it happened. I also understand there to be churches that recite the Pledge of Allegiance at Sunday services. I have always had a problem with the American flag being in a church in the first place. After all, if God exists, she presumably would not be the God of but one nation.

Because God and Country have culturally become inseparable for many, it's quite easy for them to share the same infrastructure — the same roadway. In the U.S., those with theistic/anti-atheistic worldviews often share a "mass-transit system" with those who unquestionably subscribe to American superiority. Quite frequently, these folks are the same people precisely due to this conflation. It's as if an American flag factory shares a parking lot with the church and the bus stop provides easy access to both.

A current example as I write this section of the book is the controversy surrounding Colin Kaepernick, the former quarterback for the San Francisco 49ers. In 2016, Kaepernick kneeled during the national anthem. He made it clear that he did this not as an insult to the military (which many see as being directly represented by the flag), but to draw attention to unequal treatment of Black Americans by law enforcement. President Trump's decision in 2017 to call anyone not standing for the anthem a "son of a bitch" struck a chord with many love-it-or-leave-it, so-called "patriotic" Americans, but it also came with a backlash. Trump's words only propelled the issue further into the national spotlight.

A meme spreading on social media among the reactionary, love-it-or-leave-it crowd as I write is an image of what appears to be a cowboy on a horse holding a large American flag. On the bottom right of the image is a crucifix. The meme reads, "I stand for the flag. I kneel at the cross." Granted, the cowboy is *sitting* on the horse, not standing on it, but I suppose that is a minor detail. Perhaps the meme-maker should have been clearer: "*I stand for the flag. I kneel at the cross. I sit on my horse when I try to look manly while posing for photos.*"

There are indeed other memes that express this same sentiment, many throwing a gun or two in the mix. Many show an American flag superimposed over a cross or within the borders of a cross. Either way, my point is that the God and Country connection is truly relevant and going strong today.

I played football in high school and I remember the connotations of "taking a knee" back then. Usually this would happen towards the end of the practice when listening to announcements from the coaching staff. You would *not* — as in *never* — sit down. That was a clear no-no. It was a sign of disrespect and laziness. Taking a knee, however, was not viewed this way. It was not a "snap-to-it, stand-at-full attention" mode, but it was still viewed as being respectful. It was an acknowledgement that you may be tired, but it still showed respect to your team and coaches. I read Kaepernick's kneeling protest in a similar light.

The Kaepernick protest also brought to mind lyrics to a song I wrote in my 20s. It turns out that one of my direct ancestors was the foster father (and strangely enough, father-in-law) of Civil War General William Tecumseh Sherman. After the Civil War, Sherman went on to oversee a portion of the U.S.'s handling of Native Americans in the West. Although not related by blood, I wrote a song called "Sherman's Shame" that talked of how "*my blood boils and veins are breaking*" due to shame of his actions out west. Towards the end is my favorite lyric: "*If a flag is to last, you have to see clearly the shadow it cast... always fly it at half-mast....*"

The idea I was aiming for was that we need to be able to admit our imperfection. We need to *earn* a full-mast celebration of our flag and the values we claim it represents. The strength in the idea of America for me is that we are (ideally) constantly seeking to get better. We are (ideally) always seeking self-improvement, always honing our democracy, always pushing for that "one day this nation will rise up and live out the true meaning of its creed" for which Martin Luther King Jr. openly dreamed. Until the values that the flag is said to represent (freedom and opportunity) apply to *all* in our country, we have not earned a full celebration of that symbol.

In its best moments, this nation should be undergoing continuous improvement exercises. We should not rest on our laurels. We should admit where and when we fall short of our stated goals and take corrective action. Bruce Springsteen often says that one goal of his songwriting is to survey the gap between the American dream and American reality. We need that always in mind.

Despite all this, many in the country cannot stop from "USA-USA-USA" chants followed by "We're number one, we're number one." As I write, the United States is far from top billing on education of its people, violence prevention, pollution minimization, and many other desirable qualities, but, hey, "We're number one" sure sounds nice.

Just as a theistic worldview hinges on beliefs based on faith and not evidence, national exceptionalism cannot allow for doubt to creep in, facts be damned. Both theistic and nationalistic worldviews tend to excel in certainty. I'd argue that certainty (faked or sincere) *is* the currency used to get on the shared theism/nationalism bus in the first place, and it too has "In God We Trust" written all over it.

Fast Pass in the HOV Lane

I hinted at it briefly when I mentioned section 501(c)3 of the U.S. tax code, but one result of the bromance between theism and nationalism is clear *financial* support for theistic infrastructure. I'm not just talking about financial support that one would expect to stem naturally from the social or cultural connection between the two. I'm talking about political decisions and political policy that result in cold hard cash in the hands of religious institutions. This provides an advantage to religious institutions over secular ones that is not so dissimilar from cars with a "fast pass" that are allowed access to a designated lane and can blow past the rest of us in traffic.

A 2013 analysis by *The Washington Post* estimated that U.S. governments (federal, state, and local) subsidize religious organizations to the tune of over $83 billion per year, in large part due to their tax-exempt status. Although this represented less than 3 percent of the U.S. budget in 2013, it's not a paltry sum. With the country's estimated population of 327 million, this equates to more than $250 per person, per year. I currently live in San Diego, which is, as I write this in 2018, the eighth largest city in the United States. If $83 billion were split evenly between the 10 most populated cities in the country, the amount allocated to San Diego would be more than double its entire 2018 city budget ($3.64 billion). Again, we are *not* talking about pocket change here.

Given the Unites States' history and the desire shared by many (but not all) for the separation of church and state, it's understandable that our taxation system evolved in such a way that we might be reticent for government to have the ability to impose a tax on a religious organization or church. After all, the authority to impose a tax on someone or something *implies a general authority* of the tax-imposer over the taxed.

On the other hand, government does indeed provide benefits to religious organizations, so it makes sense that they would be treated just like any other non-public organization. Churches, synagogues, and mosques all benefit from a civil police force, a civil fire department, and local water treatment plant technology. If they were to be taxed, it's not as if they would be taxed specifically because they are religious organizations. They would be taxed because they benefit from government-provided services like other organizations.

So how ought the IRS classify religious organizations? Should they have no unique classification compared to any other organization? Maybe they should be treated similarly to public schools? Public schools don't pay taxes, but this stems from them being essentially considered a capillary of greater government. Treating churches for tax purposes as if they are part of secular government seems to be a non-starter.

As it stands, churches, temples, and mosques are classified as "public charities" under the Unites State tax code. There is a laundry list of items the IRS considers when reviewing an entity's claim that it is a church (when I say "church," I also mean temples, mosques, or the equivalent for other religions). Included in that list are "a recognized creed and form of *worship*," "a distinct *religious* history," and "established places of *worship*."

This said, if I wanted to create a secular organization that might mirror many of the roles filled in the community by churches, I would not be able to check the boxes on my IRS form next to any of the items listed above. As an atheist, I do not *worship* anything or anyone. My theoretical new secular organization would also have no *religious* history whatsoever. My atheistic organization then would immediately be at a disadvantage to theistic organizations in this case.

Someone could argue in response, "What's the big deal? You still might be able to get 501(c)(3) status, just not as a church." Well, first, it's no "small deal" that theistic groups have this head start on tax-exempt status. Secondly, churches also have the specific advantage over non-religious charity organizations in that once they are classified as churches, they need not fill out and file the IRS 990 form each year.

Despite what some theists might argue concerning the United States tax code, the code provides advantages to churches that are not provided to secular charities. The very first line of the First Amendment to the U.S. Constitution is that *Congress shall make no law respecting an establishment of religion.* This favored tax status indeed implies a respect for religious groups that is not assigned to secular equivalents. Therefore, I find challenges to churches' tax status to be of considerable legal merit.

Lately, my interest in this topic has been piqued. I am writing this in July 2020, during the Covid-19 pandemic, and we just learned that the U.S. Roman Catholic Church will receive $1.4 billion in Covid-19 relief aid from the federal government. If the Church is going to be treated like a corporation when taking money *from* the government, it would make sense that it likewise be treated like a corporation at tax time, when corporations are expected to give money *to* the government.

The IRS website indicates that 501(c)3 entities are restricted from engaging in political activities that "have the effect of favoring a candidate or group of candidates." When some religious leaders essentially dictate to their congregation how to view certain societal or political issues, it's not hard to argue that they are essentially violating this requirement. From my perspective, this line appears to be crossed in nearly every election year.

Part 2: The Debate

Do You Believe in Logic?

Part 1 was intended to address the elephant in the atheist's room, which is the incredibly negative opinion that many theists hold about atheists and atheism. Without first shedding some light on this anti-atheistic bias and the infrastructure that maintains it, I felt it would be difficult to aim for an honest discussion of the topic going forward.

Part 3 of this book dives into the intensely personal emotions involved in losing my religion and the emotional break that came with the denial of my previous beliefs. Part 4 discusses the powerful and hopeful vision for the future that arose from those ashes, and a call for us to start working towards that future.

This part fills the gap between an understanding of what an atheist is and my coming to grips with the discovery that I was one. It touches on some of the "theism vs. atheism" debates that I immersed myself in during my late 30s and early 40s. It represents the steep road I climbed transitioning from being wary of atheists to being proud that I am one. This part sets the rules for the debate and touches on some of the key concepts that swayed me.

Prior to going much further, however, I would be remiss to not mention the gratitude I feel for several atheist writers who were not shy with their atheism. These "New Atheists," who took up their pens (and voices) against superstition and religion after the September 11 attacks, have significantly impacted me. These writers (Christopher Hitchens, Richard Dawkins, Dan Dennett, and Sam Harris, to name a few) boldly said what needed to be said, taboos be damned.

Many considered them too aggressive because they ridiculed beliefs that some people hold sacred. This method of delivery did not sit well with me, either. I know and love many religious people, so this blatant calling out of their beliefs as misguided struck me as rude and, if not crossing the line, at least leaning over its edge.

That said, I now believe the very fact that this approach did not sit well with me was the very reason it stayed with me. I remember thinking that all these people were doing is bluntly stating what they thought, so why did I feel threatened by it? What exactly felt so dangerous in what they were saying, and why? They opened the basement door and urged me to walk downstairs where I could remove the layers of dust covering the doubts I had shelved there for decades. They helped me bring these doubts into the sunlight for a close and an honest inspection.

Regarding these writers, I recommend that you buy their books, read their articles, and watch their debates and speeches online. If I had sensed a deference to the power religion often holds, their words might not have been as effective. They helped to snap me out of it. The title of one of Dan Dennett's book is *Breaking the Spell* and that is exactly what I feel they helped me do. I am forever grateful to them for it.

**

I'm hesitant to use the word "debate" when it comes to atheism vs. theism. A debate is defined as "a formal discussion on a particular topic in a public meeting or legislative assembly, in which opposing arguments are put forward" and this is precisely what I mean when I use the word. To many, though, the term immediately recalls the "gotcha" one-liners unleashed during nationally televised political debates. Those debates tend to be more about theater and one-upmanship than actual discussion of any substance. I am reminded of the 1988 vice presidential debate and Lloyd Bentsen's "you are no Jack Kennedy" takedown of Dan Quayle, and Donald Trump's 2016 "because you'd be in jail" comment about Hillary Clinton that inspired endless memes on social media. The utility of debate is often lost to the show.

For these reasons, I plan to use the words "dialog" or "discussion" in most cases going forward. In the event where "debate" might slip out, understand the context in which I use it. Yes, debates themselves are often held to be won or lost, but more importantly, they are held to uncover the truth, or at least they should be.

**

In Part 1, I provided specific religious texts that highlight teachings about those who do not share a theistic worldview. I provided multiple examples to hammer home the underlying bias against atheism, but those same verses serve a different purpose for me in this section. If you go back and reread some of them, you will notice something else.

- *"Do not be unequally yoked with unbelievers"*

- *"...whoever does not believe is condemned"*

- *"...see to it that no one takes you captive by philosophy"*

- *"for those, their deeds have become worthless... and those are the companions of the Fire"*

These excerpts range in tone from simple caution to something more passionate (dare I say "vicious" or even "sinister"). Regardless of the tone, however, these texts are written from a position of authority. There is no hemming or hawing. There is nothing ambiguous about these quotes.

There is no, "Hey, maybe it isn't a good thing to hang out with nonbelievers." There is "do not be unequally yoked with unbelievers."

There is no "nonbelievers who do these deeds might be wasting their time." Rather, these nonbelievers are to be "companions of the Fire," which does not mean sitting cozy by a campfire, roasting marshmallows, in case you were wondering.

These religious texts were written clearly as direction, and religious people reading these texts are clearly seeking to be directed.

Most importantly, however, they go to these books already having accepted that they are indeed texts of moral authority, capable of providing guidance. Rarely do devout believers (at least those who remain devout believers) doubt that these books should have moral authority in their lives. They take it on faith. By extension, the Ultimate Author of these texts is not questioned as *the* moral authority and *of course* the existence of that author is assumed as the *prime* article of faith.

I say all this to show that the starting point for most believers is typically quite different from the starting point for most nonbelievers. For believers, "God exists" is typically step one before anything else. To be even more precise, "God exists" is step zero. It is the blank canvas before anything has been painted. It is the understood foundation for any thing — or any life — that might be built upon it.

What this means, though, is that for most religious people, right from the start there is a belief, or at the very least, a comfort level, with the existence of the supernatural. In other words, there is a belief in magic.

Magic Mirror

When I was trying to come up with a creative subheading for these few paragraphs about the word "magic," I had a flashback to watching the "magic mirror" segment on *Romper Room,* a children's television show that ran during my childhood in the 1970s and early 1980s. At the end of the show, the host would look *through* the magic mirror (as opposed to *at* the mirror) to say hello to all the kids out there in "TV Land," saying first names in the process. I'd have to ask my father or older siblings, but I like to think I was too cool to be duped by this "magical" look across the air waves. I suspect, however, that I bought it hook, line, and sinker.

That memory spurred me to think more about these two words "magic" and "mirror" in relation to each other, and it led to a different chain of thought completely. Most of us usually have things happen in our lives that spur us to take time to be reflective and to truly examine ourselves and the wonders of the world all around us. We put *life* itself up to the mirror. During this process for me, I will often feel a rush of absolute amazement that overwhelms me emotionally. When I think of my loved ones, especially, the joy at my good fortune feels somehow transcendental — so uplifting that it could not possibly be of this earth. It is an indescribable feeling.

Because we may not have a word that captures how these thoughts make us feel, many of us assign the words "supernatural" or "magic," but there is truly no need to do so. Why must we assume that any such wonderful feeling need be beyond the natural? There is no good reason to do this. After all, I can tell you from personal experience that I have felt these "transcendental" feelings both as a theist and an atheist.

When you have that underlying assumption of God's existence, however, it is quite understandable that people would assume that these feelings must have originated from a communion with this deity — with something "magic." The term "magic," however, is so overused these days. It clearly means different things to different people.

"Do you Believe in Magic?" was a hit by the 1960s band The Lovin' Spoonful. In it, they sing of the *"magic in a young girl's heart"* that can *"free her whenever it starts."* This is followed by a lyric I particularly like: *"And it's magic if the music is groovy, it makes you feel happy like an old-time movie."* In this case, magic refers to something that seems unexplainable but makes you feel happy.

How does this "magic" compare to Harry Potter's "magic", or the magic that brought Lazarus back from the dead? What about the "magic" of magicians David Blaine or David Copperfield? What of the "magic" you see in your lover's eyes? The "magical" evening when you sit in silence and watch the stars? The "magic" of new technology that most of us lay people don't understand?

Recall that Thomas Edison was dubbed the "Wizard of Menlo Park" because his inventions seemed like magic to people in his day.

We've already dissected the hell out of connotations associated with the word "atheism" ("hell out" pun intended). The word "magic" is similar in that it can convey vastly different ideas, but it is different in that it truly does have multiple definitions, whereas the definition for atheism is both simple and singular. The confusion over the word "atheism" stems from its different *connotations*, while confusion over the word "magic" stems from different *meanings*. Magic has the following definitions:

1. *"the power of apparently influencing the course of events by using mysterious or supernatural forces"*
2. *"mysterious tricks, such as making things disappear and appear again, performed as entertainment"*
3. *"a quality that makes something seem removed from everyday life, especially in a way that gives delight"*
4. *"something that has a delightfully unusual quality"*

Raising Lazarus from the dead would clearly fit the first definition. The second definition applies to magicians. Wonder at the beauty of the night sky or amazement regarding how full one's heart can feel when with loved ones are examples of the third or fourth definitions.

This should be simple enough, but people often conflate magic's multiple meanings and then have a hard time extricating one from the other. This is particularly the case when emotion gets involved. If people are emotionally overcome by wonder, for example, they assume this *must* be due to a supernatural force or entity. Emotions that arise when thinking of *some* definitions of "magic" seem to blind people from clearly seeing the differences between *all* the definitions. They cannot look past the wonder component of magic. That is all they see reflected back. They cannot look *through* the magic mirror.

On the other hand, people who recognize the magic mirror as a stand-in for magical thinking can see well beyond it. These folks understand that one need not believe in supernatural forces to be in wonder or amazement of nature or love. This is an essential point. Richard Dawkins' book *The Magic of Reality* does an exceptional job of addressing this.

Why Logic? And What is Science?

To recap the last several pages, theists will often enter the "theism/atheism" dialog having already defaulted to "God exists" as the starting point. Theists who are not particularly dogmatic will still often default to this same starting point due to an inability to separate the idea of magic as "something wonderful or amazing" from magic as something "supernatural."

I can hear some of your thoughts right now: *"Well, they are theists after all — of course belief in God's existence is their starting point. And the starting point for atheists is that God does not exist. The two sides need to each start on their own line and see if they can come to an agreement somewhere in between or see if they can pull one over towards the other side."*

Yes, I understand this thinking, but this is not what I'm after. I'm not interested in the theatrical, cable-news "scream-a-thon" pundit debates that mimic tug-of-wars. I want to build a structure with you, and I know that it's important to build this structure on ground that we can all agree is firm. If you are going to start with a default belief in the supernatural, you are telling me that you are not interested in the geological survey. You have no interest in prodding and testing the ground to see if where we plan to set our foundation is bedrock or quicksand.

Instead, you've already convinced yourself that the land must be solid ground because you have some incredibly beautiful and emotionally satisfying architectural slopes in mind for the top of the structure. Perhaps this vision for the building was passed on to you from loved ones and is so well-defined, so intricate in every detail, that you take the true structural integrity of it as an afterthought. *After all, how can so many people enjoy this vision and obtain such beauty from this vision if it is not true? Clearly, someone smarter than me must have already determined this grand vision to be structurally sound. Why else would my ancestors have passed it on to me?* I'd argue this to be a very clear example of letting the perceived beauty of the vision override the real-world need for basic structural integrity.

So why logic? Why this insistence on pulling things to earth? After all, these visions can be useful in people's lives. Doesn't that account for something? And why such a scientific bent on things anyway? Scientists are proven wrong all the time. Why trust science, especially since we now know how bizarre and mysterious things are? At the subatomic level especially, some would say that our most basic scientific laws break down. In that realm, it appears possible for things to be at two places at the same time. That goes fully against what we consider to be logical. Why then is it any more logical to trust science than it is to trust religion?

I certainly concede this is a good and important question. Why trust science at all? I just re-watched part of Richard Dawkins' interview with Wendy Wright, the former president of the Concerned Women for America political action group. Posted online in 2013, the interview is about the evolution vs. creationism debate. It has well over 1.5 million views at the time of this writing, but I certainly hope this increases drastically. In my view, it is a near-perfect example of how people deflect away from an issue. It is a greatest-hits album for illogical thinking in general. "Why trust science?" is certainly part of that discussion and certainly a chart topper on that greatest-hits album.

To address this question, let's first talk some more about science. Wright, in her discussion with Dawkins, depicts science as just some other religion. I believe a fair paraphrasing of much of her argument is: *You have your beliefs. I have mine. We are supposed to be equal in a democracy so therefore our beliefs should all have equal footing. It follows then that creationism should be given as much time in school as evolution — "teach the controversy."*

But science is *not* a set of beliefs or a religion (aka, "Scientism"). Science is a *system* — a framework — for determining what appears to be true. It was stated previously that scientists are proven wrong all the time. This is true, but the part often conspicuously omitted is that they are proven wrong *by other scientists*. Science, by its very nature, is skeptical and self-correcting. It builds upon itself and readjusts at the core if a foundation is shown to be unsteady. Objectively speaking, there is no success or failure in science. There are simply attempts at learning — piecing together theories about the world we experience.

Science is also *not a thing*. By this, I mean science is not a trend. It isn't a social media fad. I've seen people refer to science this way (regarding global warming, for example), as if it's a meme that needs to be crowded out online. It's almost as if the thinking is *"Let's push out more 'guns-God-and 'merica' memes and then we win."*

Some theists will argue that atheists "rely on science" too much, as if science is somehow separate from our everyday experience. When someone walks across the street and trips on the curb while trying to get up onto the sidewalk, she hopefully understands that next time, she'll need to raise her foot a bit higher to avoid the same thing happening again. That is an example of learning from trial and error. In this case, the initial trip was accidental, but the experience was absorbed and learned from, nonetheless. That is science. When someone is shooting on a gun range at a target and holds the weapon in such a way as to consistently hit to the right, it would make sense to readjust slightly towards the left to hit the target. This, again, is science. It is learning from trial and error.

So, when people discuss science as if there is (1) everyday experience and then (2) "science," which is separate and somewhere else (likely practiced only by liberal elites behind the stone walls of an ancient university somewhere), they are profoundly misunderstanding what science is at its core. Science is defined as "the intellectual and practical activity encompassing the systematic study of the structure and behavior of the physical and natural world through observation and experiment."

More simply, it is experiencing our world and trying to learn about our world from those experiences.

So back to the question, *why rely on logic and science*? Because they reflect the most basic level of how we experience the world. There is nothing fundamentally different between monitoring carbon dioxide levels in the atmosphere to help us project global warming than there is with monitoring how high we need to lift our foot to avoid tripping onto the sidewalk. They are both examples of trial, error, readjustment, and trying again. They are both examples of us using our abilities to sense and understand our world.

I believe the more honest question is, "Why suspend logic?" Why use logic for so many parts of our lives but torpedo it when it comes to religion? We use it in the mundane example of crossing the street onto the sidewalk. We use it while readjusting on the gun range to home in on a target. We use it when we add money to our bank accounts and make projections about likely future income (OK, maybe not all of us do that last part very well).

We even use logic when we spend time with and teach our children. It's true there may be strong emotional reasons for doing so as well, but this does not take away the logic behind the act. We spend time with our children in part because we want to make sure they grow up feeling confident and secure. Trial and error have shown that children are typically more secure when they are not abandoned or ignored by their parents. That also is logic.

If one is going to argue that theism is logical or at least more logical than atheism, I am all ears and happy to have a respectful discussion on that topic. Ultimately, I think arguments for theism based on logic are very weak, but I can at least build a dialog with such a theist because it would presumably be founded on an agreed-upon understanding of the rules. The geological survey has taken place, we've both read it, and can agree that we are building on strong soil. Often, however, this is not the case. For many, faith itself is a virtue and there is an eager willingness to avoid certain knowledge — an eager ignorance while tripping on the curb.

Exploring NOMA's Land

NOMA 1.0 (1999)

Many theists argue that the rules are different when discussing things religious in nature. The concept of "non-overlapping magisteria" (NOMA) has increased in popularity in certain religious circles. NOMA is a view that science and religion cover different realms — different "magisteria" — and that they do not overlap and, therefore, need not be in conflict. It argues that science governs facts and the physical world, whereas religion governs the "softer" things like morals, values, meaning, and interpersonal relationships.

An objective observer might recognize the NOMA push by many religious people as a convenient — and perhaps even desperate — attempt to shield their worldview from further damage created by scientific discovery. God was high in the heavens until we took our hot air balloons, planes, and rocket ships to the heavens and did not find him there. God's vengeance was the reason for terrible plagues and floods, until we learned about viruses and hydrology/hydraulic engineering. God was the designer and creator of each individual lifeform, until Darwin developed another way to consider the evolution of life that turns out to be supported by piles upon piles of evidence. From this perspective, NOMA appears to be a shield from these punches. It aims to protect the remaining (and limited) "authority" that many people still concede to religion, but the cracks in the shield are clear and they are getting bigger every day.

In fairness, though, it is not just theists who support NOMA. There are indeed some atheists who may feel the same. Some nonbelievers, such as scientist Stephen Gould, were big proponents of the idea. In fact, it was Gould who is typically given credit for coining the term in the first place.

"Science tries to document the factual character of the natural world, and to develop theories that coordinate and explain these facts. Religion, on the other hand, operates in the equally important, but utterly different, realm of human purposes, meanings, and values—subjects that the factual domain of science might illuminate, but can never resolve... These two magisteria do not overlap, nor do they encompass all inquiry (consider, for example, the magisterium of art and the meaning of beauty)."

Indeed, in 1999, the National Academy of Sciences endorsed the view:

"Scientists, like many others, are touched with awe at the order and complexity of nature. Indeed, many scientists are deeply religious. But science and religion occupy two separate realms of human experience. Demanding that they be combined detracts from the glory of each."

It seems clear to me that NOMA is flawed at a fundamental level. Regardless of whether some people think NOMA should be held up as the ideal and that these two "realms" *should not* overlap, it must first be noted that it is demonstrably true that *they do indeed* overlap. Many religious teachings obviously infringe upon the scientific/physical realm. Claims that the earth is only 6,000 years old, or that Lazarus was raised from the dead, or that magic words can change the essence or substance of wine into blood, are all claims about the physical nature of reality — of which *science* is said to have authority.

The less dogmatic might understandably write off as metaphor all of these examples. One might think that doing so would then conceivably bring NOMA closer to a possibility, but even these folks typically still hold underlying, nonmetaphorical claims on the physical realm. For example, maybe there is no belief in a physical heaven or hell, but there is a belief that heaven is a state of being that can exist after death where one is with God for eternity. Such a claim still makes several assumptions about the nature of reality. It assumes that a spirit (or "energy of the self") exists and that it can survive death. This is a physical claim and has nothing to do with the "religious realm" of values or morals. Furthermore, it makes assumptions about the self and consciousness that are addressed by the neurological sciences and others. It also still assumes a creator God who is said to have constructed the physical world in the first place.

**

These examples are only a small sampling of the many clear instances of religion injecting itself into the realm that NOMA says is not governed by religion. But what of the "values and morals" realm that religion is said to oversee? How does religion do on this front? Is religion keeping its own moral house in order?

Well, if you focus on those people who feel inspired by a religious figure (or sacred book) to live what most would consider to be good and moral lives, you might understandably say that religion is doing its duty here. But what of those people who feel inspired by the very same religious figure (or sacred book) to focus on and lobby for the benefits of slavery, conquest, homophobia, and misogyny? The large umbrella of the "moral" religious realm of authority also allows these folks to believe that they are living good and moral lives. Many of those who kill in the name of religion believe that doing so is fully justified. This is a problem. What religion considers good morals and values is all over the map, depending on which religious teaching one is following.

The common denominator for defining "a moral act" in most Abrahamic religions at least seems to be whether or not the act is "pleasing to God." This does not simplify the issue. After all, *it is said* that God is pleased by those who stand up for and protect the marginalized, but God *is also said* to be pleased by protesting homosexuality at the funerals of gay AIDS victims. God *is said* to be pleased by self-sacrifice for the benefit of others, but God *is also said* to be pleased by the torture and genocide of whole groups of people who do not submit to certain dogmatic beliefs. It seems quite clear to me that God's intentions are defined by *those doing the saying* of what pleases God.

From my atheistic perspective, it appears obvious to me that if God exists, he must have a divine version of a multiple-personality disorder. God can be incredibly loving and self-sacrificing while also amazingly malicious and cruel. God is the loving father, but God is also the mob boss demanding payment. God, it would seem, is capable of the same wide range of actions and beliefs along the moral spectrum that we humans are. That is both interesting and telling. Claims that humans created God in our own image could indeed find support in this line of thinking.

Steven Weinberg, a Nobel Prize-winning American physicist, took it a step further in a speech at the Conference on Cosmic Design in 1999: "With or without religion, good people can behave well and bad people can do evil; but for good people to do evil — that takes religion." I'd argue that this can apply to other unquestioned belief systems, not just religion, but the point is a good one, nonetheless. This argument goes well beyond the acknowledgement that religion is inconsistent in holding high the torch of supposed moral authority. It argues that religion specifically provides a means by which the torch's flame is lowered to the ground, destroying surrounding homes in a wildfire of *immorality*. From this perspective, religion clearly is *not* holding up its end of NOMA but making things worse. I will dive deeper into claims of morality later.

In summary so far, the main anti-NOMA points made above are:

> 1. That religion does indeed infringe upon the scientific realm,
>
> 2. That religion is swerving wildly in its claimed lane of the "moral" realm, and
>
> 3. Given #2, perhaps "science" *should* take that realm under its wing. (I put "science" in quotations here because I do not consider it separate from general human experience, as mentioned earlier).

NOMA 2.0 (2008)

Remember earlier when we talked about when scientists have been wrong? In these cases, they are typically challenged by other scientists, presented with evidence and different ways of thinking, and the record is typically updated or corrected. It is clear to me that we are in the midst of that scientific "calling out" against NOMA as I write this now. Sam Harris' *The Moral Landscape*, published in 2010, is an excellent source showing a pushback against this idea from the science community.

But this pushback had already entered the public conversation, it is interesting to see a nuanced change in the explanations of NOMA by the National Academy of Sciences between 1999 and 2008. Below is an excerpt from a 2008 NAS publication:

> *"Science and religion are based on different aspects of human experience. In science, explanations must be based on evidence drawn from examining the natural world. Scientifically based observations or experiments that conflict with an explanation eventually must lead to modification or even abandonment of that explanation. Religious faith, in contrast, does not depend only on empirical evidence, is not necessarily modified in the face of conflicting evidence, and typically involves supernatural forces or entities. Because they are not a part of nature, supernatural entities cannot be investigated by science. In this sense, science and religion are separate and address aspects of human understanding in different ways. Attempts to pit science and religion against each other create controversy where none needs to exist"* (emphasis added).

To some, this might seem almost exactly like the NOMA language noted previously (whether it be the NAS or Stephen Gould). Sounds like they are saying basically the same thing, right? No. From my perspective, there are some subtle changes here that are very worthy of note. I've learned in life that the ability to distinguish between nuanced details is often very important. This is a good example of such a case.

Let's break down some key sections of the 2008 NAS statement on NOMA:

> *Science and religion are based on different <u>aspects</u> of human experience....*

In the 1999 NAS statement, science and religion occupied "*two separate <u>realms</u> of human experience*" (emphasis added). In the 2008 NAS statement, science and religion were "*based on different <u>aspects</u> of human experience*" (emphasis added). A *realm* is defined as either a "kingdom" (i.e., recall the mythical god Thor: Protector of the Nine Realms) or a "field of domain of activity of interest." It clearly implies authority. An *aspect,* on the other hand, does not infer authority. An aspect is simply a "a particular part or feature of something." In less than a decade, religion went from having authority over part of human experience to simply being part of it.

Well, OK. I'm fine with that. Religion clearly has been and is still *part* of the collective human experience. But there are other things that are also part of the collective human experience. These include mythology, fiction, and cult worship. (This last one — cult worship — has long been considered unworthy of a "civilized" society, but it's a worthwhile and perhaps eye-opening exercise to seek clear differences between a cult and "standard" religion. I'd argue that the most notable difference is simply the number of followers.)

> *Religious faith, in contrast, does not depend <u>only</u> on empirical evidence...*

The 2008 NOMA text indicates that religious faith "does not depend only on empirical evidence" and "is not necessarily modified in the face of conflicting evidence." That is quite a telling statement. I'd argue that if you can't be swayed by conflicting evidence, you don't truly rely on evidence at all. You may use evidence when it suits your purpose, but if you can eschew it so easily when it does not, I don't think it appropriate to claim that evidence is something you "depended on" in the first place (at least not with regards to truth-seeking).

Because they are not a part of nature, supernatural entities cannot be investigated by science. In this sense, science and religion are separate and address aspects of human understanding in different ways.

Yes, I agree again. Science addresses human understanding by informing it via the observation and testing of human experience. Religion might also address human understanding, but in the same way that fiction does. Huckleberry Finn "cannot be investigated by science" because he is a fictional character. He is an idea. This does not make him less important to human understanding, but the fact that he may be important to human understanding does not make him any more real, either.

(I feel it important here to reiterate a point made earlier. The claim in the text above that supernatural entities "are not a part of nature" is *not* a belief that is shared by many religious people. Christians, after all, believe that God became a flesh-and-blood man, and many followers of the Abrahamic religions agree that God physically parted the Red Sea for Moses. Even a Hindu's belief in reincarnation is making claims about the reality of our physical world.)

Attempts to pit science and religion against each other create controversy where none needs to exist.

Once again, I agree. There should indeed be no controversy between science and religion. Science helps us understand reality and ourselves. Religion *might* help some of us express parts of our human experience, but *only* in the same way that art, fiction, or myth can. I ultimately believe that religion is essentially modern-day mythology. It cannot directly help us understand reality and the idea that some people may find value in its moral teachings does not make its claims about reality true. Simply put, science is to fact what religion is to fiction. The fact that some religions claim to be *the* path to "ultimate reality" make them especially dangerous.

All this said, there does appear to be a general softening of NOMA over the last two decades and I see this as an improvement, but I still disagree with even this softer version. My disagreement rests in large part on my previously noted understanding of science. I do not consider science to be so much an *aspect* of human experience, but rather the simple observation of it. Many do not see it this way. If you say the word "science" to some people, a mental image loops in their heads of *Star Trek*'s Spock, saying, "This is illogical." They see science as a "thing" that is cold and heartless and, therefore, inherently and diametrically opposed to the warm and fuzzy feelings they may get in a church pew.

NOMA: Beauty and Meaning

Science (as an experience of life) is anything but cold and heartless for me. My experience of life has been so varied; it has been amazing, painful, joyous, and beautiful. Understanding the reasons for the colors in a sunset does not make its beauty less awe-inspiring for me. I understand that many will not feel the same. For many, there is *bonus beauty* in the idea that this sunset was *placed* there just for them by a spiritual father or mother figure who is there to specifically look out for and nurture them. There may indeed be an evolutionary reason for that perceived additional beauty and feeling of being cared for, as children who were disposed to rely on their parents for nurture and care when young likely survived more frequently than children who may have left the cave at too early an age to attempt the dangers of the hunt on their own.

Before leaving NOMA, I want to quickly touch on "meaning," as NOMA seems to still put it in religion's wheelhouse. Religion is said to deal with the common "meaning of life" question. Instead of asking that question, however, one might do well to first ask the path-less-travelled version: "Why is meaning needed?" Or an even more honest question: "Is meaning needed?" These are fundamental philosophical questions that are scary for many to ask. Many fear death and the idea that their short existence may have no predetermined meaning. Religions typically provide pre-made answers for the "meaning" question, and this can make them quite attractive for some. I will discuss meaning in more detail in Part 4 of this book.

Addressing the Charges

I find it necessary in laying out the ground rules for an "atheist vs. theist" discussion that some of the key charges against atheists be clearly addressed and dismissed. I've already written extensively about the enormous image problem atheists face with many (if not most) theists. There would be limited value in repeating it here, but for my repeated experiences of people being unwilling (or unable) to separate charges against atheists from the discussion regarding whether God exists. Despite rules of logic, ad hominem attacks against atheists are somehow considered by many to be justification for theism. If we are going to use logic in this debate, such obvious logical fallacies must be checked at the debate door.

Even if I were to concede that every charge about atheists is true (which I certainly will not), this would still have no bearing on the truth claims made by theism. It is of vital importance that this point be understood. This said, given the near omnipresence of these allegations against atheists, I will now recap and respond to a few of the common charges.

Charge 1: Atheists Have No Morals

It's not difficult to find theists who feel that atheists are immoral. Within a few minutes of searching online I found an article with an accompanying picture of presumably Christian teens helping little old ladies across the street from a church. The pro-theism article conceded that there may be some atheists who act better than theists, but the clear inference is that this was likely the exception and not the rule. The author went on to essentially advise atheists to not be so arrogant and to show remorse for evil done when some "atheistic" regimes have held power.

The reference to evil atheistic regimes is a common talking point among some theists. It is notable that the article makes no mention of the 9/11 attacks, the Spanish Inquisition, the Crusades, IRA attacks in Ireland, and countless other wars or conflicts throughout history that are clearly motivated by religion. The counter from theists always seems to include Joseph Stalin (Soviet Union), Pol Pot (Cambodia), or Adolf Hitler (Germany), although claims of Hitler's atheism are frequently challenged. Ultimately, I see no value in a morbid "who-killed-the-most" contest. Obviously, atrocities were committed throughout history by the religious and irreligious alike. My main point here is that the religious have no standing to consider theistic belief as a moral differentiator. Immoral behavior under theocratic governments throughout history attests to this.

Moral Relativism

It's quite common for theists to claim that atheists have no "real" (aka, "absolute") morals because without defined rules regarding good and evil (presumably written in a centuries-old book), morality is a free-for-all and can only be described in terms relative to each individual's worldview. I've seen debates where a theist will spend significant time building to this point and then gleefully release it as an apparent mic drop moment. Perhaps I'm undercutting someone's Cloud 9, but claiming your debate opponent believes in moral relativism is not a mic drop moment. It is an empty point and basically an irrelevant argument.

Moral relativism is an obvious fact of life. To say that only atheists live in a world of relative morality is demonstrably false. Different theistic groups clearly have different understandings of what constitutes moral action. For example, one theist thinks it's important to protect groups such as homosexuals from ridicule or assault, while another theist believes it's important to throw these people off rooftops. Both are theists, yet their relative interpretations of morality are startlingly different.

Many theists will claim that religious teachings are the basis for what they consider to be good morality. Thankfully, however, despite these many claims, it appears that most theists actually hold a morality separate from religious teachings altogether. This independent morality decides which teachings to focus on and which to gloss over or ignore. If this were not the case, many in the Abrahamic religious traditions would likely still find it acceptable for a person to be killed because she was found working on the Sabbath. The *Good News Translation* of Exodus 31:14 reads as follows:

> *"You must keep the day of rest, because it is sacred. Whoever does not keep it, but works on that day, is to be put to death."*

If this is the "good news" translation, I'd hate to see the "bad news" version (cue punchline drumbeat). Thankfully — at least in many places in the world — I need not fear being hacked to death for mowing my lawn on a Sunday afternoon. Many Christians will argue that Old Testament verses such as this are outdated because Jesus came and his sacrifice somehow released us from the "old laws." To them, I'd only ask, "So if Jesus didn't come yet, would you kill your neighbor for working on the Sabbath?" I hope very much that the answer to that would be "no."

Theistic "Bad Morality"

The reality is that there are still plenty of theists who would approve something heinous because the supposed "absolute morality" in some religious text demanded it. This is evident in the uncomfortable poll results cited by Sam Harris in a 2017 episode of HBO's "Real Time with Bill Maher," in which he infamously got into an argument with actor Ben Affleck while discussing the results of a 2013 Pew Research Center survey taken in majority-Muslim countries. The percentage of Muslims polled who agreed that death (actual physical death; not some metaphorical death) was the appropriate punishment for people who left the Muslim faith was far from zero, and therefore horrifying.

Andrea Yates was a Texas woman who drowned her five children in 2001 because she thought God told her to do so. Although she was ultimately found not guilty by reason of insanity, it is worthwhile to note that Abraham — the (likely mythical) figure given credit for being the earthly starting point for Judaism, Christianity, and Islam — is said to have planned to kill his son Isaac because he believed God had told him to do so. Nearly as disturbing, however, is the eager willingness with which many followers gloss over the story of Abraham and Isaac as a simple lesson to be loyal to God. There is no discussion of Abraham being clinically insane. In fact, God rewarded Abraham for his willingness to murder his own son. I recall being in church on a Sunday hearing this read aloud and it finally clicking for me. *"What a sick notion!"* I thought. *"Either this guy had major mental issues or God is one sadistic creature, or both."* As I understand it, the Muslim holiday of Eid'l Adha specifically celebrates this story, although Isaac is replaced with a different son in the Muslim version of the story.

I give these examples to show that there are people who will blindly follow religious teaching as "absolutely moral," even if some of those teachings strike most of us as heinous. In these cases, theists clearly lose the supposed moral high ground that they claim to have. Such a claim is of course based on my own personal understanding of morality, but I like to think that most people would agree that setting to kill an innocent child is a terrible thing. Is it an "objectively" terrible thing? Well, no — it's obviously not objectively terrible for *everyone* or the Abraham story would not be celebrated as it is. Thankfully, enough people share my assessment that such an action is morally wrong that laws are written to protect against it.

Defending God; Defending "Bad Morality"

I also need to address those who, while reading this, might feel offended. I basically just said that a God who would demand that someone prepare to murder his own child is a God that I find dreadfully evil. You'd think that such an opinion would be universally agreed upon, but I can recall a time in my life when I would have felt the need to defend God against such allegations. One might reasonably question why an all-powerful ruler would need a bag of carbon water like me rushing to his defense. It makes you wonder what exactly is being defended anyway, but I digress — for the time being at least.

There is a comfortable "his ways are not our ways" knee-jerk reaction that some theist readers may have to defend what most would consider indefensible. I expect so because I vaguely recall leaning on such a crutch. "God works in mysterious ways" is another one that comes to mind.

Imagine someone murders a man in the middle of the day in front of the man's family and a thousand other witnesses. The murder was captured on video, the victim's blood is all over the murderer, and the murderer's fingerprints and DNA are all over the weapon and the victim. Now imagine a defense in court for the killer: *"No, I am not pleading insanity. I actually loved this man, and I was doing something nice for him. What? You don't understand how my killing him was a good thing? Well, I work in mysterious ways. My ways are not your ways. You simply don't understand."*

What juror would accept such nonsense? Yet, this is essentially what is being done. God has an infinite number of free passes to do whatever the hell he wants for whatever reason. If this is your belief, I ask that you please recognize this and snap out of it. This may be difficult to realize about yourself at first, but it should become easier if you come to the same conclusion that I did — that God is likely fiction in the first place.

Theistic "Middle-Ground" Morality

In discussions about theism and atheism, it's quite common to go to the extremes. I've already discussed the murdering of children as one extreme. Various murderous regimes were also discussed. These extremes are used to make a point. Once a point is made related to an extreme condition, parameters are thought to be set based on those foundational points. But what of "middle-ground" morality?

I think most would agree that it is more immoral to kill a gay person for being gay than to openly protest homosexuality at the gay person's funeral (such as has been done frequently by members of the Westboro Baptist Church). I find such protests abhorrent, but relatively speaking, I'd take them over murder. So, in these circumstances, one might say it's their right to protest and at least they're not being violent. One might even conjecture that perhaps they're trying to use tough love to shock the gay-supporting funeral-goers back onto a "righteous path." But this, too, I argue, is preaching a "morality" that many would not have if they weren't raised in a religion that claims homosexuality is unnatural. An objective study of nature shows that it's quite natural in the animal world, and humans aren't an exception.

Fortunately, Westboro Baptist Church protests are considered extreme by many Christians. Perhaps this is not the best "middle-ground" example. Let's stay with the gay theme, though, because it's an easy example, but let's use a more common scenario: a co-worker in her early 20s confides in you that she's gay and is terrified to tell her abusive father.

What is the moral thing to do? For me, it would be to support this woman and let her know that people love her as she is, that homosexuality is natural, and that I'll help her find a support group that could better assist her with dealing with these emotions. I would see that as the kind thing to do (at minimum).

What might a Christian fundamentalist like former U.S. Vice President Mike Pence do in this case? Perhaps he would also aim to support this woman. He might tell her that God still loves her and that homosexuality is an abnormality likely sent by the devil to test her faith in God. He might immediately pray over her and find her a Christian conversion "support group" to help her with her "affliction." He would also likely see his actions as consistent with moral behavior.

So, what's the difference? Both Mike Pence and I may believe we are acting out of kindness, and we both may even feel true compassion for the young woman. The main difference is that the Christian fundamentalist perspective is based on religious teachings with an eye towards a likely fictitious "afterlife," while my approach is based on an objective understanding of nature with a focus on what's best for the woman in *this* life.

This is a perfect example of how morality is entwined with belief in God. Religious morality is typically based on an afterlife. Numerous stickers on car or truck windows in the United States tell the story. Jesus is "NOTW (Not of This World)." The focus is nearly always on making the cut to the next life. If Pence is focused on the next life and truly believes homosexuality may prevent admittance to it, it's understandable that he would consider recommendations for conversion therapy to be the kind way to go. The importance of this cannot be overstated.

To any religious people who still might be reading this book, please understand that atheists as a group are not immoral. Many of us simply make ethical decisions based on what we think is good for people in *this* life because we do not believe in the heaven/hell afterlife as presented to us by religion. As I discuss later, there is good reason to be skeptical of such religious beliefs.

Lastly, it's important to reiterate that most theists are not throwing gay people off roofs or protesting at a gay person's funeral. But the focus on meeting religious requirements as the moral basis to enter the afterlife is the same. I believe most theists are melding their own morality with the morality dictated by their specific religion, resulting in a hybrid morality. How each person chooses to interpret religious teaching is key.

What Guides Interpretation?

There are clearly many people who chose to interpret religious text as fully true in every way possible. Ken Ham, founder of the Christian Fundamentalist group Answers in Genesis and the Creation Museum in Petersburg, Kentucky, argues for a literal interpretation of the Bible. Case in point, his group took great pains to literally interpret biblical text to build a full-size, accurate "replica" of Noah's Ark as a tourist attraction.

But, increasingly, readers of religious text recognize conflicts between the text and their life experience. They appear more open to viewing some of the events in the text as metaphor. Numerous religious people, for example, no longer refute evolution. Others take Moses' parting of the Red Sea as a story about God's willingness to take care of *His People*, as opposed to Moses calling upon God to install a magical, invisible temporary dam.

Likewise, many people are more open to different interpretations of religious teachings. As a former Catholic, I know that fasting rules for Lent have changed over time. At one point, you were supposed to undertake a rather severe fast on Fridays, but this eventually changed to not eating meat (other than fish) on Fridays. By the time I became an adult, I had sat through homilies teaching, *"Yeah, maybe don't eat that hamburger, but God doesn't really care too much about that. God doesn't so much want you to give something up for Lent, as he'd prefer you do something nice for Lent."*

So how did we go from imposing harsh fasting requirements to "do something nice for someone"? What is causing the shift in how religious texts are interpreted? It's clear that there is a decision-making process *outside* of the religious text that allows one to choose how to interpret that text. This outside process is evidence of a personal morality *separate* from the religion. Fortunately, as stated earlier, most religious people do not stone their neighbor on the Sabbath because the Bible tells them to.

**

In summary, morality need not be tied to religion, and luckily, for many (if not most) religious people, it's not. Religious text is simply a canvas on which one can paint her own morality via brushes of interpretation. If you are a kind person, you will likely focus on the kinder passages. If you are not, you may instead focus on passages about retribution. The whole idea of absolute morality from a holy book goes by the wayside. Some Bible verses are OK, and some are not. How is that decision made if not by a morality independent of religion and religious dogma? We each have our own moral compass. Whether we acknowledge this and whether we let the compass guide us depends on the person.

Again, though, please don't confuse what I'm saying here. There are indeed people who will keep their compass in their pocket and allow their view of right-and-wrong to be dictated by religious teaching. I've known many good religious people, and thankfully I don't think any of them would support stoning their neighbor over religious differences. But I also don't want to gloss over some of my real concerns. It's my hope that those who follow all religious dictates without question are few and that they decrease in number, and that those who follow the "softer" religious dictates without question begin to question.

I hope this section has convinced you that arguments for inherent immorality in atheism are false. Good theists simply happen to believe things that I do not. I see them as good people independent of those beliefs, not because of them. Good atheists simply happen to share some of my views. I see them as good people independent of our shared nonbelief, not because of it. It is my hope that theists can come to view atheists as standing on equal moral ground. Throughout human history, attempts have been made to lock morality into the confines of religious dictates and superstitions. This writing hopefully does a small part to help break it free from this jail.

Charge 2: Atheists Have No Purpose

Underlying much of the "atheists have no morals" charge is the idea that atheists have no morals *because*:

> *(a) when you do not believe in an afterlife to strive for where you meet your creator,*
>
> *(b) this life becomes unnecessary as a means to prepare for an afterlife; and therefore,*
>
> *(c) this life has no real purpose or meaning at all because*
>
> *(d) you just live and die and that's it.*

This is the root of nearly all "atheists have no purpose" arguments. There is much fault in this reasoning, and I aim to refute it here.

Conflating God and Purpose

As a husband and a father of two, I frequently wonder if I'm doing my best in my relationships with my wife and our boys. In my free time, I'll often wander through self-improvement-type websites. I came across one the other day that listed 10 goals for dads.

Goals 1 through 9 were predictable, seize-the-day-type goals, and ones that I certainly support. They included being financially secure and physically fit. Goal 10, however, was different. It argued that I needed to develop my faith in God, and if I did not do this, any progress made on Goals 1 through 9 was meaningless. All was meaningless if there is nothing "greater than" me.

I found this to be a good example of how people conflate the idea of purpose with the idea of a creator God. The unmistakable inference in Goal 10 was that the greater purpose is, and must be, God.

As I'll discuss later, I find deep purpose in my life and I am also an atheist. I am first-hand proof that you can have purpose without believing in God. The comedian Ricky Gervais has a quote that is appropriate here: *"It's a strange myth that atheists have nothing to live for. It's the opposite. We have nothing to die for. We have everything to live for.*"

I don't agree that atheists (inherently) have nothing to die for, but the general idea of an atheist's ability to treasure life is something I experience daily.

Purpose at Any Cost?

This is a good time to bring up what I consider to be an obvious question, but one I feel I must ask because many do not: Will *any* purpose do?

Aside from being incorrect, the claim that "atheists can have no purpose or meaning for their lives" infers that purpose is a necessity and that atheism fails because it does not have a well-defined, step-by-step guide towards purpose. But is purpose truly a *necessity*? Is it a goal in and of itself? What if a person's purpose is to become the most ruthless serial killer in history? I'd hope that most people would agree it would be far better for that person to have no purpose than *that* purpose. Having a purpose clearly does not inherently imply "good morality."

I moved to San Diego in the summer of 1997, just months after the 39 bodies of Heaven's Gate cult members were found in an affluent San Diego suburb. Led by Marshall Applewhite, these people felt that their purpose was to commit mass suicide in order to free their souls to take a trip on a UFO that they believed was following Haley's Comet. As police found no signs of struggle, this was a purpose they each apparently believed in. This certainly was a group of people with purpose, but I see no reason to hold this purpose high as a model for others to follow.

Optimistic Nihilism

I had a brief writer's high when the term "optimistic nihilism" flashed in my head. Nothing would be better, I thought, than coining a new and meaningful phrase in my first real attempt at a book. After a quick search online, though, I learned I was too late to that party, as the term was used at least as early as 2017. Given that this book has been a multi-year effort starting in early 2015, this is a bit painful as perhaps I could have coined it if I had been more diligent with my writing earlier on. I still do like the term, though, and there is a comfort in seeing that there are others sharing these same thoughts with me. Still, I am tempted to find some hairs to split and then coin "hopeful nihilism," "meaningful nihilism," "purpose-driven nihilism," or some other seeming oxymoron.

Nihilism is "the rejection of all religious and moral principles, often in the belief that life is meaningless." The root of the word is both Latin with "nihil" meaning "nothing" and English with "-ism" being a suffix "denoting a state or quality." So at its root, nihilism can be interpreted to mean "the state of nothingness." This state might refer to nothingness with regards to existence itself, implying that existence is a mirage. More commonly in the atheist vs. theist discussion, however, it tends to refer to the "nothingness" of moral absolutes, which we covered when we discussed moral relativism.

Optimistic means "hopeful and confident about the future." Combining the terms "optimistic" and "nihilism," therefore, can mean a "hopeful state of (moral) nothingness." Put differently, it acknowledges that there may not be an "absolute" morality that is commonly accepted, but it is hopeful that some perceived "good" morality may at some point win out over humanity. At the very least, it's the individual's decision to allow it to win out. It essentially minimizes the likelihood of an *objective* moral purpose while opening eyes to the immense opportunity for a *personal* moral purpose to take seed in life experience and flourish.

I appreciate that optimistic nihilism is honest with the potential predicament we find ourselves in — that there is likely no objectively true, absolute morality or purpose. Frank honesty like this can be hard to come by nowadays. This philosophy does not sugarcoat anything. It does not force our perceived experience of what is true through rose-tinted glasses. Instead, it accepts our predicament and highlights those things that may still be in our control as we live our short lives on this tiny ball in a vast universe.

Now to provide some additional background to "atheists have no purpose," let's look into how the perceived need for "purpose" originated in the first place.

Evolution of Purpose

It makes sense that our sometimes-frenzied seeking of an "objective purpose" may simply be the result of our brain's limited ability to understand the world as we evolved. I will periodically check various "atheists vs. theists" debate groups on social media and, as you might expect from any anonymous debate forum, the quality of conversation is not always top-shelf. That said, someone asked a question the other day: *"What came first, atheism or theism?"* Simple as it was, the question did force me to think.

Atheism must have come first. As we evolved, we needed to make sense of the world around us in order to survive. Atheism would be the natural state for most evolving animals because the most rudimentary concept of a "God" required for theism would likely have been beyond our initial ability to imagine. Our survival as a species in large part depended on our brain's ability to develop as a pattern-seeking machine. If we did not evolve to see the pattern that a quickly moving shadow in the brush could mean danger, our species would likely not have survived. If we did not see the pattern that striking flint rocks together over dry brush could lead to sparks and a fire, our species would likely not have survived. This development of our pattern-seeking capabilities was essential to our continued intellectual development.

As our brains became more capable of self-reflection and of asking abstract questions, we still sought patterns. It is hard-wired in our coding from these earlier successes. Once we started applying the cause-and-effect pattern recognition to more abstract ideas, we started to theorize that because the sun rises every day and goes down at night, there must be some being that moves the sun across the sky. Likewise, there must be some being that throws terrifying lighting and screams thunder. You can see how the cause-effect theorizing can accelerate and build upon itself.

1. "There is very scary lighting and thunder that I don't understand." *What caused this?*

   "There must be a powerful being creating this."

2. "This very powerful being is scaring us with this lighting." *What caused this?*

   "It must be angry."

3. "This powerful being is angry." *What caused this?*

   "Perhaps we did something to make it angry."

4. "We want this being to have its anger pacified." *What could cause this desired effect?*

   "Perhaps we should continually honor it in every way possible so that it is not mad at us."

5. "We want this powerful being to feel continually honored." *What could cause this desired effect?*

   "We must make it our clear *purpose in life* to worship this being continually. Our survival literally depends upon it."

A cause-effect chain such as this is rather likely in my view. It shows that the whole perceived need for a theistic purpose may have evolved from our brain's limited ability to understand nature and abstract ideas in the first place.

Charge 3: Atheists Have No Humility

I've always found the charge that atheists are inherently arrogant to be interesting and telling. To be fair, many theists, when pushed, will begrudgingly concede, "Well, OK, not *all* atheists," but the inference is abundantly clear. Atheists are perceived by many theists as being more arrogant than their theistic counterparts.

First, let me be clear how I feel about this topic. Generally speaking, I believe that people tend to be fundamentally arrogant or fundamentally humble, wholly independent of whether they believe in a god. That must be said clearly and loudly. There are countless examples of both arrogant and humble atheists and theists. I will concede that the theistic and atheistic perspectives discussed in this section can be strawman arguments, but they are not so in every case. There are many people who ascribe to these views, so it's important that they are stated and considered. There are of course many variations on the spectrum, and I for one do not doubt the humility of many good theistic people.

Perspectives of Theism

Argument for Theistic Humility

While being raised to be a good Catholic, I learned the Hail Mary and how Mary (Jesus' mother) confessed her joy to be a simple "handmaiden of the Lord." There seems to be a collective admiration of the humility associated with this handmaiden image of Mary, even among Protestants and Muslims. My best friends growing up were sons of a Protestant minister and I became part of their church's youth group. I saw firsthand how Protestants deeply respected Mary's "handmaiden humility." In fact, it was the only time I ever saw Mary propped up as an example for anything by Protestants. I also understand that some Muslim women wear a hijab in part to emulate the humility of the Virgin Mary (as she is often depicted in art with a head-covering).

Clearly, humility is a trait that is prized among many theists. Some will take it further, though, arguing that humility is in fact *inherent* in theism. After all, God is the Almighty Creator. He made the dust and breathed His Life into it to create us. Without Him, we are just dust and dust cannot be proud. Theists recognize this subservient position to God. As the song goes, they *"humble thyselves in the sight of the Lord."*

Listen to any evangelical preacher's sermon and you will soon hear that we are just lowly sinners without God's grace. Without God's grace, we are a *dirty wet rag in the gutter.* Even lower, *we are a wet, mildewed, and torn rag in the earth below the gutter.* Even more, *this rag is soiled by thousands of defecating maggots, each with some terrible maggot diarrhea disease.* Having had years of exposure to the stereotypical "Catholic guilt," I believe I could continue along this line of thinking for some time, but I will spare us, as I believe my point is made. Many theists believe that we are worthless — and, therefore, necessarily humble — before God.

Argument for Theistic Arrogance

My wife and I were on our honeymoon, touring the ruins of the Mayan port city, Tulum, in Mexico in the spring of 2002. The tour guide eloquently described humanity's incredible loss with the near destruction of the Maya people during the Spanish conquest. I loved how he knew the stories associated with the many carvings among the ruins. He told us the Maya creation story and how they believed that the first people originated from corn, a dietary staple in the region.

"We came from *corn*? That is ridiculous!" The loud voice was from an older Caucasian man on the tour. His accent sounded Texan. While I processed how shockingly rude he seemed, the tour guide didn't miss a beat.

> Guide: *"Do you have a creation story that you believe sir?"*
> Man: *"Yes, I do. I am a Christian, so I believe the Bible."*
> Guide: *"OK, so you believe we came from dust?"*
> Man: *"Yes... I...."*
> Guide: *"... and not corn?"*

The man nodded yes, but it was a slow nod, and my hope at the time was that he was understanding the guide's point. I remember thinking that at least corn gave us nourishment.

Although this man may have considered himself "humbled in the sight of the Lord," he clearly did not act humbly in relation to the guide who expressed a different belief. The self-righteousness in the man's voice was unmistakable: "*Corn?* Ha!" By definition, an arrogant person deems himself to be "superior." This "humble" Christian was clearly displaying arrogance.

Now, Christian apologists may simply argue that the man wasn't being arrogant, he was just being right. This, of course, is the same argument that some atheists may make when told they are arrogant. It again comes down to whether you believe your beliefs are "correct." And of course you do; why else would you believe them? (Let's hold onto that question for later in the book, as it's not intended to be a rhetorical question.)

Christianity's claimed focus on humility can lead Christians to believe their religion is humbler than other religions. As humility is typically deemed a good thing, this ironically has the practical effect of giving Christians another reason to view their religion as superior.

Extending this thinking, it's clear to see how "humble theism" claims superiority over "arrogant atheism." "*My God has chosen me.*" "*I heard God's voice.*" "*What? You haven't heard God's voice yet? Perhaps you are too arrogant, and you therefore are not capable of hearing it.*" See Part 1 for all the connotations associated with those who do not "hear" God's voice.

I can understand that theists view themselves as humble before an almighty God, but since I see this God as likely fictitious, that humility means much less to me. I care about humility and respect between people.

As a quick aside, I recommend that readers search online for "Kenneth Copeland, Jesse Duplantis, defending their private jets." These two televangelists spend several minutes discussing how their work is so important that they need private jets. They would have done well to end it there, but instead they argue that they cannot be *agitated* by sharing a plane with the "dope-filled world" or be in a "long tube with a bunch of *demons*." Call me naïve, but I'd think that this would strike many as a bit arrogant, to say the least.

Perspectives of Atheism

Argument for Atheistic Arrogance

The theistic argument that atheists are arrogant seems to stem from the fact that atheists don't have a God before whom to humble themselves.

Some theists will argue that atheists see themselves as "gods." In fairness, "I am my own god" is indeed a phrase I have seen in some atheistic circles online. But while theists may interpret this as atheists assuming the "throne of the Almighty," it is clear to me that atheists who use that terminology do so to convey simply that they see themselves as the masters of their own decisions, without feeling the need to follow some guidebook.

Interestingly, there are similarities here with theists who believe God has given them free will, which I expect is most theists. God allows them to make their own path. The difference is that theists believe they will be judged on how closely their path stays within the boundaries of the pathway prescribed by religious teachings.

This is an important distinction. Both atheists and theists make decisions based on what they think is the best way to live their lives. Period, end of sentence. Arrogance has nothing to do with it. Humility has nothing to do with it. The only difference is that some folks believe there is a guidebook authored by an all-powerful creator. So again, it is not a question of arrogance or humility. It is a question of belief or nonbelief.

Atheism and Intelligence

Recent studies show a negative correlation between religiosity and intelligence, and a reasonable conclusion, therefore, is that atheists tend to be smarter than theists. Although there have been attempts by theists to contest or qualify these studies, I've seen nothing that directly undermines them. This correlation, understandably, makes some theists uncomfortable. Who, after all, is eager to agree with a study that questions their own intelligence? A common defense is to consider the other (more intelligent, and usually more educated) group as condescending and therefore arrogant. It is a means to hit back.

If someone "crosses you over" (a basketball term for luring a defender one way and then dribbling past her the other way) on the basketball court, you might feel foolish and embarrassed. If you are a mature person, though, you respect the other player for the great move, pick yourself up, and watch the other person like a hawk to learn what made her so good on the court. If you're not a mature person, you may claim that you were fouled or that the other player cheated.

When possible, some people proactively try to avoid embarrassment. Keeping with the basketball theme, it's been customary for winning sports teams to meet with the president for a ceremony at the White House. When the Golden State Warriors won the NBA championship in 2018, several players spoke openly about their dislike of President Trump. Trump decided to purposely *not* invite them to the White House to avoid embarrassment in the event the team declined the invitation. It was Trump proclaiming that he was not interested in asking the homecoming queen to the prom because he knew darn well what the answer would have been.

Similarly, some theists use comparable measures to "proactively" hit-back. Atheists are frequently lumped in as the "politically elite," the "educated elite," or simply as "elitist." I believe this name-calling is frequently a knee-jerk reaction for people who might not feel comfortable with their own educational standing.

Some folks have such low self-esteem that they, by default, view people who are more educated as being arrogant or condescending. Instead of recognizing *"I know about topics a, b, and c, but maybe I don't know that much about topics x, y, or z,"* or *"Maybe I was not able to go to school to learn certain things, so it makes sense that there will be certain things that I do not know,"* the response, instead, is, *"Who do these fancy people think they are acting like they know all these things? Just because I might not be book-educated, I know plenty, and I have street smarts."* In truth, there are plenty of arrogant educated people, but the reverse is true as well.

Being arrogant does not equate to being incorrect. I could be the most condescending jerk in human history, but this still would have no bearing on whether I'm right or wrong on an issue. The rightness or wrongness would be based on a reasonable assessment of demonstrated facts. It may very well be that many atheists do consider themselves generally smarter than most theists. As just discussed, there is evidence that supports that assumption. As a former theist and a current atheist, I'm often amazed that some people still believe what they believe. Does that make me a "liberal elite" or an arrogant person? I don't think so. I think it just makes me someone with an opinion.

Argument for Atheistic Humility

I think I'm a fairly good example of atheistic humility. I recognize such an assertion may seem paradoxical, but the truth is I don't think I am very different from the average atheist in this regard. While theists might feel the need to "humble themselves in the sight of the Lord," I believe most atheists are humbled by nature or even existence itself. Physically speaking, I am a carbon-based bag of water like everyone else and that certainly is humbling. That I am a carbon-based bag of water that can feel awe is even more humbling.

I am writing this in the afternoon of Christmas Eve day in 2018 in Lake Arrowhead, California, watching the sun sparkle off the pine needles on the 50-foot-tall trees above me. The briskness in the air and the silence of the birds are both invigorating. It's just one more opportunity to take a moment and let it sink in — that I am alive. The fact that we are here (or we at least "appear" to be here, but that is for another discussion) is astonishing. So many things needed to happen perfectly for us to exist, from Jupiter's gravity protecting Earth from the brunt of asteroid hits, to the fact that it did not protect us from the one asteroid that killed the dinosaurs and allowed mammals to thrive and evolve. It truly is amazing.

In short, awe — even transcendent awe that lifts us to bliss — in no way requires belief in a creator. I have experienced this humbling awe as both a theist and an atheist. The mere recognition of existence is enough. We are tiny specks of dust on a speck of dust floating in an infinite universe. That is incredibly humbling. Yet, we are aware of ourselves and that we truly are part of the universe. In fact, we *are* the universe discovering itself. This last thought is emotionally invigorating and provides a sense of even greater awe and humility. How fortunate we are to be alive and how incredible it is to know it. I can take no credit for the evolution that led to me, but I am grateful for it.

Charge 4: No One to Thank

My gratitude for existing is perhaps a perfect lead-in to this next "charge" against atheists. In truth, though, it's much less a charge as it is an apparent means to pity them.

As I mentioned in the introduction, I went to a Catholic university and I was actively involved in campus ministry activities. During this period, I had what many religious people would call a pretty significant test of faith. I was pained by cracks in my faith and thoughts about them took up significant headspace for some time. I attended prayer groups and talked with many people about it.

During this period, I was exposed to the following G.K. Chesterton quotation:

> *"The worst moment for the atheist is when he is really thankful and has nobody to thank."*

I recall exactly where I was on campus when this quote popped into my head. The beautiful, tree-covered trail, often frequented by squirrels and birds, was one of my favorite parts of the walk back from class to my dorm on the southern part of the campus. I remember that it was a nice day and that I did, indeed, feel thankful. At that moment, the quote was seemingly enough to reinforce my theism. After all, how could someone be thankful if there was no God to thank?

I currently see this quote as completely irrelevant to the existence-of-God debate, so I'm somewhat surprised that it shored up my theism at all. I think the difficulty of testing my faith was taking a toll on me at that time and this quote (and others) gave me a nice mental break from the doubt. It was comfortable and peaceful to just be thankful for my life and my default was thanking God.

As an atheist today, I am thankful all the time for many things. I just don't necessarily have a specific recipient of my gratitude. This is a non-issue for me. "Thankful" is defined as "pleased or relieved." It doesn't require an object or being as its focus. I may simply be thankful for a circumstance. I see a parallel with the "humility" discussion earlier. Just as I need not be humble *before God* in order to be humble, I need not be thankful *to God* in order to be thankful. Some theists may claim to have a monopoly on humility, but no such monopoly exists. The same can be said for thankfulness.

My Conversion

Now that we've covered some ground rules for an honest theism vs. atheism discussion, it makes sense to now go through the thoughts and arguments that led to my conversion. I am 45 years old as I write this. I was around 40 when I recognized I was an atheist, so this change was not that long ago. That said, it also was not yesterday and the precise order of thoughts that got me over the hump would be difficult to pinpoint. As I'll discuss later, my struggle to accept my atheism was emotionally taxing and it took some time. The underlying arguments for atheism itself though were clear and they made so much sense to me that I rather quickly found them convincing once I was fully open to them. This chapter attempts to capture some of these major revelations.

"Standing Up in the Cosmos"

If memory serves, we started our Netflix subscription in 2010. With my movie-watching hobby no longer tethered to a DVD or Blue Ray, other streaming services soon followed. This big bang explosion of on-demand video options not only provided entertainment, but also made viewing recommendations based on an algorithm-based assessment of my likely preferences. Many of these recommendations were scientific documentaries, often addressing some of the deep and existential questions of the universe. I inhaled these documentaries and was spurred to find more. These shows stirred a wonder in me. My awe at the incredible vastness of the universe was awakened and further imprinted in me, even if true understanding was always just beyond my reach.

If you have not done this before, I recommend that you go online and search for "size of universe video." There is no shortage of mind-blowing videos that test our ability to comprehend the scale of infinity. The earth is a dot in the solar system. The solar system is a dot in our galaxy. Our galaxy is a dot in our galaxy cluster. Our galaxy cluster is a dot in the universe, which itself may be a dot in a multiverse. One can't help but see the photos looking outward at the universe on a macro-scale and see similarities with the photos that look inward at our cells or atoms on a micro-scale. I have not taken hallucinogenic drugs, but I imagine that some of these seemingly transcendental thoughts are akin to observations while high. Space folds upon itself, into itself, out of itself. Scale is its own dimension. The immensity of infinity awes.

Carl Sagan launched the TV series *Cosmos* in 1980 and its update with Neil deGrasse Tyson appeared in 2014. Both were outstanding at fostering this wonder and awe. The phrase "standing up in the cosmos" comes from this series. Sagan's poem "The Pale Blue Dot" is especially effective in portraying our own fragility and the delicate nature of our little place in the universe. The "standing up in the cosmos" theme in the series is an honest acknowledgement that although we are indeed floating on a small ball in space, we are still alive, and we can stand up and look around us and marvel at this life. We can do this without having to sacrifice or suspend our reasoning and cognitive abilities.

Once in this mindset, the idea of a creator God who purposefully made this planet so he could populate it with beings specifically made in his image becomes suspect. For me, it started to seem incredibly unlikely and eventually ridiculous. The geocentric model of the universe had been kicked to the curb by Copernicus in 1543. Everything did not revolve around the Earth, but the Earth itself revolved around the sun. The Earth, therefore, was not even the center of its own neighborhood.

If the creator of the universe was truly looking to find a spot to house his most special creations, you'd think he would have chosen a more prominent piece of real estate. I'm envisioning a *huge* planet in the exact center of the universe that would have all stars and planets circle around it. Brush aside the incorrect belief in a flat earth, and such a vision is essentially what most people imagined prior to Copernicus. This is understandable, as it fit what they already believed at the time and challenging what you believe (or were told to believe) wasn't in fashion.

New Geocentric "Arguments"

This is not to say that some people aren't still trying to make a geocentric model work. Unbelievably, there appears to be an increase in conspiracy theorists who question the sphere-like nature of Earth. These flat-earthers got a notable boost from basketball player Kyrie Irving in 2017 when he went public with his doubts about a round Earth. He (sort of) walked his comments back in 2018, but it was too late to prevent some people from basking in their purposeful ignorance all over the internet.

I was back on the East Coast with family about this time when a particularly religious family member and I got into a discussion. He was aware by then of my atheism and he would periodically strike up a conversation about it. I believe we had stumbled on my awe of the immensity of the universe and he responded that "science now shows the Earth *is* in the center of the universe." He went on to say that he didn't totally follow it all (an important admission), but that scientists had determined that the Earth was the center crossing point of detected natural radio waves in the universe and therefore, to him, this meant the Earth was the universe's center.

This sounded ridiculous, but I figured it made sense to research it. In case you were wondering, here is a summary of my findings:

1. Scientists sent out three satellites over a multi-year period to detect and monitor cosmic waves in the universe. Each subsequent satellite had improved technology.

2. In 2013, partial results of a combination of data from the three satellites seemed to indicate that the Milky Way and

other galaxies may be aligned on the same plane. This plane has been referred to (tongue-in-cheek) as the astronomical "axis of evil."

3. Jumping headfirst through giant holes in logic, some people chose to go further and interpret this to mean that the Earth was indeed the center of the universe. This was not helped when a "documentary" film took a quote by famed physicist Lawrence Krauss out of context, making it seem as though Krauss somehow gave credence to the geocentric universe concept. Krauss has actively attacked those who've misused his words.

4. Remaining analysis of the sample data was published in 2016. This more complete picture strongly refuted the initial claims made by people who reviewed the partial data.

In short, the whole "axis-of-evil"/geocentric argument rests on a weak hypothesis based on incomplete data and a quote from a scientist that was taken so fully out of context as to imply the exact opposite of what was intended.

So, what do you do when the dots don't connect and the authority in your appeal to authority disowns your argument? If you're a conspiracy theorist who doesn't care that your position has a near-zero chance of being true, you apparently just continue with the propaganda. Despite the latest evidence, you can still go online and find this stuff preached as if it were a sacred, revealed truth.

Earlier in the book, we talked about NOMA (non-overlapping magisteria) and how people claim there should be a dividing line between the "mystical" and the "scientific." This is another great example of how easily some people trample that line if they think science supports their beliefs. Once the scientific record is clarified and their beliefs are shown to be wrong, many of these folks quickly hop back over the line. Others, like the continued purveyors of this geocentric theory, simply pick and choose their facts and don't care what side of the line they're on.

God vs. the Universe

While some people disregard scientific consensus when it suits them, many theists simply adapt their post-Copernicus worldview so that God still has a place. A frequent argument is God made the conditions of the universe just right so that we could exist in it. These folks, however, conveniently do not discuss how drastically inept we are at surviving in the universe outside of our own little bubble.

We take a small trip out of the Earth's driveway into the cul-de-sac of the earth's own orbit and, if exposed, we suffocate, burn, freeze, or even slowly explode due to pressure differentials. If God created a universe just for us, why not make it so we could more easily travel throughout it? Instead, we appear to be suited for this single planet alone. Scientists who understand the evidence for Darwin's arguments would conclude that this, of course, is the case.

Recognizing our small and seemingly insignificant place in an infinite universe is powerful. It was powerful enough to almost completely shake me from the theistic belief system I had nodded along with for decades. My paradigm shifted completely. New thoughts came to me that highlighted the conflicts in my head. *Why would God choose just this one planet? Was God a cosmic farmer spreading his seed on different planets to see which would take root? Are there other planets — potentially billions — where God created other beings in "his image"? Are there billions of prophets preaching in billions of otherworldly deserts? Perhaps there are billions of Gardens of Eden, maybe even some with the apple remaining unbitten?*

After some time with these thoughts, I noticed that this all started to sound less like something real and more like fiction, perhaps a good *Star Trek* episode. Arguments for a God who specifically looked after this little speck of dust in space with intense interest began to seem like a fairy tale — a feel-good story. Recognizing the unlikeliness of a personal God in the face of this immense universe was one side of the sword that did me in as a theist. The other side was an intellectually honest review of my own religion and the likely influences in its development. For this, I needed to turn even further inward.

Leery of Evolution

It was a slap in the face to recognize that God as a philosophical concept no longer made sense to me. Realizing that the Jesus I loved and relied on for so much of my life might not be as advertised, however, was much more of a gut-punch. My "breakup" with Jesus was difficult for personal and complicated reasons that I will discuss more in Part 3. In this section, I'm focusing on the head as opposed to the heart and things I learned that helped me look at the figure of Jesus more objectively than I had before.

**

A 2019 Pew Research study reported that 18 percent of the roughly 325 million people in the United States believe that humans did not evolve, but rather have existed in our present form from the beginning of the Earth's existence. This represents ~ 60 million people in the U.S. alone who reject human evolution as a reality. The same study found that certain Latin American countries and some highly populated, predominately Muslim countries reject human evolution at even higher rates.

I bring this up to show that although Darwin's theory of evolution is now considered as close to fact as many scientists will allow themselves to get, it is not a foregone conclusion that acceptance of Darwin will eventually take hold everywhere. And with so many people still not accepting the evolution of physical life, it is a tall order to expect that these same people will acknowledge that ideas evolve over time as well.

As I absorbed more arguments for and against theism, the idea that religions themselves evolve and adapt became so thick in the air that I could not see beyond it. I had long known that certain Christian holidays (such as Christmas and Easter) were influenced by pagan beliefs, but the idea that the core teachings of Christianity themselves may not be unique was new to me, and it scared me to consider it.

The Evolution of Religions

In 2004, my wife and I were fortunate enough to take a vacation to Italy before we started our efforts to grow our family. Our travel started in Rome, and it was Disneyland for me. You could not walk 10 feet without passing something of historical significance. I planned the trip for months in advance and the engineer part of me shone brightly, as I created multiple spreadsheets to ensure we took in all the things we wanted to see. (I say "we," but I must admit my wife was not as eager as I was to cross the city to see some of the more obscure items on our list. She would have happily traded some of that time for more people-watching while sipping a limoncello in a local plaza. I definitely still owe her for that.)

One of the lesser-known highlights was the Basilica of St. Clement. Only a few blocks east of the Colosseum, it is understandably overshadowed by its colossal neighbor of a tourist attraction. Nonetheless, this church — which appears quite unremarkable from the outside — fascinated me more than its neighbor. The ground-level, 12th century church was beautiful, but nothing to write home about when compared to other churches in the area. What differentiated it from others was what lay beneath. It was built on top of a fourth century church, which in turn was built upon a first century pagan temple dedicated to Mithra.

Once in power, it was common for Christians to destroy pagan temples and build upon them as a means to root out paganism. To stop analysis here, though, would be wrong, as it might imply that only a pure "seek-and-destroy attitude" was in play. The situation was likely much more complicated and nuanced. Did Christians destroy pagan temples? Of course; the evidence is undeniable. Did Christians absorb some of the beliefs or customs of religions that it looked to dominate or destroy? The answer is also quite clearly yes.

(In a short aside here, I want to stress that I am not implying that Christian history is unique in its attempts to destroy competing religions. Other religions have done the same. Go no further than the Taliban's destruction of religious artifacts and structures.)

I see striking parallels between the clashing of religions and the clashing of "modern" vs. "non-modern" humans. Until recently, scientists have debated whether "modern" humans killed off Neanderthals, interbred with them, or outlived them due to superior planning skills and mastery of tools. With current DNA analysis, we have learned that most people of European descent do indeed have some Neanderthal DNA. This is proof that interbreeding appears to be at least part of the answer. Most likely, however, all three scenarios probably occurred.

Similarly, when religions meet, there can be a mixture of dominance/destruction and domestication. There are indeed examples of pure destruction of "weaker" religions, but there are also examples of efforts to bring the beliefs of the "weaker" religion under the roof of the "stronger" religion. New religions can be adapted to better serve the needs of people in a given area at a given time. The "spiritual competitiveness" of one religion can leave other religions at a disadvantage and ultimately depleted of members. If your religious differentiator is then adopted by the new religion in town, you may have just lost whatever remained of a competitive advantage. Just as the evolution of modern humans may have been messy, so too was the evolution of many religions.

There are extensive writings about Catholic efforts throughout history to destroy anything that challenged its power (including other religions). One only need to glance at the Crusades and the Inquisition for evidence.

In 2014, my family and I travelled to Godafoss Falls, the beautiful "waterfall of the gods" in Iceland, where in 1000 AD, Christianity was adopted and statues of pagan gods were tossed into the falls. I've heard multiple versions of the "tossing of the idols" story. One version implies it was forced and one implies it was not. Either way, this is another example of how the destruction of the old ways was welcomed by the church.

A Mythical Jesus?

While researching for this book, I came across critiques of Christianity that went far beyond anything I had heard before. Chief among them is the claim that Jesus may not have existed at all, but rather was a byproduct of the mixing, adaption, and evolution of religious belief — and that he was more likely a combination of several mythical and non-mythical figures, including, but not limited to, Mithra, Krishna, Buddha, and Horus. As an active Christian for decades, this seemed utterly ridiculous to me.

In the face of this seemingly outlandish claim, I did some research. I have a real problem with people propagating conspiracy theories and this struck me as just that. I read sources for and against the "Christ as a myth" theory and found evidence for both sides. In truth, I'm not an expert in this matter, and it's not always clear to me which sources can be trusted. I watched what I thought was a rather convincing documentary that argued Jesus was simply one more mythical character in a long line of solar-god-myth iterations; but I then watched the follow-on documentary from the same group and it argued an unrelated, but well-known and disproven conspiracy theory, thereby losing significant credibility with me.

For the record, I've since further researched the arguments made in their first documentary and it appears that many (but, importantly, not all) were misleading at best. Misinformation such as this harms the search for truth as much as the initial untruths it may seek to counter.

As strange as it may seem, though, in this case, it almost doesn't matter to me. Whether Jesus truly existed is not central to the points I'm making in this book. My "breakup" with Jesus is basically the same whether he's a myth or was a real person who's had mythical, divine, or magical properties assigned to him.

Just as I counsel friends and family to acknowledge what climate scientists say about climate change, in writing this book I'm taking my own advice. It appears that the consensus among experts is that *a Jesus* likely existed, so I'll continue under that assumption. The debate going forward will be on *which* version of Jesus existed.

First, though, I think it's important to address a common response to claims of a purely mythical Jesus: *How can approximately 2 billion people worship a person as their God if that person didn't exist?*

I thought this was a good and challenging question initially. Then I realized that the same question could be asked of any god who's believed to have, at some point, taken a physical form, whether it's Odin, Hercules, or Krishna.

Imagine, for example, if the Vikings maintained their pagan beliefs, were not defeated at the Battle of Stamford Bridge in 1066, and then went on to conquer all of Europe and take economic, military, and cultural control for centuries. During this period, they absorb from the conquered the importance of the written word and decide to write a Viking "bible" of Norse religion. A unified "Viking Pagan Church" is created, and its writings are transcribed and passed along throughout the known world and taught to young children of the greater Viking Empire.

Those who contest these teachings are punished or killed. Then, one day, a Viking version of Christopher Columbus decides he wants to retrace the voyage of Leif Erikson and the Viking Empire expands westward to the "new" world. In such an alternate history, who's to say that 2 billion people today would not be followers of a Norse pagan religion? Thor might still be a god to many, considered as truly having existed within our physical realm. There would be no "Thor" superhero and Captain America would need a new sidekick. Under these circumstances, perhaps Jesus would be available for the role.

In short, people believe in Jesus today in large part because "Christianity" and "empire" were intertwined for centuries. The religion was connected to political power. (A strong argument can certainly be made that this connection still exists today in the political lobbies of many Christian groups in the United States.) Without this connection, it's likely that Christianity would have died out with other nascent beliefs. The original definition of the word "Christendom" was meant to capture this marriage between heavenly and earthly powers. For centuries, Christians had what some Islamists now call for in a worldwide caliphate: a sacred combining of religion and geopolitical power.

A Partially Mythical Jesus

So how did this version of Jesus who performed miracles survive to today? I argue this occurred due to a mixture of political power and cultural influences.

Let's start again with the political power.

Political Power and Nicea

In the early days of Christianity, there were varying and competing perspectives regarding what followers of Christ were to believe. Was Jesus a man who had a connection to God, was he in some way on par with God, or was he God himself? Was his birth miraculous? What is the Holy Spirit? Where did Jesus go after he died, and will he come back?

In 325, in what is now Iznik, Turkey, Emperor Constantine called the Council of Nicea to address these types of questions. The result, "The Nicene Creed," is familiar to anyone who's attended a Catholic mass. It starts with, "I believe in one God, the Father almighty, maker of heaven and earth." It goes on to lay out required beliefs for Catholicism. Although religious belief was the focus, one can't help but notice the political implications of this council. On one level, the Nicene Creed is similar to a modern-day political platform. It acts as the guidebook for what a particular group believes.

There is an enormous power in people having a common set of beliefs. A saying attributed to the philosopher Lucius Annaeus Seneca seems appropriate here: "Religion is regarded by the common people as true, by the wise as false, and by the rulers as useful." It seems that Constantine may have agreed. There is evidence in his own writings that he didn't seem to care too much what exactly the unified Christian beliefs were to be — just that they were unified. He wanted agreement. In the book The Life of the Blessed Emperor Constantine, the author Eusebius includes a writing from Constantine himself where he explicitly states this: "My first concern was that the attitude towards the divinity of all the provinces should be united in one consistent view."

It may be up for debate whether Constantine was a spiritual man, but it seems he was a practical one. Obtaining consensus appears to have overridden any concern he may have had for obtaining actual truth. This focus on consensus enabled Christianity to unify and adapt. There is strength — and political power — in the tribe, and Christianity's tribe was fortified in Nicea. It was also filtered in Nicea, as dissenting writings about Jesus were largely confiscated or sent underground. The idea of Jesus as described at this council has survived to the present day.

**

Nicea represents a milestone in Christian history as many things were decided about Jesus at that time. But what understandings of Jesus influenced these decisions? How did these ideas about Jesus develop in the first place? How did people know stories about Jesus' childhood? How did they know of his early miracles before he was well known? Of course, a Christian might say these ideas are known because it all happened in the Bible just as it says. (To this I would ask, "Which book of conflicting information in the Bible am I to read?" But this leads to a separate argument about internal biblical conflicts that has been made many times. I'm not interested in going into this any further, as the conflicts are numerous, obvious, and others have already adequately argued these points elsewhere.)

The similarities between the Christ story and the story of other perceived deities are quite stunning. I'm typically skeptical when people seem to stretch a theory beyond credibility, but from what I can tell, there is plenty to support the idea that the Jesus story is not unique. The idea that the Jesus story — and, in turn, Christianity — may have been influenced by other beliefs at the time seems quite clear. I'm interested to find out how the historical Jesus (assuming he did exist) became Jesus the Christ.

Cultural Influences

The Silk Road Exchange

It's commonly accepted that the four gospels in the New Testament were written decades after Jesus died. I'm not aware of any confirmed first-hand accounts of Jesus' life. Many Christians proclaim that God himself oversaw the writing of the Bible, so the accounts must be accurate. Forgive me, but that is not adequately convincing. Taking this "on faith" is no longer on option for me. Not to mention that if God were the overseer of the Bible coming together as it did, it may have done him well to enlist the services of a holy editor, as the repetition and incongruities are many.

So, if the writings about Jesus' life came long after his actual life, is it not possible, even likely, that stories about his life may have been influenced by other stories or beliefs circulating at the time? We've all played the telephone game when we were children where one person whispers something in someone's ear and it's repeated down the line from ear to ear. It nearly always ends up with some change from the original message. Now apply this same principle to decades of storytelling in a time when literacy was not common. Does it not seem likely that stories by the campfire might get modified slightly — or exaggerated, perhaps? Does it not even seem likely that aspects of different stories might entwine themselves with the Jesus story?

Trade routes active during Jesus' time did more than enable the exchange of goods. Ideas were perhaps the most important exchange. The Silk Road trade route (and some of its predecessors, such as the Royal Persian Road trade route) had already connected the world. When Rome conquered Egypt mere decades before Jesus' apparent birth, the floodgates of this exchange between "western" Rome and "the East" (including the Middle East, China, and India) opened even further. As is clear in biblical and non-biblical accounts alike, Judea (Jesus' purported region of upbringing) was already controlled by Roman forces. Therefore, it's easy to imagine that ideas from the recently expanded world would have been on the collective mind, consciously or otherwise, largely as a result of this Roman presence. This area at the time would have likely been traveled and even populated by some of these "easterners" (i.e., Buddhists) with whom trade was so attractive. In fact, evidence of Buddhists in the area at this time is not contested by most scholars.

When I first heard of Eastern beliefs (such as Buddhism and Hinduism) having possible influence on Christianity, I thought it absurd. Those ideas were so "eastern" in my mind that it seemed ridiculous from the beginning. That was until I realized that Christianity itself *is* an eastern religion — at least it started out that way. The subsequent history of Christianity has certainly leaned westward (especially with the rise of the Catholic Church in Rome and the conquests in the "New World"), but its origins are clearly in the Middle East.

St. Paul is said to have travelled 10,000 miles on his evangelistic missions after his conversion. Keep that in mind while realizing that the distance from Judea to India was merely 1,500 miles and the travel routes were well developed. The distance from Judea to Persia (aka, Iran) was a mere few hundred miles. The idea that Jesus may have travelled to India might be unlikely, but it certainly would have been possible at that time. These travel routes changed everything.

The Raglan Scale

In 1936, Major FitzRoy Richard Somerset (aka, Lord Raglan) published a 22-point scale based on common features from stories of heroes throughout European and Asian cultures. The points range from being born of a virgin to having a unique death and/or burial. Some of the similarities between stories are stunning.

Healthy criticism of the Raglan Scale exists, including that interpretations need to be quite loose for certain characters to fit the mold (e.g., "virgin" may simply refer to a young, unmarried woman). I find the general framework, however, to be undeniable in multiple cases.

I strongly recommend researching the Raglan Scale as it relates to multiple characters, including Mithras, Oedipus, Mithridates VI of Pontus, Theseus, Romulus, Heracles, Perseus, Moses, Zeus, Apollo, and Jesus. Each character gets one point for each similarity. Many characters score high on the scale and similarities between some come to light rather quickly. Depending on interpretation, Jesus seems to score between 18 and 20. This means his story is approximately 85 percent similar to the "standard" Raglan hero story.

Religious Syncretism and Christianity

There is so much information available nowadays regarding different religious entities' perceived similarities with Jesus that unless you're formally trained in these matters, it can be a challenge to understand which sources can be trusted. I admit here once again that I'm not an expert in comparative mythology or religious syncretism. I am, however, generally cautious in my research and do not take unsubstantiated claims as evidence. A majority of what I've written in the following pages is supported by multiple source documents and by experts in the field. There are other instances where I might mention a possible syncretism, but I will highlight it as a claim in which I have less confidence. I have also completely left out multiple examples of some syncretism claims that may be true, but I did not find them convincing enough to include in this writing. Ultimately, I strongly recommend that the reader do her own research if this is a topic of interest. Either way, the examples that I could verify left me with the strong general impression that the Christian story is clearly influenced by other stories.

Christianity and Hinduism (Indus Valley)

Jesus and Krishna

Below are some notable commonalities between the stories of Jesus and the Hindu god, Krishna. Note that Hinduism is centuries, if not at least a millennium, older than Christianity.

Death of the innocents:

Krishna: King Kansa was warned that the child Krishna would threaten his kingship. Kansa in turn sought the death of all the children of Devaki (Krishna's mother). Vasudev (the husband of Devaki) received a message from fortune tellers to flee with the young Krishna for his protection.

Jesus: King Herod was warned that a child born in Bethlehem would threaten his kingship. Herod in turn sought the death of all children that could be this child. Joseph (the husband of Jesus' mother) received a "divine message" in a dream to flee with the young Jesus for his protection.

The Trinity:

Krishna: Although it can be argued that Hinduism does not officially preach of a "trinity" as three Gods in one, they do have three major gods who split up the divine works of the universe. Brahma is responsible for primary creation, Vishnu (of whom Krishna is an incarnation) maintains creation, and

Shiva controls the realm of destruction. It is significant to note, though, that the *trimurti* is a representation of these three Hindu gods in a single form with three faces. This is not universally accepted in Hinduism, but similarities to the Christian trinity are obvious.

Jesus: The Christian trinity of God the father, Jesus the son, and the Holy Spirit is considered a mystery by which all three entities are the same entity. But each has its own focus in the divine works of the universe. God the father has a focus on creation, Jesus the son has a focus on salvation, and the Holy Spirit has a focus on reconciliation and ongoing spiritual guidance.

Transfiguration:

Krishna: In Chapter 11 of Bhagavad-Gita, Krishna revealed his godly form (Vishnu) to his follower, Arjuna. Arjuna recognized this and was "disturbed by fear."

Jesus: In Chapter 9 of Mark, Jesus revealed his godly "transfigured" form to his followers Peter, James, and John. Upon hearing God's voice, the apostles trembled in fear.

Other Similarities

Hindu texts dating approximately 700 years before Christ teach of the nonviolent concept of *ahimsa*. This principle of not injuring others is shared with Buddhism, but it is also clearly aligned with teachings attributed to Jesus, who told his followers to put down their swords when he was being arrested.

Hinduism believes in the concept of multiple lives. If you live a good life as a rabbit, for example, you might come back in the next life as a human. If you live a bad life as a king, you may come back in the next life as a beggar. The term "karma" refers to actions one can take that impacts your chances of coming back as a "higher" or "lower" form of life in your next life. Today, "karma" is often used in a more immediate sense to imply that there will be consequences for bad actions in this life. The term in its purest sense, however, refers to a continuation of life after death.

While Christianity doesn't include a belief in reincarnation, it does teach about life after death and that there are consequences for the actions you take in your current life that manifest themselves after your death.

Both religions share an end-times prophecy. Certain sects of Hinduism believe that Kalki, the final avatar of the god Vishnu, will appear on a white horse to help bring about the end of the age. Hindu art frequently depicts him holding a bow, arrow, and a sword. While Hindus don't believe in a final end times, as there is much more focus on the cyclical nature of time, Kalki certainly ushers in the end of an era.

The Book of Revelations in the Christian Bible reflects similar imagery. Jesus is prophesized to come back in a glorified form, followed by the "four horsemen of the apocalypse." One of the horsemen rides a white horse and carries a bow and arrow. Another carries a sword. Just as there have been people who've claimed to be the "second coming" of Jesus, people throughout history have claimed to be the prophesied Kalki.

Christianity and Buddhism (Ganges Valley)

Jesus and the Buddha

There are notable similarities between the stories of Jesus and the Sigghartha Gautama (also referred to as the Buddha), the founder of Buddhism. Note that Buddhism is centuries older than Christianity and that many of the Jataka stories (Buddhist texts) date back to the fourth century, before Jesus.

Tempted (three times) by "the evil one":

Buddha: Before his enlightenment, the Buddha is tempted three times by the demon Mara in a natural setting (under a bodhi tree). He is tempted with desires of the flesh (sexual temptation of Mara's daughters), possibility of facing death (physical attack of Mara's army), and social status (sense of duty to be a prince).

Jesus: Before his baptism, Jesus is tempted three times by Satan in a natural setting (desert). He is tempted with desires of the flesh (turning stone to bread), possibility of facing death (jumping from the temple), and social status (become ruler of all kingdoms of Earth).

Because Buddhism predates Christianity by centuries and the story of the Buddha's enlightenment (which is intrinsically tied to the story of his temptations) is so central to Buddhism's teachings, it seems highly likely that the stories of the Buddha's temptation influenced the Gospel stories of Jesus' temptation (and not the other way around).

Multiplying food:

Buddha: Jataka 78 describes dough for a single cake rising continuously until 500 people are fed from it.

Jesus: Matthew 14:13-21 describes a meager number of loaves and fish multiplying miraculously until 5,000 people are fed.

Eat of this flesh:

Buddha: In Jataka 316, the Buddha tells a parable of the self-sacrificing hare. In the story, a hare is willing to offer his own body so that others may eat and live. The hare says, "*If any beggar shall appeal to me, I shall have to give him my own flesh to eat.*" After telling the story, Buddha makes it clear that it was his own flesh that was in the pot. Referring to himself in a previous life, he says, "*I myself was the wise hare.*"

Jesus: Jesus often spoke in parables, but in John 6:55-56, he is quite direct: "*For My flesh is true food, and My blood is true drink. He who eats My flesh and drinks My blood abides in Me, and I in him.*"

I'd expect that some would argue the similarities are a stretch. After all, one is the story of a hare sacrificing his body so that beggars can eat, while Jesus suggests more of a spiritual feeding. This may be true for some interpretations, but recall that the official Catholic teaching about the Eucharist is that (via transubstantiation) the bread and wine truly become the body and blood of Jesus (or, at the very least, the "essence" of Jesus). A teacher willing to *sacrifice his own flesh* seems like a memorable enough concept to have influenced early Christian belief.

Other Similarities

While in college at Villanova University in the early 1990s, I developed a friendship with a guest professor, Father Daniel Berrigan. Dan and his brother Phillip were famous/infamous for their very active protest of the Vietnam War, so much so that they made *Time* magazine's January 25, 1971, cover with the caption "Rebel Priests: The Curious Case of the Berrigans." Both brothers eventually went to prison due to their protest activity and Dan used much of that time to develop a craft for poetry that I connected with during college.

Dan, like his friend and fellow writer Thomas Merton (another Catholic priest), had an interest in the overlap of Christian and Buddhist thinking. I asked him about this during a lecture and he responded that he'd frequently have an image come to him of the Buddha on the cross and Jesus sitting under the bodhi tree. I recall him saying that the Buddha in Jesus' place and time may have been crucified and Jesus in the Buddha's place and time may have spent vast amounts of time meditating under a tree.

If you were to do even minimal research comparing the teachings of the Buddha and Jesus, you would come across several sources that claim to make the comparisons easy. I became a bit suspicious of some of these sites as I was not able to find all the texts attributed to the Buddha in the original Buddhist source documents. This does not mean that the Buddhist texts listed on the sites is wrong or nonexistent. It could be that the sites simply didn't provide enough information regarding text location, or it may be that I'm not well enough versed in Buddhist documents to know where to find the specific texts.

Either way, the text that I could verify makes the point sufficiently. The similarities between the teachings — even the similarities between sayings attributed to both Jesus and the Buddha — are startling. The following are some teachings that I was able to verify:

> Buddha: *"Hatred is never appeased by hatred in this world. By non-hatred alone is hatred appeased. This is a law eternal.... Overcome the angry by non-anger; overcome the wicked by goodness; overcome the miser by generosity; overcome the liar by truth." — Dhammapada Chapter 1, Verse 5 and Chapter 17, Verse 223*

> Jesus: *"Love your enemies, do good to those who hate you, bless those who curse you, pray for those who abuse you." — Luke 6:27-30*

> **

> Buddha: *"If anyone should give you a blow with his hand, with a stick, or with a knife, you should abandon any desires... utter no evil words... abide compassionate for his welfare, with a mind of loving-kindness, without inner hate.'" — Majjhima Nikaya 21:6*

> Jesus: *"If anyone strikes you on the cheek, offer the other also." — Luke 6:29*

Buddha: *"Easily seen is the fault of others, but one's own fault is difficult to see. Like chaff one winnows another's faults, but hides one's own." — Dhammapada Chapter 18, Verse 252*

Jesus: *"Judge not, that you be not judged... And why do you look at the speck in your brother's eye, but do not consider the plank in your own eye?" — Matthew 7:1-5*

**

Buddha: *"Don't speak harshly to anyone. If you do people will speak to you in the same way." — Dhammapada Chapter 10, Verse 133*

Jesus: *"Do to others as you would have them do to you." — Luke 6:31*

**

Buddha: *"...So one should cultivate this bondless love to all that live in the whole universe." — Sutta Nipata 149*

Jesus: *"This is my commandment that you love one another as I have loved you." — John 15:12*

**

Buddha: *"Whoever would tend me, he should tend the sick..." — Vinaya, Mahavagga 8:26*

Jesus: *"Truly I tell you, just as you did not do it to one of the least of these, you did not do it to me." — Matthew 25:45*

**

Buddha: *"Happy indeed we live, we who possess nothing. Feeders on joy we shall be, like the Radiant Gods." — Dhammapada 15:4*

Jesus: *"Blessed are you who are poor, for yours is the kingdom of God." — Luke 6:20*

Buddha: *"Go now... and wander, for the gain of the many...Preach... the doctrine which is glorious... in the spirit and in the letter... if the doctrine is not preached to them, they cannot attain salvation...."* —*Vinaya Mahavagga 1:11.1*

Jesus: *"Go therefore and make disciples of all nations, baptizing them in the name of the Father and of the Son and of the Holy Spirit, and teaching them to obey everything that I have commanded you."* — *Matthew 28:19-20*

**

What is so interesting to me here is not that Buddha and Jesus are saying similar things. After all, if they both said it was important to get a good night's sleep, there would be little to discuss. Instead, many of the things they said were anything but ordinary for their time. In fact, many of these sayings were diametrically opposed to the prevailing thinking. *Love your enemies. Turn the other cheek. Do not judge.* These were radical teachings. The fact that the similarities are so clear on *these types* of teachings is significant.

It's also noteworthy that they both make a plea for their followers to spread their teachings. Recall that evidence of Buddhist teachings exists in the general area of Judea at the time Jesus is said to have lived. Given Buddha's missionary call, this is not surprising.

**

One Buddhist story that is stunningly similar to a Christian story relates to walking on water.

Jataka 190 includes this text about a follower of Buddha: *"... as no boat could be seen at the landing-stage, and our friend's mind being full of delightful thoughts of the Buddha, he walked into the river. His feet did not sink below the water. He got as far as mid-river walking as though he were on dry land; but there he noticed the waves. Then his ecstasy subsided, and his feet began to sink."*

Matthew 14:29-30 reads as follows: *"'Come,' he said. Then Peter got down out of the boat, walked on the water and came toward Jesus. But when he saw the wind, he was afraid and, beginning to sink, cried out, 'Lord, save me!'"*

It would be difficult to read both of these texts and still believe that there is no connection between the two. One might try to argue that the Christian story influenced the Buddhist one, but given that Buddhism is significantly older, I find this unlikely. Unless there's clear evidence that this particular Christian story came before this particular Buddhist story, it seems rather safe to assume that the Buddhist story is the original.

Another similarity are the stories of old wise men recounting their visions about newborn saviors. In Buddhism, it's Asita (*Bhagavatprasūtih,* Book 1, Verse 62*),* and in Christianity, Simeon (Luke 2:25).

**

Speaking as a westerner, it was initially difficult for me to consider an Eastern philosophy such as Buddhism as having any real impact on Christian teaching. (I know I've touched on this before, but it's worth repeating.) I think many of us see Buddhism historically as from the far, far east, way over huge mountains and beyond long deserts. In our heads, it might as well be "in a galaxy far, far away." In truth, though, Christianity's origins are eastern (albeit Middle Eastern). After seeing the similarities in teaching, I now see it as much more likely that Buddhism had a direct influence on Christian teaching than not.

Christianity and Greco-Roman Religions

Jesus and Heracles (Greece)

Heracles was born of a mortal woman (Alcmene) and a god (Zeus). The goddess Hera attempted to have him killed when Heracles was an infant. Heracles spent significant time performing miracles in order to obtain forgiveness for his sin. After his death, Heracles ascended to Olympus to be with his father, Zeus.

Similar to Heracles, Jesus was born of a mortal woman (Mary) and a god (Jehovah). King Herod attempted to have Jesus killed when he was an infant. Jesus spent a significant amount of time performing miracles, and his greatest miracle (resurrection after death) allowed for the forgiveness of all sin. After his death, Jesus ascended to heaven to be with his Father.

Note that the Heracles story was documented in writing and art several centuries before Jesus'.

Jesus and Orion (Greece)

Orion, the son of the god Poseidon, had the ability to walk on water, due to his father being the god of the sea. Jesus, the son of God (Yahweh), was said in the gospels to have walked on water (see: Mark 6:49).

I include this because although water-walking seems like a unique ability, researchers will argue that it's not an unusual superpower among deities. Orion's water-walking is even written in the stars. The Eridanus constellation, which is frequently represented as a river, lies at the feet of the Orion constellation.

Jesus and Romulus (Rome)

Romulus was the son of the god Mars and human mother Rhea Silvia, a vestal virgin — a young woman who took a vow of chastity as part of her work maintaining religious rituals in Rome. Rhea Silvia was born into a royal lineage as the daughter of King Numitor.

Jesus was the son of God and human mother Mary. Whether Mary was a virgin at the time of Jesus' birth is up for debate among some Christians, but the birth itself is believed to have been a "virgin birth" (that is, brought on via miraculous means and not via sexual intercourse). Mary was born into a royal lineage as a descendant of King David.

Like Jesus, Romulus and his twin Remus were seen as a threat to the King at the time (Amulius), who sought to have them killed. The twins escaped and were raised by a foster father; likewise, Jesus was raised by his foster father, Joseph.

Romulus founded and built *a special new city*, Rome. Jesus is described as ushering in *a special new "city,"* the New Jerusalem, a heaven on Earth (Revelations Chapter 1).

Other Similarities

It would be a disservice if I didn't mention the obvious influence that Greco-Roman religions have had on Christian art. The imagery of the Christian God the Father throughout history is all but indistinguishable from Greco-Roman art depicting the ruler of the Greco-Roman gods, Zeus (Greek)/Jupiter (Roman). Zeus' home is high above his people on Mount Olympus, while God the Father resides "on high" as well.

Christianity and Zoroastrianism (Persia/Iran)

Jesus and the Saoshyant

Zoroaster (the founder of Zoroastrianism) is believed to have lived anywhere from the 15th to the sixth century BCE. There are notable similarities between the stories of Jesus and those of the still-to-come Saoshyant of Zoroastrianism.

The mother of this Saoshyant is prophesied to be a virgin impregnated miraculously by the sperm of the prophet Zoroaster, which was (is being) preserved for years in a lake.

Both this Saoshyant and Jesus play similar roles in a final judgement scenario. The Bundahishn (Zoroastrian scripture), Chapter 30: 27 says: "Then Saoshyant by order of the Creator will give reward and recompense to all men in conformity with their deeds." In Revelation 22:12, Jesus says, "Behold, I am coming soon, bringing my recompense with me, to repay everyone for what he has done."

Zoroastrianism has its roots in Iran/Persia, which was only a few weeks' travel from Judea in Jesus' time. Note that while Zoroastrianism (or at least the roots of it) likely predates Jesus by a full millennium, many of the writings associated with it date to the first century CE or later. In fact, some writings (e.g., Bundahishn texts) may have come several centuries after Christianity. Some Christian apologists will latch onto this to argue that perhaps Zoroastrian writings were influenced by Christianity. Religious syncretism can go both ways, but given the importance of the dualistic, good vs. evil, view of the world at the heart of Zoroastrianism, it seems unlikely that the final parsing of good from evil, and the figure essential to that parsing (Saoshyant at the "end of the world") were wholly an afterthought created many centuries after the religion.

This does not mean that older Zoroastrian writings did not exist. It just means that they did not survive into the hands of modern archeologists to date. As stated earlier, it was (and sadly still is) common for members of some religions to destroy artifacts or scriptures of competing religions.

Other Similarities

Just as there is a clear connection between the Abrahamic religions (Judaism, Christianity, and Islam), some scholars see Zoroastrianism almost as a prequal to the three. Many of the concepts that Christians take for granted today appear to have roots in Zoroastrian teaching. These include the strict good vs. evil duality, the concept of free will — and the importance of aligning your actions with good — the "restoration" of the dead, and the final judgement at the end of time.

Some scholars will argue that Zoroastrianism may have been the first monotheistic religion, even predating Judaism, which frequently claims to have been the first. This appears to be a complicated analysis that depends on whether you consider the Amesha Spentas, seven "god-like" beings in Zoroastrianism, to be actual gods, or sub-divine beings. If you don't consider them gods, you'd be inclined to consider Zoroastrianism as monotheistic. If nothing else, it seems that Zoroastrianism influenced, or was a precursor to, monotheism.

The seven Amesha Spentas can't help but draw comparisons to the seven archangels in Christianity; the Zoroastrian beings called the Fravashi seem to correlate with the Christian concept of guardian angels. Beings called Yazatas seem similar to Catholicism's patron saints. I find the level of detail involved with the story of each "yazad" of interest. For example, just as the Catholic Saint Fiacre is the patron saint of medicinal plants, a yazad named Haoma oversees a specific plant with medicinal properties.

Spenta Mainyu is the Zoroastrian version of the Holy Spirit. Fire is a symbol of the divine in Zoroastrianism, and its influence on Christianity seems likely, given the symbology of the Holy Spirit coming to the apostles as "tongues of fire" on Pentecost (Acts of the Apostles 2:3) and the "Holy Fire" Easter ritual in the Greek Orthodox church.

Mithraism, a Roman religion in practice at the time of Jesus, is believed to be at least loosely based on the Zoroastrian yazad Mithra. Mithras (the name for the Latin version of this character) is discussed later.

Christianity and Egyptian Religion

Jesus and Osiris

Below are some notable commonalities between the stories of Jesus and those of Osiris. Note that the worship of Osiris is believed to predate Jesus by more than three millennia.

Rising from the dead:

Osiris: Osiris was killed by his brother Set. He came back to life (for a short period) in order to father Horus. (Note that there are varying versions of this mythology.)

Jesus: Jesus was killed and rose from the dead three days later.

I suspect some Christians would claim that similarities between Osiris and Jesus rising from the dead are a stretch. The general concept of some sort of physical resurrection is important to note, however, as is the recognition that the concept had likely existed for millennia before Jesus.

The underworld:

Osiris: Osiris is the Egyptian judge of the dead and god of the underworld.

Jesus: For the three days between his death and resurrection, Jesus is said to have descended into hell (the underworld) to judge the dead and free good souls from hell.

Other Similarities

Egypt had significant political power in the ancient world, so it's understandable that its culture would have far-reaching influence. The concept of the afterlife is one of the most noticeable similarities with Christianity. Egyptians believed that the real journey began after death, when you navigated the pathway to the next life.

The Egyptian Book of the Dead is not what you might think. It's frequently and incorrectly portrayed as ancient Egyptian religion's equivalent of the Christian Bible. But it's almost exclusively an afterlife guide for the dead — a step-by-step instruction manual for the next life — and not a book of moral teachings for this life. The writings that make up the book were found on tomb walls or on illustration-filled papyrus next to the deceased.

Included in these writings are special words (i.e., spells) that one might say to certain entities encountered in the afterlife. I find the whole concept of "magic password"-type language to be interesting and I see comparisons with Christian prayers, including those said by priests during the Catholic sacrament of last rites.

**

In 2018, my son and I went to see a traveling King Tut exhibit at the California Science Center in Los Angeles. The statues of the Egyptian guards were a highlight. I don't recall if they were intended to guard the dead king on his post-life journey, or if they were guards for the Egyptian gods themselves. Either way, I thought immediately of the Christian image of St. Peter guarding the entrance to the gates of heaven, checking to see who's on the reservation list.

Also prevalent in the exhibit were smaller statues that accompanied the dead king. Upon the king's arrival to the afterlife, these servant dolls were believed to magically grow to normal human size, come to life, and get to work serving the king. (I much prefer this "magic doll" custom to the "kill-your-real-life-helpers-so-they-will-help-you-in-the-afterlife" custom.) The idea of people ready to assist the newly dead is similar to imagery I had grown up with of Catholic saints welcoming the dead into heaven.

**

Egyptian art is also replete with images of the goddess Isis with her young son Horus on her lap. I discuss Horus in more detail later, but the image of him with his mother is iconic and strikingly similar to Mary and Jesus as the "Madonna with child."

Goddess worship is something found throughout history. The feminine, and particularly a mother's ability to bring life into the world, was worshiped by ancient people. One can therefore understand the Catholic Church's decision to thrust Mary into the spotlight. She's not officially worshiped by Catholics, but the reverence for her might have been just enough to scratch the goddess itch for goddess-worshipping pagans as they transitioned to Catholicism.

Years ago, my wife and I received some difficult medical news. The hospital was in a beach neighborhood, so we decided to go for a walk outside to absorb the news in the fresh salt air. As we walked the streets, we came across a church and decided to go in and sit for a moment. The name of the Catholic church was Mary, Star of the Sea. Even with the grief that we were dealing with at the time, I remember having the distinct thought: "What the heck does Mary have to do with the sea?"

I have not felt the urge to spend much time studying the origins of this title for Mary. After some research, though, I understand that this might have arisen out of a transcription error centuries ago. It is of note, however, that among her many roles, the Egyptian goddess Isis was also a "goddess of the sea."

Christianity and Judaism

It should go without saying that Christianity was enormously influenced by Judaism. Jesus, after all, was Jewish, as were nearly all of his disciples. Christians consider Christianity to be Judaism's sequel. For them, it represents the realization of the Jewish wish for a Messiah.

Christianity is inseparable from Judaism, and the term Judeo-Christian is prevalent largely due to this fact. Christians believe Jesus fulfills Jewish prophecy found in the Old Testament. But, of course, the writers of the New Testament had the Old Testament documents available to them, so writing in fulfillments of the old prophecies would have been quite easy. It's worthwhile to stress this point.

Potential Astrological Influence

As indicated earlier, some people argue that Jesus is simply another iteration of astrologically drenched, sun-god mythology. I don't claim to have adequate knowledge to support or deny such a claim, but I do find interesting similarities between the astronomical/astrological cycle and certain biblical stories.

In noting the sun's passage through the different "astrological ages" in the constellations, it's hard to miss the connected symbolism in biblical text. The timeframes associated with the beginnings and ends of astrological ages can differ by hundreds of years depending on interpretation. For this reason, I won't list specific dates, but they do generally seem to coincide with certain biblical stories.

The Age of Taurus (the bull)

Moses' anger at the worship of the "golden calf" (a bull) in the book of Exodus can signify the stepping away from the ancient gods (symbolized by the calf/bull), which may have been worshiped in conjunction with the astrological age of Taurus.

The Age of Aries (the ram/sheep)

There are references throughout the Old and New Testaments to rams/lambs being sacrificed or shepherded.

There are also biblical stories of bulls being sacrificed during this period, so sheep were clearly not the only option. 1 Kings 18:20-40, for example, tells the story of how Elijah's god was more successful at igniting a sacrificial bull than priests of the god Baal. Baal is frequently associated with a bull and is at times depicted with bull horns. The priests' inability to have Baal ignite the flame of sacrifice might imply the death (or at least impotency) of the bull-god by this period.

The Age of Pisces (the fish)

Jesus himself may act as an astrological symbol for the transition from the Age of Aries to the Age of Pisces. He is the "good shepherd" of the lamb, but he is also symbolized in early Christianity by the fish, as he makes his apostles "fishers of men."

**

It's also worth noting that Jesus had 12 apostles, just as there were believed to be 12 "astrological ages." Jesus also rose after three days, which happens to be the approximate time that the sun seems to stop its move southward during the winter solstice before it rises towards the north again. This is dependent on the location of the sun-viewer, but it would be the case for someone in the area of Galilee.

The Bible is replete with references to specific stars and/or star formations (see: Job 38:31-33; Amos 5:8; Acts 7:42-43). Most notable, perhaps, is in Matthew Chapter 2, which includes the story of the magi (Greek for "wise men") following the "star in the east." Most educated people today consider astrology a mixture of pseudoscience and bad entertainment. At the time of Jesus, however, this was clearly not the case. The "wise men" of the time paid close attention to the stars, planets, and their formations, and sought to find meaning in them.

The astrological symbolism of both Christmas and Easter are also quite clear, as these times of year were celebrated throughout the ancient world long before Christianity. The winter solstice and spring equinox have been central to religious belief for ages. Multiple gods/saviors were said to be born on or near the winter solstice (e.g., Jesus, Horus of Egypt), and the astrological connections to some religious beliefs seem to be more than coincidental. I can see the draw in assigning the birthday of a savior to the day when daylight begins to get longer and hope and life return with the warmth of the sun.

Other Possible Syncretism Concerning Jesus

There is controversy regarding similarities between Jesus' story and some of these gods, mythical figures, and related belief systems. In researching for this book, I came across arguments that seemed quite substantial, only to read something else shortly afterward that would cast doubt on the points I had just found so convincing. I specifically sought arguments from Christian apologists, and many did indeed walk me back from making claims that I could not comfortably support. Below are some of these cases where similarities with Christianity may exist, but I felt the evidence was weaker than in other cases.

Note that this separate break-out of these examples are based solely on the subjective review of my own research. Although I did feel it necessary to make this break in order to distinguish between what I felt to be stronger and weaker claims, I acknowledge also that some of these were close calls with regards to whether I tagged them as "weaker" or not. I'm inherently skeptical about some of the astrological claims, for example. Either way, I want to reinforce the importance of maintaining a healthy skepticism when reviewing claims based on ancient information.

In cases where I mention that I did not locate a primary source, please don't interpret that to mean no source exists. I have a keen interest in these older religions, but I don't consider myself an expert, despite the significant research I have done. If interested, I recommend the reader do her own research and draw her own conclusions based on the information available, which is what I'm doing here.

Jesus and Mithras

Mithraism, a religion that has interesting overlaps with Zoroastrianism, was long popular in Persia and a version of it developed in the western Roman world from approximately 100

BCE to 300 CE. Both Mithras and Jesus were "savior gods" who performed a sacrifice for the benefit of their followers. They both offered a version of life after death, they both stressed the importance of doing good works, and they both were assigned the winter solstice for a birthday. They also had ritualistic meals associated with their following — for the initiated only.

St. Justin Martyr (~100-165 CE) expressed the concern of many Christians regarding the similarities between Mithraic and Christian practices, accusing Mithras' followers of being "wicked devils" for essentially copying the Christian practice of sharing the eucharist. Clearly, Mithraism predates Christianity, but as both religions existed side-by-side in Rome, it's quite possible that one (or both) could have influenced the other.

Was Justin Martyr correct in arguing that Mithras' followers adopted rituals like those associated with the Christian eucharist in order to mock Christians? Is that why he was so upset? Or were Christians eager to demonize and stamp out Mithraism because they feared the obvious parallels between the two religions would become more widely known, along with the understanding that Mithras came first? Mithraic rituals were notoriously mysterious and held in secret by the initiated, so it may indeed be unlikely that we will ever find out which ritualistic meal came first. The secretive nature of their religious services is another thing that followers of Mithras apparently shared with the early Christians.

As discussed earlier, Christianity ultimately gained power and its leaders suppressed Mithraism by doing things like building churches on top of Mithraic temples. The Basilica of St. Clement in Rome is Exhibit A.

Jesus and Dionysus

Dionysus is another god who's been compared to Jesus. A Greek god, he appears to have been worshipped for more than a thousand years before Jesus' birth. Like Jesus, Dionysus was born of a male god (Zeus) and a female mortal (Semele). He was brought to trial, like Jesus and, in a manner of speaking, killed and then brought back to life (although the circumstances are significantly different). After researching the Dionysus-Jesus connection, I ultimately found most of the parallels relatively weak.

The ritualistic meal associated with Dionysus (called the *omophagia*), however, does strike me as particularly interesting. The term refers to eating raw flesh, as live animals were said to be consumed by the Cult of Dionysus. The meal included wine and the belief was that by partaking in it, followers were taking in the essence of Dionysus who also happened to be the god of "ritual madness" and "religious ecstasy." This communion with Dionysus is notable in light of the Catholic perspective on the eucharist.

Among other things, Dionysus was the "god of wine" and is said to have turned water into wine, although I have not found a primary source that supports that claim. Considering Dionysus' connection to wine, I find Jesus' miracle at the wedding at Cana even more suspect than I had as a child growing up. At Cana, Jesus is said to have turned water into wine for wedding guests.

Perhaps due to a puritanical streak in the brand of Catholicism I grew up with, the idea that Jesus would essentially help people get drunk didn't square with my image of him. I can see, however, how such a story appealed to those who appreciated Dionysus for his "god of ecstasy" moniker. It almost seems like this is the start of the "cool Jesus" meme. *"Yeah, I'm the savior of the world, and you do need to repent and all that, but hey, I'm also not against a fun party, so lighten up, chill out, and drink up."* I can see this being an attractive side of Jesus for followers of Dionysus who may have been considering a leap to Christianity.

Jesus and Horus

I learned of the apparent Horus and Jesus connection via the 2008 movie *Religulous*, a documentary featuring comedian and renowned atheist, Bill Maher. This movie was quite impactful in getting me to think differently about my religious beliefs and the part of the movie that discussed apparent similarities between Jesus and Horus was particularly influential.

After further research, however, I was disappointed that I could not locate a primary source that corroborated many of the Jesus-Horus claims. I say "disappointed" not because I wanted there to be a connection, but because the movie inferred that there was a clear link. It appears that many of the claims of syncretism are based on questionable interpretations of the record. My apologies to Bill Maher if clear connections do indeed exist, but I couldn't confirm many of them and I certainly attempted to do so.

From what I could find, Horus and Jesus both are said to have been conceived in unique manners and both have been linked to light as a metaphor. A unique conception or birth is common among many mythical heroes, and light as a metaphor in contrast to darkness is common as well.

Despite what I've written, I still recommend *Religulous*. I found other parts of the movie to be effective in examining religious beliefs from a perspective that people with a religious upbringing might be unwilling (or unable) to consider otherwise.

It's important to maintain objectivity as much as possible when challenging and/or accepting claims as true. Further vetting is often required, and this is certainly the case when you plan to propagate challenged ideas. Regarding *Religulous*, there are plenty of clearly justifiable challenges to religious claims. It does not appear that Maher had stuck with these alone, and I wish he had. By not doing this, he runs the risk of people dismissing his movie outright without considering its many valid points.

Jesus and Apollo

Apollo was a Greek god who was the son of the greatest Greek god, Zeus. Jesus is considered by Christians to be God and also the son of God. Both Apollo and Jesus were known to have been healers. One could argue that there are other similarities between them, but these two seem to be the most obvious. I bring up Apollo for a different reason, though.

In 2004, my wife and I toured the Necropolis underneath St. Peter's Basilica in Vatican City. This spot is arguably the global epicenter of Catholicism and it was a fascinating place to tour, even if it required my wife and I peeling ourselves from our beds in the early morning after our first night in Rome. For those who might not know, the Necropolis is a cemetery dating back millennia where people at the turn of the first century AD were buried. St. Peter is believed to have been buried there, and his namesake basilica was built on this perceived holy spot.

As is the case with many places in Rome, history builds upon itself layer by layer. Although the level underneath the main basilica floor was interesting because the remains of many former popes are kept there, the older cemetery underneath that level blew my mind. It was heavily climate controlled with technological sensors and *Star Trek*-type automatic doors that confused the visitor with a mix of futuristic and ancient.

As we walked through this old cemetery, the guide would show us how there were changes in the artwork decorating the graves as we got closer to what is thought to be Peter's final earthly resting spot. Some changes were blatant in that they would explicitly mention Peter, but many changes were more subtle.

While many of the graves featured artwork that reflected non-Christian religious beliefs of the day, there were signs that some of the art may have had a hidden Christian meaning. Apollo, for example, was at times depicted as having the sun behind him, as a sign of his connection to the sun in Greek mythology. Many graves included such imagery of Apollo. As we walked closer to what's believed to be St. Peter's grave, there were similar images of a figure with a sunlike halo behind him, but there were also subtle Christian symbols, such as a fish, off to the side. The guide pointed out that this was likely a way for Christians to provide Christian imagery without everyone knowing that it was Christian. He mentioned that these images are considered to be some of the earliest artistic representations of Jesus, even though ancient observers may have understood them to be depictions of Apollo.

Disguising Jesus as Apollo would be understandable at a time when Christians were persecuted in Rome, and this gravesite art doesn't shed light on how the idea of Apollo may have influenced the idea of Jesus. That said, the overlapping imagery does underscore how it's possible that the two figures may have been in some way conflated — and well before the Christian line of consensus was drawn in Nicea in 325 AD.

Other Evidence of Religions Evolving

Similarities between religions and myths aren't unique to Christianity. There is evidence of similarities between Egyptian and Indian myths, such as both Isis (Egypt) and Ganesh (India) having their heads replaced with the heads of animals, a cow and an elephant, respectively.

Stories of brothers in conflict can be seen in Horus vs. Set (Egyptian), Romulus vs. Remus (Roman), Cain vs. Abel (Judeo-Christian) and Jacob vs. Esau (Judeo-Christian).

The infant twins Romulus and Remus were put into a basket and sent down the river, similar to the story of the infant Moses (Judeo-Christian) being put in a basket in the river (Exodus 2).

The story of a great flood is shared via Noah in the book of Genesis, which is believed by scholars to date back to nearly 1000 BCE. *The Epic of Gilgamesh* from Mesopotamia, however, dates back to approximately 1800 BCE, and its story of Utnapishtim being told by a god to build a large boat to protect his family and the animals of the field during a huge flood has more than an uncanny similarity with Noah's story. They both even reference birds being released from the boat to find signs of dry land.

Roman religion all but commandeered Greek religion, changing the names of some of the gods and little else. There may have been some nuanced differences, such as beliefs about an afterlife, but there's no doubt the Romans hijacked Greek mythology.

Religious syncretism is certainly not a one-way sign pointing at Christianity, as Christianity has influenced other religions like Islam and Santeria, and there are scholars who believe it impacted certain aspects of Norse mythology as well. I am confounded, though, by Christians who might acknowledge syncretic influence *from* Christianity, but refuse to acknowledge syncretic influence *on* Christianity, especially with the many examples cited here.

I find it hard to deny that Christianity was impacted by pagan religions as it spread. The Celtic goddess Brigid, for example, has striking similarities with Saint Brigid of Kildare, a co-patron saint of Ireland with Saint Patrick. Likewise, the Roman Catholic Lady of Guadalupe may have helped many in the new world transition away from some of their own history of goddess worship.

Final Thoughts on Syncretism

These comparisons are intended to be thought-provoking, but they most certainly are not intended to be taken as an exhaustive review of religious syncretism. Volumes and volumes have been (and continue to be) written on the topic. What I have written is primarily meant to make the reader aware that religious syncretism exists.

Until I had done this research, I knew little about it myself. After starting into the research though, the sheer quantity of examples of similarities between religions stunned me. There are many other examples that I did not include, either due to the lack of source documents or the fact that I felt the need to continue on with other topics.

Even if some of the claims regarding Christian syncretism are eventually disproven, I suspect I would still remain convinced of religious syncretism. Even if, for example, new information determines that the communal meal in Christianity influenced the communal meal in Mithraism (and not the other way around), that doesn't mean that Christianity was formed in a bubble. In fact, it supports the opposite claim. If Christianity influenced Mithraism, that would be an example of religious syncretism. There is no reasonable explanation that it exists for all religions except Christianity.

I'm a U.S. citizen and whether you think "melting pot" or "mixed salad" is the more appropriate term for the United States, it's clear that there are ample opportunities for different cultures to mix and influence each other. As an example, one of my wife's favorite bands is Sublime, from Long Beach, California. She knew the lead singer, Bradley Nowell, who died in 1997 from a drug overdose. We frequently play their music and their song "Santeria" came on the other day. While listening, I couldn't help but be struck by the confluence of cultures the song represents. The band members were "surfer dudes" of mostly European descent; their music was a mixture of reggae, ska, punk, and rock; the religion referenced in the song has roots in Africa, Spain, and the Caribbean.

Although communication was certainly slower two millennia ago, there is no reason to doubt that a similar mixing of ideas took place in the area where Jesus was believed to have lived. As already mentioned, the trade network had opened significantly in Jesus' time, and Judea would have drawn travelers from afar with different customs.

In the face of religious syncretism, a Christian might feel a bit cornered and respond defensively: *"Well, OK, so maybe some of these stories weren't totally true. So what? No big deal. That doesn't mean it's all fake."*

Well, of course that's true, but once certain parts of the religious canon are shown to be false (or at least heavily shaded), why would one think that other parts would automatically hold up under scrutiny? Where would you draw the line, and why feel the need to draw a line at all? Let it play out. Do the research yourself.

Whether Jesus was made up or a real man draped in mythology from across the known world, it seems clear that there's little about the Jesus story that's unique. For what it's worth, I think Jesus is likely a mixture of Greco-Roman, Persian, Indian, and Egyptian gods; he shared spiritual teachings similar to the Buddha, but adapted to his place and time.

The pathways via which these stories split, merged, or evolved over time are hard to pinpoint now. Much of the written record has been destroyed. The destruction of the Library of Alexandria in Egypt nearly two millennia ago is perhaps the single most damaging event in the quest to seek the truth. Nonetheless, the evolution of belief systems seems clear.

The God Dilution

During moments of doubt in my religious faith, I was frequently comforted by 1 John 4:8, which reads: "Whoever does not love does not know God, because God is love."

God is love. God. Is. Love. That was all I really needed to hang on.

Engineer that I am, I remember having the revelation in college that I could use the transitive property in mathematics to seemingly solve my faltering faith in Catholic dogma.

As any good sophomore civil engineering student knows, if A=B and B=C, then A must equal C. It is fact. It is indisputable. It makes sense.

Likewise, if God *is* Love and I still felt love for people and strove to connect with people, then, in some way — even if I couldn't explain it — I was OK. If I lived in love, I lived in God. It was the transitive property. It was the "Love Equation."

1 John 4:12 even added the clarification for me: "No one has ever seen God; if we love one another, God abides in us and his love is made complete in us." John was making it clear. My doubts were OK. I was still covered.

So, yeah, I was cloudy about some of the religious mysteries that didn't really make logical sense. Maybe it wasn't right to lean so hard towards the side of logic anyway, right? My doubts were OK, right? It was probably all too hard to understand anyway. As long as I loved, I was still safe as a believer.

This way of thinking was incredibly comforting to me at the time and for much of my life. *It meant I didn't have to throw it all away.* These verses almost single-handedly allowed me to hang on, and I loved them dearly for it.

I'm not sure if it will surprise the reader, but I see these verses from a wholly different perspective now. I needed them and trusted them before, but now I see them as a *very betrayal* of my trust.

This section is intended to go hand-in-hand with — and be an extension of — the previous "Leery of Evolution" argument in this book. Hopefully, the arguments made and evidence provided so far have been successful in convincing you that religions evolve and adapt over time.

When followers of an old religion believe in a man-god who is the son of the great god and a mortal woman (i.e., Hercules), it's helpful for a new religion (i.e., Christianity) to include similar dogma so that believers in the old religion will be able to better relate to the newer religion.

When certain teachings from an old religion highlight a day of judgment that has proven effective in guiding behavior in a culture (i.e., Zoroastrianism), a new religion (i.e., Christianity) may evolve to include this concept in its own teachings. It makes the transition from an older religion and the draw to a newer religion more palatable and powerful if there are commonalities.

I'm not saying that someone purposely decided to steal a little of 'a' from the Greek gods, a little 'b' from Buddha, and some 'c' from Zoroastrianism to make religion 'd.' Just like animals don't make a purposeful decision to evolve, I suspect most religions evolve similarly. Certain adaptions simply increase the chance of survival.

And the psychology of religious leaders need not be nefarious in this process, either. People will believe many things if it helps them keep their worldview intact. I suspect that many changes to religious belief were made in sincerity. This doesn't negate the effectiveness of the adaptions or the underlying evolutionary process.

But conflating God with love, in my view, takes us to a whole new level. I believe a focus on this conflation corresponds with the threats the Enlightenment and the rise of science posed to Christianity.

Yes, of course the "God is love" text from 1 John was written long before the Enlightenment. The draw to make God indistinguishable from powerful emotions is certainly not new. After all, what religion wouldn't benefit from hitching its wagon to a thing so powerful as love? If you can conflate the idea of God with the power of love and goodness, you've likely converted a believer to a life-long believer. Who among us wants to live without love? Who wants to feel that they're living an immoral life? If you believe that love is truly inseparable from God, you will be more inclined to embrace God (dogma in tow).

But as scientific knowledge increased, religion took some punches to the head.

- God isn't zapping lightning at earth out of anger. A stream of electrons is simply following its natural path from positive to negatively charged particles under certain conditions.
- God's curse doesn't wipe out thousands with disease. Bacterial or viral infections that can be viewed through a microscope do that.
- The stars are not homages placed by God to his good followers. Using telescopes, we can see that stars are balls of burning gas, light years away in what's believed to be an infinite universe.

As these hits to the concept of a bearded God in the sky grew stronger, the response was to focus on a softer, more diluted, idea of God. This image was easier to defend. *Remember, God is love! It even says so in the Bible!*

This discussion tracks closely with the "God of the gaps" concept that I'll touch on a bit later. I've already addressed the "non-overlapping magisterial," or NOMA, arguments previously, so I don't want to repeat too much of that here. I do want to emphasize, however, that the dilution of God from an all-powerful bearded man in the sky to broad concepts of love, morality, or even energy is thanks to those who sought the truth and questioned assumptions. If not for scientists and the scientific method, we might still be ritualistically sacrificing each other in hopes of appeasing God. Unfortunately, and in truth, some of us still are.

When I discuss the dilution of God, I hope I am being clear about what I mean. I watched a religious movie the other day. I won't name it here as I suspect the producers would not appreciate it being used to make my point. It followed the pattern of many religious movies and arguments for theistic belief. The main character experiences a series of terrible events and his belief in a caretaker God is put to the test. Although he seems to be questioning God's existence, he nonetheless decides to pray to the entity that he questions. He struggles in anguish, but when he reaches the end of his rope, he unburdens his concerns onto this hoped-for entity in a moment of surrender and acceptance. He feels a huge relief with this unburdening and he's able to take a moment in the silence to acknowledge the wonderment of life and the universe. He feels a loving connection with all of life that bursts from within him.

Although the character drew a connection between his feeling of love for the universe and what he perceived to be God, I argue that he confused the two. His unburdening led to a moment of relief and quiet contemplation, which then led to his feeling of oneness with the universe. *A person in the midst of a struggle doesn't need to place her burdens onto what is likely a fictional character.* She can simply set her burdens to the side. I have felt these moments of awe and wonderment myself, both as a theist and as an atheist. I can attest that the idea of a God entity is not required.

These moments of awe truly are powerful. You feel at one with everyone and everything. You feel the shared kinship with all life, with all matter and energy. When I was a theist, it was clear to me that God indeed was this power. God was love, after all. God was this wonderment. God was in me and in you. God was in the trees and the mountains. God was that energy in all things. God was even in my coffee cup, in the Windex bottle on the counter, in the ping pong table. God was in all things and was all things. God was not just love; God was the universe itself!

I didn't know it at the time, but this was a shift from a theistic worldview to something more like a pantheistic worldview. "Pan" means "all," so pantheism literally means all-god-ism. In other words, "all is God." All is God and God is all.

As an atheist, I've come to recognize that such a definition is useless. If "God" is diluted to essentially mean everything and anything in the universe, what's the point of the word in the first place?

Personally, I find it helpful to go back to math to make the next point. The symmetric property of math declares that if A=B, then B=A. In other words, if God is love, that means love is God. If God is goodness, then goodness is God. If God is kindness, then kindness is God. If God is the universe, then the universe is God.

All these things are meant to be "God," yet they each already have their own distinct definitions. God has been diluted to the point of essentially having no clear definition at all. This doesn't make sense. Therefore:

> Love is not God. Love is love.
>
> Goodness is not God. Goodness is goodness.
>
> Kindness is not God. Kindness is kindness.
>
> The universe is not God. The universe is the universe.
>
> Wonder is not God. Wonder is wonder.
>
> Connection is not God. Connection is connection.

For those who might not be familiar with Richard Dawkins, the title of this section, "The God Dilution," is a nod to his influential book, *The God Delusion,* which I highly recommend. In truth, I don't consider the dilution of God into these softer definitions to be particularly problematic in itself. After all, if everyone essentially worshiped love and connection with one another, the world would likely be a better place. Importantly, though, many believers do far more than simply dilute God.

The problem, in my view, is not so much a God dilution as a God expansion. For many, God is love, morality, goodness, and the energy in the universe — all while miraculously remaining the personal, loving father, caretaker God, floating in some other dimension, peeking in on our lives. God, for many believers, is all the good emotions and ethereal qualities we appreciate about life while still holding onto his very real and solid, dogma-producing, Zeus-like qualities handed down by religious evolution.

This embedment and entwinement, this soaking in and then hardening of the softer definitions of God into the standard dogmatic versions has merged the two in a manner that can seem inseparable to many believers. Many don't see it as two separate elements (love and God) being mixed together, as if in a sandbox. Instead, the two notions are chemically bound and inseparable. For many, the very possibility of separating the two is simply beyond imagination.

This expansion of God represents compartmentalization in perhaps its most common form. Although the believer may not acknowledge it, there clearly is a conflict. If God exists, it's either God as the universe and all of its loving and connecting energy *or* it's God as a unique entity, one who cares even about small things, such as whether you stole ten dollars of quarters from your brother when you were eight years old, felt guilty about it, and then threw them all under the couch because you didn't want to get caught.

God is either one thing or God is everything. This is a conflict.

I see two common defenses in response to this conflict. First, some will simply double down on God as a unique entity who wants a personal relationship with you, and they will seem to write off the pantheistic thinking as satanic eastern weirdo stuff, like that "sneaky evil" practice of yoga, for example. (If you don't believe me, I recommend you go online and search for "is yoga satanic?" I suspect you may be intrigued by what you find.)

But even many of these religious folks who seemingly dismiss the softer definitions of God will still invoke them when needed. The religious movie I wrote about earlier is an example. Emphasis on "God is love" comes back when it suits them.

Other believers seem to take a different approach. Simply put, the response is that it's just a mystery. I don't know if I was ever fully the first type of believer, but I did spend time with many who were, and I wasn't shielded from their influence. But for at least my years as an adult believer, I was more of the second type.

It didn't make complete sense to me that God would be both a unique entity and also love or the underlying energy connecting the universe. But instead of turning back on that idea to inspect it with a magnifying glass, I simply wrote it off as being beyond my understanding. On a certain level, I just accepted it.

As a Catholic, I had the Trinity to lean on. God the Father was an entity, albeit perhaps not a physical entity. God the Son (Jesus) was definitely a physical being as he walked among us a full man. And I always liked to envision God the Holy Spirit as the love and the connection between the father and son, something that certainly was not part of the material world. This mixing of the real and the ethereal as my understanding of God was a strong foundation on which to compartmentalize.

For me, and for quite some time, I could live with this incongruity and I accepted it as something that didn't make sense to me, but perhaps made sense on a higher level that I couldn't understand. Maybe it made sense on God's level, and perhaps when I died, my soul, my energy, would understand it.

For many theists that I know personally, I think this is where they are. There is so much about life that is not understood. I recall feeling that perhaps this mystery is a good thing because it can lead to wonderment and awe, which make us feel alive — and feeling alive is perhaps the best thing about being alive. I even wrote a song when I was younger about the importance of "preserving the mystery."

Preserving the mystery is just one part of the thinking, though. Speaking for my younger Christian self, there is also a real connection to the stories of Jesus' sacrifice and compassion that I feared would get lost if I were to lose faith in God. These stories of loving others, of caring for the poor, of sacrificing for the greater good — they were, and are still, pure gold. I didn't want to lose them. I think this was the harder problem for me.

A eureka moment came to me one day while listening to the song "Eye in the Sky" by the Alan Parsons Project. I was probably nine years old when I first heard it and it brought back great memories of jumping around in our New Jersey basement (where "the kids" had their own record player) listening to music. At that age, I perhaps cared more than most of my peers about things like lyrics, but I didn't make the connection to these lyrics that I do now as an adult. One lyric in particular stands out: *The sun in your eyes made some of the lies worth believing.*

I don't know the backstory about the lyrics. I expect that the song is about a relationship gone bad. That single line, though, was a revelation to me.

There are some things, some ideas, that are so beautiful, it's difficult to turn away from them. The idea of God loving us so much that he was willing to be tortured and then sacrifice his own life to save even the most forgotten among us is an incredibly powerful and beautiful idea. It's the hero king caring about the lowly. It plucks the strings of our soul. It speaks of that connection between us and that stirring energy that we can feel in quiet moments of reflection. These most definitely are the "sun in the eyes" of a lover. Many of us are so overcome by that beauty that we overlook things we don't care to see. We'll even find excuses — do mental and spiritual gymnastics — to accept what we deep down know must be untrue. For some of us, the lies are simply worth believing in light of this beauty. I understand this, or at least I used to, and I understand why it would be hard to break away from this thinking.

The problem with this, though, is that falling in love with these noble ideas of sacrifice and love as seen through the "eyes" of the Christian story (or story of some other religion) continues the merging of the ideas of love, compassion, and spiritual energy with the dogmatic stories and teachings. This is not necessary, but I believe many of us don't see this.

In today's ultra-political and tribal world, we often talk about people "moving the goal post." Folks make certain claims and then when the claims don't match reality, these same folks redefine what they meant by the claims, they add a nuanced change, or they make a new claim out of whole cloth and act as if it's their original claim. The goal line to prove them wrong continually gets pushed back.

In this case, however, it's far beyond pushing back the goal post. Folks are tearing it down and reforming it into a basketball hoop, yet they believe they are still playing the same game. One game is whether a creator God exists. The other is a game about the importance and the power of things like love and compassion. The compartmentalization is amazing.

Cracks in the Armor and Nails in the Coffin

For me, a full conversion away from theism was two-fold. First, there was the mental acceptance. Second was the emotional acceptance. So far, I've been discussing the mental part of my conversion. To recap, this includes:

- Recognizing the immensity of the universe and how unreasonable it seems that a creator of such a universe would focus its energy on our tiny blue speck in space.
- Recognizing obvious similarities between religious belief systems and how they've clearly influenced one another and evolved over time.
- Recognizing that despite religion's ownership claims of concepts such as love and morality, such ideas exist independent of religion.

Before diving into the emotions, I first want to touch on some of the other lines of thinking that assisted the mental acceptance of my atheism. As someone who wants the truth, I've made a significant effort to seek out counterarguments from theists that I found believable. To date, I have found none. But I felt it important to address these arguments in more detail. I've already touched on some; others I'm bringing up for the first time.

Which God?

It's impossible to count the deities who've been worshiped throughout human history. Whether they number in the few thousand or tens of thousands, the obvious question is: which god is the right god to worship? As many competing gods lay claim to the same creation, mutual exclusion dictates that not all of these claims can be true.

What makes believers so sure of their God/gods? Major world religions see Zeus and other older gods as myth, for instance, so what's the difference between these mythical characters and the God/gods of today? I hope I've been successful in showing that the similarities between today's God/gods and those of yesteryear are many. Or, as comedian Ricky Gervais puts it:

> *"There have been nearly 3,000 gods so far but only yours actually exists. The others are silly made-up nonsense. But not yours. Yours is real."*

Modern-day believers in a single God have refuted the thousands of deities of myth and legend. A common saying among atheists is that we simply "go one god more."

Some will argue previous believers were mistaken and they'd follow the one God and his teachings if they were alive today. That's easy to say, but it's clearly not even happening now. Differences in religious beliefs still frequently lead to violence.

If there really is only one God (and all the others are false), why wouldn't God just make it clear and take the guessing out of it for us? No more whispering secrets to people in the desert who haven't eaten in 40 days. No more relying on ancient stories that make little sense with what we know today. No more conflicting documents that each claim to be God's word. For God, this would presumably by very easy to do. It would be a snap of the fingers. Instead, the conflicting beliefs continue, and people ultimately die because of it. It doesn't make sense that an all-good God would allow this.

God of the Gaps

I've touched on much of this already in this book, but want to quickly recap it. There is a sequence of events associated with the idea of God that go something like this:

1. God's existence is assumed; this perceived existence provides an explanation for things that are not understood.

2. As knowledge evolves, it becomes clear that there's an explanation for things previously attributed to God.

3. Because so many of us have such an emotional tie to the God concept, the focus is shifted to those things that we still don't fully understand, and God is once again the explanation for gaps in knowledge.

4. Repeat #2 and #3 many times.

5. The idea of "non-overlapping magisteria" (NOMA) is then introduced, proclaiming, with a tinge of desperation if you ask me, that certain phenomena are simply in God's realm and beyond our understanding. This leaves the assumption of God's existence intact.

NOMA shields religious belief from a more honest assessment and a deeper inquiry. But why on earth would you want to defend yourself against an honest assessment of anything? Subconscious or not, trying to defend yourself from honest inquiry should be a blaring alarm bell that your worldview may require reassessment.

Pascal's Wager

Blaise Pascal (1623-1662) was a mathematician, scientist, and philosopher. He's credited with discovering details concerning hydrostatic pressure (Pascal's Law), developing Pascal's Triangle to help visualize mathematical truths, and he's even recognized as the inventor of the syringe.

Clearly, Pascal was a brilliant man. I do not claim to relate to Pascal on an intellectual or professional level, but I do relate to him in a more personal way, at least in one regard.

Having read some about his life, I can relate to Pascal having suffered hardship, as well as his attraction to religion. In the introduction to this book, I wrote that my head is an engineer, but my heart is a poet and philosopher. I'm curious about how things work and how they can be useful, but I also ask myself the bigger questions of meaning. It appears that Pascal was similar in this regard.

Pascal attempted to mesh these two parts of himself by applying statistics and mathematical probabilities to philosophical and theological issues, and Pascal's Wager was born. Pascal's Wager argues that people should live as though God exists because the benefit of doing so — and the loss for not doing so — could be infinite, while only minor sacrifices are required to obtain eternal life. The argument continues that if God doesn't exist, not much is lost because in that case, we were all going to disappear into darkness anyway.

Putting Pascal's Wager into stock market terms, choosing to believe in God is a low-risk, high-return proposition, while choosing not to believe is a high-risk, low-return proposition.

Now let me offer my criticism. As brilliant as Pascal may have been, he, like all of us, was influenced by his time and place. He lived in a largely Catholic country well before key scientific discoveries. He assumed God existed and believed in heaven and hell.

He speaks nothing of the possibility of other religions worshiping the correct deity. These were simply not on the table for consideration in 17th century France. The "wager" could be tweaked to apply to some non-Christian god. In that case, Christians are suddenly on the losing end of the deal. As these gods are considered to be mutually exclusive, the whole premise of the wager falls rather quickly.

Importantly, Pascal's Wager doesn't prove or disprove God's existence. It only states that we might benefit from living "as though" God exists.

Please consider the following and forgive me if you find it offensive:

> *A man is approached by the mob and told to each day pick up an envelope from one location and tape it underneath a different park bench as directed. He is told that if he complies, he and his family will be protected and showered with wealth and opportunity for as long as he follows these directions. If he does not comply, he and his family will be kidnapped, one by one, slowly tortured, and then killed. There is a clear benefit to agreeing to the mob's demands and severe consequences for saying "no." These consequences make it easy for the man to*

tell himself that becoming a pawn for the mob was the right thing to do.

One might argue that there's no harm in "choosing" to believe in God. In my view, this is akin to "choosing" to believe that there's no harm in distributing those envelopes throughout the city. One might claim ignorance or engage in mental gymnastics to justify certain actions, but deep down, something doesn't feel right. The truth is that just as the items inside those envelopes are likely not harmless, the disregard for reason in favor of magical thinking is also not harmless.

This God/mob boss metaphor limps for a few reasons, but one in particular is that organized crime is indeed a real thing. There are real people who commit real crimes. God, on the other hand, is a concept. "Evidence" of God tends to be intangible things like awe, human connection, or the power of nature. The chance of God making good on a promise of eternal protection or torture is extremely low.

Another problem I have with Pascal's "living as if God exists" approach is that it's rooted in the concept that one can indeed *choose* to believe in God/gods.

For some, "living as if God exists" may simply mean being moral and kind. I take minimal issue with these folks, as we share common goals for the world. For people in Pascal's time — and, I'd argue, for most people today — "living as if God exists" includes following dogmatic teachings. The whole wager is based on teachings about heaven and hell, with God as the decider. To "live as if God exists" inherently assumes an underlying belief in this decider God.

For me as an atheist, then, to follow the advice of Pascal's Wager, I only need to *choose* to be a theist. *Well, why didn't you just say so?* That's easy enough, right? Of course not.

In my experience, belief is not a thing that one arrives at by choice. I have a set of experiences and my beliefs stem naturally from these experiences. Because I'm generally a curious person, I do actively seek opposing perspectives. If I find these sources trustworthy and their experiences or arguments convincing, my beliefs on a given topic may indeed change. *But I don't choose to make that change. It happens naturally in the convincing.*

Who among us would step off a skyscraper because we're told that we can fly if we choose to believe it? Who would step in front of a bus because we're told we can pass right through it unharmed if we choose to believe it?

Fortunately, there are few who would put their lives in danger after being told to believe something for which there is no evidence. Yet many people who'd refuse to jump off a skyscraper are the same people who will believe things with equally poor evidence just because those things bring them comfort.

Christians are indeed told (quite conveniently, I might add) that they will be blessed if they can believe without seeing. John 20:29 makes this clear via the example of the apostle Thomas, who refused to believe that Jesus had risen from the dead until he could see and touch his body.

Being a "doubting Thomas" indeed has negative connotations among the religious, but I don't know if I can think of a higher compliment. Thomas couldn't just choose to believe. He had to be convinced. Presumably, belief came after.

There is another option: one can *pretend* to believe.

Pascal's "living as though God exists" sounds strikingly similar to *pretending* that God exists. Pretending that God exists doesn't make God real, just like pretending doesn't make Santa Claus or the tooth fairy real.

Living as though God exists as recommended by Pascal would require herculean pretending for many of us. One can pretend Santa Claus exists with children, enjoy the story and the excitement, and then tell the children the truth about Santa as they grow.

Imagine attempting to hold on to a belief in Santa well into adulthood. You see people ordering packages online for their spouses on Christmas, yet you have to assume that these are not the "real" Christmas presents from Santa. Perhaps you may still be telling yourself that the many Santas at the malls are Santa's helpers, even though you know that your neighbor is one of them and he tells you that he hates the snow. You have to think to yourself, "*Well played, neighbor. Suuuure you don't like the snow. Wink-wink. I get it. Suuure.*"

For most of us, pretending about Santa would be untenable, yet theistic religious belief is so woven into our social and psychological fabric that pretending about God is much easier.

I'm not saying that most people who claim to believe in God are pretending. I think the opposite much more likely. That said, some folks who say they believe in God, but truthfully don't really think about it all that much, may simply be going along with the flow. Why rock the boat? If I look under the rug, I might see something I don't want to see. Best to simply go along with the stories and focus energies elsewhere.

Pascal's Wager argues that one needs to sacrifice little ("just" an obligation to believe in God and to live as the Church dictates) in order to get infinite reward in heaven if God is real (and as imagined by the Catholic Church). I argue that the sacrifice is hardly small.

In fact, this "minor sacrifice" is none other than your very integrity. It's your honesty and reason. It's your willingness to observe the world with truth-seeking in mind. If you're not willing to experience the world around you clear-eyed, then what's the point? You are living your life by someone else's dictates. In other words, you are living someone else's life. You are sacrificing the very heart of yourself. What greater sacrifice is there than the truth? What God worth worshiping would lead us to abandon the search for truth?

Simply put, Pascal's Wager is a recommendation that *truth-seeking be sacrificed at the altar of things wished for*. I recommend instead "Steve's wager," which is the following: *Seek the truth and let the chips fall where they may*. If a creator God does exist and is not appreciative of truth-seeking, such a deity is not one I'd be interested in worshiping anyway.

Lastly, let's talk about probability. A big part of my day job involves risk assessment. This largely involves attempting to analyze two things: the probability of an event occurring, and the anticipated impact of the event occurring. For example, the probability of getting in a fender-bender is far more likely than getting hit by a large meteorite. The consequences of either event are drastically different, too. One may get you a bloody nose, while the other might obliterate you and everything nearby.

Because fender benders occur so frequently, we plan for them. The auto insurance industry is testament to this. And, thankfully, we also have experts searching for asteroids in space that could harm us, precisely because the consequence of a collision would be so drastic.

What we do not have, though, are groups of researchers looking for where an army of leprechauns may attack. Such a research effort would not only seem ridiculous, it would also divert attention from real items that need our focus.

In Pascal's time, the perceived likelihood of God's existence may have fallen somewhere on the spectrum between fender-bender and a meteorite hit. Given what we know today, though, I argue it is far more akin to the attacking leprechaun army. We simply have more important, and far more likely, things to focus on.

Evil, Suffering, and Excessive "Punishment"

Many, if not most, theists believe in an all-good God. This was certainly the case for me during my time as a theist, having received religious instruction from both Roman Catholics and evangelical Protestants while growing up.

The concept of evil can be tricky. Evil is defined as a "profound immorality and wickedness, especially when regarded as a supernatural force." In practice though, it's incorrectly — yet still frequently — conflated with anything that causes suffering. Murder would be viewed by most as an obvious evil. But what about a flood that kills thousands and destroys homes? This clearly causes suffering, but no one person is responsible for it. Putting the human impact on climate change aside for a moment, this suffering is simply the result of a natural event.

Whether that event is considered evil, as God's punishment for evil, or simply nature being nature depends on individual perspectives. The suffering, however, remains the same and God — even though he's said to have the ability to prevent it — allows the suffering to take place. This seems more evil than good. God presumably could stop the suffering of the innocent, yet he sits on his hands.

The problems of evil and suffering appear to be some of the most effective arguments challenging western theology. There is no shortage of people who lose their faith in a loving God when they lose a loved one or go through some other awful life experience. For some, this jolt is enough to snap them out of it.

It's a challenge for some theists to square the circle. How can an all-good and all-powerful God allow evil to exist in the world? How can an all-good and all-powerful God allow an innocent child to be killed, whether by cancer or a kidnapper?

A common back-pocket answer stems from the idea that Adam and Eve disobeyed God in the Garden of Eden and thus allowed evil and suffering into the world. The Bible tells us, for example, that their disobedience resulted in the suffering of all mothers during childbirth. And even a seemingly innocent child who dies in some horrible way wasn't really innocent because she'd somehow inherited original sin from her biblical ancestors.

Theologians have tried to let God off the hook for such tragedies, but these explanations can be difficult to swallow when it's your own child or family member who is lost. Yet many believers still believe them anyway. They don't want to believe their loved one was abandoned by God, so they employ other psychological tools. Such a tragedy can, in some cases, actually reinforce their beliefs.

Believing that a loved one was lost for no reason can be too great a sorrow to endure.

There are whole courses in Christian apologetics that attempt to address the problem of evil. Typically, these focus heavily on the idea of free will and God's desire to be a bit hands-off out of respect for individual choices. This hands-off approach allows us the "freedom" to choose evil or choose good. But it's funny how people who hold these beliefs will readily summon God to, say, blow a field goal far right.

There were awful wildfires in Australia in 2019 and 2020, and dozens of firefighters were tragically killed. A religious friend of mine took to social media to post how people's prayers were answered because two firefighters in a specific group were not killed. As respectfully as I could in the situation, I responded by asking if the prayers for the dead fire fighters and their families were simply not answered. Somewhat surprisingly, my friend's response inferred that perhaps those people didn't pray. I found this odd because people clearly prayed for them as "pray for Australia" was trending on social media during the fires.

I guess that's one way to answer the "evils" of a natural disaster: you simply didn't pray hard enough to avoid it.

Punishment for evil acts also creates problems. Free will says we can choose evil or good, but what of the punishment for choosing evil? (Given that some people consider birth control on par with murder, "evil" and "choosing evil" are loaded terms.) Regardless of how one defines "choosing evil," the choice to accept or commit evil clearly is a finite crime. Condemning a perpetrator of a finite crime to eternal punishment seems like a step too far for an all-good God.

Another apologetic response to the problem of evil is that while God is all-good and all-powerful, he is also all-just. The argument goes that if God establishes a law and people (with their free will) choose to break the law, then enforcement of a "just consequence" is indeed "good." But, again, one wonders how an infinite punishment in hell for a finite crime is a just consequence. But

who am I to question the reasoning of the almighty? *Oh wait —*
that's right. I'm a normal person who can and should do just that.

It also makes no sense that a "just consequence" like a famine,
flood, or plague is doled out as a divine means to punish specific
people who may not even be directly affected by the punishment.
As I write today in 2020 during the Covid-19 pandemic, some
religious leaders are once again leaning on a surprisingly common,
yet still ludicrous, explanation: the outbreak is not due to
pathogenic evolution, but instead it's God's angry response to
homosexuality.

Oh brother. Can we stop with the anti-gay stuff, please? According
to some, gay people are to be blamed for almost any natural
catastrophe. It seems to me that if God didn't like gay people, he'd
stop making gay people. Gay people still exist, so God must be
cool with the gays. (Whether God exists, though, is another story.)

The Maybe-Not-All-Good God

Another answer to the problem of evil is that maybe God is not
always good. Such a belief system would seem to be more
consistent with our everyday experience of good and evil. Ancient
gods, after all, were not always good. Many were simply
authoritarian. If you were on their good side, good for you. If not,
bad for you. Hence, this thinking led to countless sacrifices of our
four-legged cousins — all attempts to stay on different deities'
good side.

A review of the Old Testament supports a strong argument that the
early Israelites didn't believe in one god initially but rather
multiple gods (see: Judges 10:6). They did eventually settle on
their one God, Yahweh, but even then, there was no accompanying
belief that Yahweh was much different from the previous
authoritarian gods. There are some notable exceptions, but the
general rule still applied. Do what he says and you're OK. Don't
and you're not. The concept of Yahweh as what we'd today
consider an all-good entity did not seem to apply.

A reading of Numbers 31 should make this clear. God commands Moses to war against the Midianites, in which soldiers are told to kill all males, including boys, but to "keep alive for yourselves" all virgin females. One hardly needs to read between the lines about why the virgins were "spared." Despite what apologists will argue, the virgins were clearly treated as spoils of war, to be *used* as the conquerors saw fit. A god that allows, let alone supports, such action is certainly not all-good in my book and is definitely not a god I'd be interested in worshipping. After reading verses like this, I can understand why Richard Dawkins sums up the Old Testament God as "arguably the most unpleasant character in all fiction."

When did the God of the Abrahamic religions became all-good? Clearly the Christian narrative that God sacrificed "himself" for us helps that perception. It was also helped by the writings of St. Augustine (354-430), who drew from Plato and other Greek thinkers to find ways to shed a favorable light on the Most High.

Augustine, an early proponent of the concepts of original sin and free will, didn't specifically blame the devil (Satan) for evil in the world. He believed that humans, through our original sin, allowed evil into the world and we are therefore responsible for both its existence and also our individual decisions to avoid or succumb to it. He frequently stressed his and our own weaknesses in the fight. Clearly he was a fan of Romans 3:23, which states, "for all have sinned and fall short of the glory of God." Studying all this now is like watching the evolution of self-bashing Catholic guilt in real-time.

It's important to note that while Augustine rests the blame for choosing evil on weak humans (meaning the consequences of such a choice fall on us as well), the existence of evil predates humanity. This pre-existing evil, in the Abrahamic religions at least, goes hand-in-hand with the character of Satan.

The question of why an all-powerful God would allow such a terrible thing to exist in the first place — on earth or anywhere else — is frequently skirted by many who've bought into the "evil is our fault" line of thinking. It's as if the theistic response is, "*Hey, we gave you answers to the evil problem — original sin and free will. Now let's just move on to something else, please.*" Never mind that the logic to the argument has gaping holes. Some apologists go steps further into defenses of this thinking, but these become more ridiculous to me the deeper they go.

It's understandably convenient for theistic apologists that the character of Satan would emerge in answering evil. *It's not God's fault. God is all-good after all. It is God's lesser half, his little bratty brother, and/or his fallen angel Satan who's causing all the problems for humans. What a shame it is that humans seem to find him so persuasive.*

While the blame for "personal" evil, such as the decision to commit murder, would clearly fall under free will in the Augustinian model, blame for random suffering or "objective/natural evils" — when not seen as just-consequences or a test of faith from God — often ends up at the feet of the devil. Examples could be if your five-year-old daughter gets cancer or if a tornado destroys your town and kills your husband. These are not personal decisions. They are things that happen to you. Many believers see these as Satan causing suffering to test theists' faith.

I will never forget a Christian concert I attended in the late 1990s where the singer's voice kept cracking. Incredibly, instead of just getting through the song, he stopped after each crack and told the crowd that Satan was attacking his vocal cords and we all needed to pray Satan away. He then led a prayer and when he finally finished the song, the applause reflected the audience's sense of assisting in a divine intervention.

For theists like those who attended the concert, I suspect the general belief is as follows:

- *When something good happens, it's God's doing.*

- *When something bad happens, it's Satan's doing.*

- *When someone does something evil, it's their own fault because they succumbed to temptation and God is not to blame.*

Even for theists who envision Satan as an ambiguous negative force, the same general belief typically remains, and God's omnibenevolence stays intact. God fills the gap for those looking for someone to thank, while Satan fills the gap for those looking for someone (or something) to blame.

Pawning off evil on Satan is convenient, but it has obvious problems. It's as if God created us as children, built a sandbox for us, then poured toxic chemicals all over the sandbox. If you believe in original sin, perhaps us children found the poison under the kitchen sink and poured it into the sandbox — as our parent, God, watched. When we go play in the sandbox and some of us get sick from the poison and die, God washes his hands of all blame. In courts today, this would at minimum be gross negligence, if not involuntary manslaughter, if not voluntary manslaughter, if not murder. Once more, the concept of God being all-good is a difficult one to defend.

The Omniscient Excuse

Now we come to the final backflip of the mental gymnastics competition: God is all-knowing and we're not.

Theists show your score cards. Yes, of course, a perfect 10.

The argument is that God is not only all-good, all-powerful, all-present, and all-just. He's also all-knowing. So, yes, God allows Satan's influence out in the world. He permits hardship and suffering because it's all part of "God's Plan." My goodness, how many times have I heard that term? The *Master Planner God* allows suffering because he is forging the sword of your soul. The heat and fire of the forger's work may cause anxiety and torture, but you are being forged into a beautiful sword for God. You are being made a soldier for God. Suffering in this light should be celebrated.

In this scenario, you are to thank God for the good, but also thank God for the bad (because somehow it's really good, and we just don't understand). Clearly, this is a no-lose scenario for theism.

Other justifications include: *"His ways are not our ways"* or *"God works in mysterious ways."* Think about what is happening here. We don't know the future, so many of us rely on the idea that an unseen entity who cares about us knows the future and is pulling certain strings so this will all work out in the end, at least for you and the ones you care about (and, notably, perhaps not so much for your jerk of a boss or that ex-girlfriend who cheated on you).

So much for free will in this case as someone is clearly directing the show in this scenario, but theists will just push that off to the side — seemingly without a thought — until free will is needed again in some other argument. Again, mental compartmentalization is required here. The ideas conflict. Either someone is pulling the strings to enact some pre-ordained master plan, or you have free will to affect your destiny. Which is it? Consistency in thought does not allow both.

Comedians such as Jim Jefferies and Ricky Gervais have found fodder in the "mysterious ways" of God argument. In no other aspect of our lives would we accept such an obvious non-answer. *Why did you cheat on the test? Because I work in mysterious ways. Why did you rob the bank? Because I work in mysterious ways. Why did you push that person off a cliff? Because I work in mysterious ways.*

The "mysterious ways" defense for evil doesn't hold up in court and it shouldn't hold up anywhere else. I hope the reader can see by now what I consider to be the ridiculous nature of some of these defenses of God regarding evil and suffering.

There is a simple way out of this ongoing need to mentally reshape your reality in order to fit the narrative you've been handed. Instead of endlessly being on guard for new excuses you'll need to make in order to justify the belief in a likely fictitious entity, why not finally admit it's indeed likely fictitious? It can be quite freeing to unburden oneself of such a heavy weight. I suspect many theists don't even recognize that they're carrying it until they put it down. Once down, they may wonder why they held onto it for so long. This was the case with me.

The "natural evil" of the storm that destroyed your house was not sent by God so you could believe in him or so you could be honed for battle. The storm was not sent at all, but simply grew as a result of a temperature differential in our atmosphere.

I understand the desire to want things to have a unique and personal meaning and purpose. I understand the comfort that can provide, and I think this more than anything is why people still hold onto what they must know at some level does not make sense.

This is a Test

I'm writing this section still in the midst of the worldwide horror of the Covid-19 pandemic. With this backdrop, I wanted to check in with the televangelists to see their take on things, so I turned on the television on a Sunday morning in April 2020. I was happy to see that no mass groups were gathered, which would directly conflict with the Centers for Disease Control guidelines, but this hasn't stopped some churchgoers from believing that God will protect them.

On one show, the host told viewers that Satan had brought evil to our door and if we follow God, he will protect us from those evils. To me there was a clear inference that God will not protect you otherwise. I could easily see how some viewers could interpret the sermon as a test of faith.

Ah, yes, the "this is a test" argument for theism! The idea that God is up there testing you to see if you can maintain your belief in him, despite what your logical brain may tell you. It contends that no logical argument about the nature of God will hold sway because God may be putting these arguments there just to test you. You can't debate people who hold onto this belief, because the more rational your argument, the more they see the need to refute it because it's a sneaky "trick." The more logically based, the sneakier it is, and the defenses go up.

I will remind you of 2 Thessalonians 2, which includes the lovely text: "Therefore God sends them a strong delusion, so that they may believe what is false, in order that all may be condemned who did not believe the truth but had pleasure in unrighteousness."

So not only is it a test; it's a test full of trick questions! You need to discard things that you thought you knew about reality and somehow that gets you points. Discard your honesty. Discard your integrity. Just keep doubling down on this way of thinking in spite of all that. That's how you get points in this game.

This is a conspiracy game I'm not interested in playing. I seek the truth. It should be obvious that the *this-is-a-test* argument is not an argument for theism at all, but rather a panicked denial that seeks to fend off weakness in the narrative.

Dying for a Lie

When I was still a theist looking for reasons to hang onto my theism, I took comfort in equating God with love. I also relied heavily on what appeared to be a more concrete Christian argument. It said that Jesus' apostles would not have risked their lives by preaching that Jesus rose from the dead if he indeed didn't rise from the dead. In short, they would not have "died for a lie."

I think I found this convincing simply because I imagined myself in the apostles' place. I like to think I'm a relatively logical person; I wouldn't risk my life for something that I knew to be false. In fact, the "die for a lie" argument comes up frequently in theism vs. atheism discussions. Clearly, I'm not the only one who'd been swayed by this argument.

This said, I want to make sure to spend some time breaking this argument down, as I used to consider it one of the stronger arguments for the Christian version of theism. I now find it quite weak, but I still think it's worth exploring in some detail. The following are several possible counterarguments to the *"they wouldn't die for a lie"* claim.

Apostles as Myth?

First, we ought to acknowledge that the very existence of the apostles is in doubt. We discussed previously that some scholars question the existence of Jesus himself, so it would logically follow that the idea of his apostles is also in doubt.

I'm more inclined to think that Jesus was likely a real person but with mythical stories attached to him. I suspect that the same could be the case for some of his apostles as well. Recall, for example, the story of Peter walking on the water and its uncanny similarities to a Buddhist story. The evolution of myth need not be solely focused on the main protagonist of any story. It can impact the co-stars as well.

Much of what is written about the initial twelve apostles comes from religious sources. With possibly a few rare exceptions, the apostles are not mentioned in secular documents at the time. It should be clear that having to solely rely on religious documents written by people who want you to follow their religion is problematic.

Obviously, if the apostles didn't exist or they are clothed in heavy myth, the "die for a lie" argument doesn't even get out of the gates. Also recall that the Acts of the Apostles (the book in the Bible immediately after the gospels) was, like the gospels, written decades after Jesus' supposed death, so stories of the apostles' hero-like courage to preach the gospel in the face of persecution could certainly have been added years afterwards for effect.

They Believed, But Were Wrong

If one is to concede for argument's sake that Jesus and his apostles were real people, and that the apostles did preach of Jesus' resurrection after his death, we are faced with another option to consider, and that is that the apostles believed that Jesus rose from the dead, but were mistaken.

Clearly, Christian believers will balk at this immediately. What of the risen Jesus appearing to the women in the cemetery, to the apostles behind closed doors, to the men on the road? Did Jesus also not appear to the crowds? Again, all of these stories are from the religious source documents, without significant credible historical backing.

But what of St. Thomas probing the resurrected Jesus' side and hands? Surely, this story is so detailed that Jesus must have physically risen. But perhaps the story is written precisely for the detail — to convince the reader. Thomas, after all, was the skeptic among them. What better way to convince a skeptical person of something, but to demonstrate a case where skepticism is transformed into belief? It attempts to build credibility. You might notice that many Christian apologists today who take part in debates about theism always seem to have some back-pocket, atheist-to-theist conversion story for this very purpose.

All this said, let's still assume that the apostles did exist and they did believe Jesus rose from the dead. Why would they believe this if it wasn't true? The answer will seem simple and overly trite, but it's still the likely answer nonetheless: *They believed it because they wanted to believe it.*

I don't know if I've ever come across a more poignant and truthful lyric than in the Simon & Garfunkel song "The Boxer": "*A man hears what he wants to hear and disregards the rest.*" I see this lyric play out almost daily in normal life. This is especially noticeable as I write in 2020, during the age of President Trump, where every single iota of news seems to be run through a pro- or anti-Trump lens.

If you unabashedly support Trump and have invested your energies (and reputation) into that support, you will be looking for things that help justify your support. "*Look how tough he is on China, on the libs, etc.*" When this "toughness" backfires (negative effects of the tariff war with China, North Korea talks breaking down, etc.), supporters will simply dismiss it and find a more favorable tidbit of news to highlight.

Let me preface these next few paragraphs with a clear disclaimer that I am not equating Jesus with Trump. I find a good portion of teachings attributed to Jesus to be redeemable and admirable. In contrast, I would hardly say that Trump has any real teachings at all, but rather rantings of narcissistic self-worship. While the harshest of Christianity's critics would argue that Jesus, too, is guilty of narcissistic self-worship, I will place that discussion to the side.

Instead of focusing on Jesus and Trump, let's focus on their followers. There are some similarities that are worth pointing out. Followers of both saw charismatic leaders who seemed to speak to them directly. They saw leaders who said things that they may have thought or felt but that they had not heard expressed so openly before. They became emotionally attached. They supported these leaders and at times felt persecuted for doing so. Granted, no Trump supporters have been fed to lions, but the sense of persecution still exists. This "persecution" spurred a sense that they were "in this together" with their leader. The sense of solidarity strengthened.

Generally speaking, Jesus's followers were likely invested in their leader even more than some serious Trump supporters are invested in Trump. In the apostles' case, they essentially gave up their entire lives to follow Jesus (as Jesus required), leaving their families and professions behind. It is understandable, therefore, that it would be hard for them to let go, and that they would want — even expect — a return on such a large emotional investment. It's also understandable that they would not take bad news well. They may dismiss it. They may deny it. Instead, they'll search for the good news they want to hear — the good news they want to believe.

We may never know whether there's any truth to the stories related to events after Jesus' death. Did women really go to a tomb to look for Jesus' body and not find it? Did Jesus' body, in the supposed care of Joseph of Arimathea, even get buried in the first place, or was it likely left to get picked at by animals, as was customary for many Roman crucifixion victims as a means of further humiliation? Perhaps his followers were told that he received a decent burial to make them feel better, while in reality he was thrown in a pit with other perceived criminals. Such a scenario is believable and would explain the lack of a body in the tomb.

Perhaps the man that the two apostles met on the road to Emmaus (as told in Luke 24:13-35) was truly just a kind man who shared a meaningful meal with them, and not a risen Jesus in disguise. Perhaps the "hearts burning within" them were due to them making a connection with a stranger, as Jesus would have likely done or taught. Of course, thinking that it was the risen Jesus in disguise is far preferable to people who had so much invested in Jesus as a savior.

I can understand how different stories like this could have, in aggregate, convinced some followers that Jesus had risen, especially when they so eagerly wanted that to be the case. And as the stories built upon each other, and the people closest to Jesus began to lend credibility to these stories due to their own hopes, I could see how these rumors may have solidified into a communal belief. Any new Jesus-sighting rumor was added to the pile of "evidence" with little regard for, or understanding of, confirmation bias. They believed it because they wanted it to be true.

This is as good a place as any to point out something obvious once again. Instead of posing as a stranger in a cemetery or on a roadway, instead of magically appearing and then disappearing a moment later, a risen Jesus presumably could have done something else entirely. He could have gone immediately to local secular scholars and historians of the time and discussed the details of his resurrection and plans for salvation. He did not make this choice, however — instead putting it on his followers and others to believe without such credible evidence. Once again, it is a "test of faith." Convenient indeed.

More modern examples of people "dying for a lie" are unfortunately plentiful: the 9/11 attackers who expected to meet their 72 virgins in paradise upon waking from their "sacrifice," the Jonestown followers who quite literally drank the "Kool Aid" in 1978, and the Heaven's Gate followers, some of whom had themselves neutered before killing themselves in preparation to be carried away on a spaceship that they believed was following the Hale-Bopp comet in 1997. While I would argue that these folks died for a lie, some would counter that they simply died for their religious beliefs, to which I would respond that this is a distinction without a difference. Religion's ability to clothe lies in protective garb is precisely why I find most religious belief so dangerous.

Metaphorical Resurrection

I remind the reader once more that I'm making several assumptions about the apostles. If they did exist, I expect that stories about them were exaggerated. And some of them may have continued to preach about Jesus' resurrection even though they didn't believe it.

Some followers of Jesus may simply have viewed the resurrection in a metaphorical sense only and this hugely important point has been lost in the stories about their teachings. It was the radical teachings of Jesus that outlasted his death, not his physical body. His teachings showing the worth and dignity of the poor and downtrodden would live on in the teachings of the apostles and other followers. Recall that during the debate regarding which writings would be included in the official books of the Bible, several that made no mention of Jesus' physical resurrection were left out.

A more modern example of metaphorical resurrection can be found in the liberation theology movement in Central America that gained popularity in the mid-to-late 20th century. The movement focused on the impoverished and Jesus' call to help the poor. When listing the names of martyrs for the cause, such as St. Oscar

Romero, groups of believers would shout out *"presente"* in response. These martyrs were not dead, but they lived on — *they were present* — in those left behind to continue the struggle. It's an emotional connection to the dead and one that inspires courage going forward.

Liberation theology is helpful in illustrating this nuanced point about the predicament some of the apostles may have found themselves in after Jesus' death. Whether or not an individual follower believed Jesus physically rose from the dead, she or he may undoubtedly have still held onto the importance of Jesus' teachings, many of which focused on the poor and would have been considered politically and socially radical at the time.

Just as the spirit of liberation theology martyrs lived on in the fight against economic oppression in Central America, the spirit of Jesus may have lived on in the teachings of the apostles after his death. Apostles may simply have viewed the fight for social justice and the moral teachings of Jesus as something worth dying for.

**

Given this seriousness in purpose, it's understandable that some might have gone along with the stories of Jesus physically rising from the dead as pragmatically useful to the cause even if they didn't believe it themselves. The stark reality is that such powerful stories of one among us overcoming death could give hope to people who had been oppressed for years in a way that simple calls for social change would not. Hope is an essential ingredient to any political movement as it brings people together in common cause. The stories, whether true or not, were useful. They were effective in building up a base of followers, something that would be necessary to reach larger goals.

Some apostles may have seen the goals of freeing themselves from establishment leaders (Romans and the Jewish Sanhedrin) and establishment thinking as an end that justified many means. Some may have thought that allowing the stories of physical resurrection to propagate was akin to telling a white lie that could be forgiven because of its effectiveness. They might not have really believed it, but they may have been willing to die for it because they thought it could lead to better things.

**

Let's consider more current times. I suspect most suicide bombers tend to believe they are fulfilling religious duties, but there have been groups that openly support terrorist acts and make a point of publicizing that "martyrs" for the cause would be celebrated and their families taken care of. In such cases, new motivations enter the picture.

What if you're an oppressed and poor person who can't provide for your family? Perhaps you don't believe the religious stuff at all, but your depression has you near suicide as it is, and you see dying this particular way as having a silver lining. Clearly, there may be many motivations for one to "die for a lie" under these circumstances.

What if you were a Branch Davidian, a follower of David Koresh in Waco, Texas, in 1993? Perhaps you cut all ties to your earlier life and you believed that Koresh was the person chosen by God to break one of the "seals of the apocalypse." Perhaps over time your belief in him waned, but when federal agents surrounded the compound, your deeply held belief in religious liberty over governmental mandate took hold. Perhaps you had an opportunity to leave the compound, but you stayed to protect your rights and because you were emotionally connected to many people inside.

When all is said and done, will your death be counted as one who believed in Koresh and died for your faith? Was it a death for religious liberty? Were you held back due to threats and pressure from inside? Or did you simply love several people who wouldn't leave the compound? Once again, the point is clear. Motivations for seemingly "dying for a lie" can be complicated. There's no reason to think differently in the case of the apostles.

The Prosperity Gospel

There is an inherent respect for the apostles that comes with being raised in a Catholic family. Their sainthoods are revered, and their lives are raised high for all to emulate. As the stories about the apostles (the original twelve and those thereafter) took hold in my imagination as a boy, the respect seeped further into my blood. I recall being proud to be named after St. Stephen, who was not one of the original twelve, but he was the "first martyr" for the faith so that certainly was worth something. I myself could think of no better way to die at the time than a Christian martyr's death.

With my many years of built-in respect for the apostles, you might understand why even now I find it difficult to write about another possible reason why they may have continued preaching about Jesus' resurrection. Hope, as we just discussed, is a powerful motivator in bringing people together. But hope, as it turns out, is also a powerful business opportunity.

Go no further than your remote control to see a business side of Christian hope today. Televangelists ask for private jets to preach the good news without having to be *bothered* by those folks to whom they would presumably be preaching. Some teach of a "prosperity gospel" that melds Christian teachings with modern capitalism. It teaches that God wants you to be rich in this life, and riches may indeed be considered a sign of God's favor. Who knows how the apostles in Jesus' time would compare to these preachers today? Similarities could certainly be argued based on available religious writings.

Acts of the Apostles 4:33-35 sheds some light on the prosperity involved:

> *"With great power the apostles continued to testify to the resurrection of the Lord Jesus. And God's grace was so powerfully at work in them all that there were no needy persons among them. For from time to time those who owned land or houses sold them, brought the money from the sales and put it at the apostles' feet...."*

I find the fifth chapter of the Acts of the Apostles to be downright disturbing with how it relates to those who gave to the young church. The couple Ananias and Sapphira sold land and gave only a portion of their proceeds to the apostles, keeping some for themselves. Ananias was chastised for not giving it all to the church and died immediately. Sapphira later lied about how much the land was sold for and she died suddenly as well.

I can't help but read this story and think of a mob boss telling a lackey how awful it would be if something happened to the man's daughter. The story of Ananias and Sapphira seems quite useful as a veiled threat to those who didn't financially support the apostles as fully as expected. If not an outright threat, it was at minimum severe peer pressure.

Given these stories, it seems clear that continuing to teach people about Jesus' resurrection could be a lucrative venture. These apostles had left their homes and careers, but what incentive would there be to go back to the fishing nets when they may have found something far more profitable?

So, one might argue: *OK, maybe they could make some money continuing to preach what they did, but why would they continue in the face of threats to their lives?* Presumably, someone who is doing something just for the money is not typically someone who would die for a cause.

Again, in this case, we're only considering the motivating factor of money as a reason to teach of Jesus' resurrection. There are other, more lofty possible reasons for doing this. And perhaps a mix of factors motivated them.

Apostles who were motivated by money simply might not have realized that their teachings put their lives at risk. After all, Jesus had been killed and perhaps the Romans and the Sanhedrin expected that the social unrest related to him had been squashed in the process. Rome certainly had other things keeping it busy, such as battles with barbaric tribes along the edges of the empire. Perhaps the balance between making a profit and staying off Rome's radar wasn't something the apostles considered enough.

Once back on that radar, it may have been too late for them fade into the background.

There's also the opposite possibility that the apostles were doomed anyway, regardless of what they said or did after Jesus' death. Assuming the Romans in the area were not preoccupied elsewhere and/or the Sanhedrin kept their eye on suppressing the "Jesus-is-the-Messiah talk," perhaps the apostles were never able to evade attention. Perhaps plans were made early to make a strong example of them.

Benjamin Franklin is credited with saying, after the Declaration of Independence had been signed, "We must, indeed, all hang together or, most assuredly, we shall all hang separately." History tells us that the signatories didn't all sign the Declaration at once in 1776, but there is little doubt that when each man did sign, he knew he was signing his death warrant in the case of a failed revolution. There would be no forgiveness from King George at that point. They were beyond the point of return.

Likewise, it's quite possible that if Jesus was truly considered dangerous (which, apparently, he was), the plan could have been to stamp out any of his followers to prevent similar uprisings in the future. Rome, after all, was often ruthless against revolt. If you don't believe me, consider the 6,000 slaves that Rome crucified along the road between Capua and Rome for fighting alongside Spartacus several decades earlier.

In other words, it might not be that the apostles bravely stared down death to preach of Jesus' resurrection. It could simply be that they were not going to be spared anyway — that they would be hunted down and killed regardless. And if someone is hunted down and killed, it certainly sounds better for his sake if people believed that he had faced that scenario with courage and grace from God.

The Apostles and Occam's Razor

As I mentioned earlier, when I was a Christian, I took comfort in the idea that the apostles had been divinely strengthened and inspired to preach of Jesus' resurrection, even in the face of death. After all, why would they lie about such a thing if it could mean their own necks?

I hope the reasoning discussed in this section helps the reader understand why I no longer find such an argument convincing. To quickly recap:

1. There is little secular historical evidence that many of the apostles existed. It seems likely that some may have been purely mythical, and others may have been real people whose stories were bathed in myth. In such a scenario, the argument for their strength in the face of death is a non-starter.

2. It seems quite possible that some apostles so desperately wanted to believe that Jesus rose from the dead that they convinced themselves it happened. Examples of confirmation bias or people seeing only what they want to see are on full view as I write this during the presidency of Donald Trump. There is no reason to believe that human psychology was vastly different 2,000 years ago.

3. It's quite plausible that some apostles may not have believed that Jesus physically rose from the dead, but they went along with the story because it was useful in giving hope and bringing people together who had been so influenced by Jesus' teachings. They may have viewed it as acceptable, partly because they felt an inspirational, albeit metaphorical, resurrection — or rebirth — of Jesus' teachings in themselves.

4. Biblical stories in the Acts of the Apostles describe how people would sell their possessions and give the proceeds to the apostles. Given these stories, it seems that teaching about Jesus' resurrection may have been a lucrative business opportunity.

5. Lastly, it's also possible that, like Jesus, his apostles had already been deemed dangerous by the Roman Empire and their fates were decided. Given what we know of Rome's ruthlessness in clamping down potential uprisings, it's plausible that the apostles would have been targeted for execution and hunted down to be made examples of, regardless of their actions after Jesus' death.

Any one of the five arguments above seem strong enough to refute the "they-wouldn't-die-for-a-lie" argument. Stronger still is the possibility that there is some truth to each of these reasons, creating a mixture of motivations and realities. This would undermine the glorifying stories that end up in the Catholic pamphlets I read as a young boy about the apostles courageously facing down death due to an unshakable belief in Jesus' resurrection.

Many know the concept of Occam's razor, which says that the best explanation for something tends to be the simplest explanation. Interestingly, this concept is credited to a 14th century friar who used it to defend the concept of divine miracles. In his world, explanations for thunder, disease, and drought were easily explained by a single assumption: God did it. It was the ultimate "God of the gaps" argument. The gaps in human understanding at that time were so huge, it's understandable that "God did it" would have seemed the obvious and most simple explanation to many.

But so much has changed since the time of Friar William of Ockham. Occam's razor comes up often in scientific discussions as a means to advance scientific thinking — and, in the process, refute magical thinking. It can certainly be used in the case of Jesus' claimed resurrection.

What's more likely to have occurred?

> A man (who may have been purely fictional, but whose life at least was certainly bathed in myth) found a way around all known laws of physics and biology to die and then rise again days later, because his invisible father wanted it to happen. This resurrection was a reward from the father to the son for abiding by the father's wish that the son be tortured and killed as recompense for the eating of a piece of fruit by people who were said to live thousands of years prior. This physical resurrection occurred in secret, or at least far from those who would document it.

> OR

> A charismatic leader and teacher came on the scene in a time and place where myth was frequently enmeshed with reality in people's minds. People were drawn to him and likely were distraught upon his death. Still believing much of his moral (and political) teachings, some of these followers may have chosen to continue the general teachings. Some may have even so desperately missed their friend and leader that they convinced themselves he'd returned from the dead. This teaching of their risen leader seemed to solidify a movement that they had long hoped to build — and it may have been profitable to boot.

As the second option is quite believable given our understanding of human experience (not to mention that it doesn't refute laws of nature), it clearly passes the Occam's razor test, while the first option does not.

**

As an important afterthought for this section, I should at least mention one option I've not yet discussed: Jesus may have *survived* the crucifixion. The medical cause of death for many crucifixions was suffocation. It's not crazy to imagine that someone might have passed out due to limited oxygen and then be believed dead, especially with the limited medical understanding at that time. Some Christians I know like to stress that Jesus was stabbed in his side to ensure he was dead, but even if that happened, being stabbed in the side after passing out wouldn't guarantee death. Some Muslims, for example, believe that Jesus survived his crucifixion (and/or he wasn't even crucified in the first place). Such a scenario could explain post-death sightings.

The Illogical Story of a "Perfect" God

Hopefully, the Occam's razor discussion helped to highlight what I see as a clearly illogical thought process that goes along with theistic belief. When one can take a step back and — dare I say, "snap out of it" — the absurd nature of theistic belief exposes itself. At least it did in my case.

To stress the point, I will once again dissect certain Christian beliefs as I'm most familiar with these. Let's look at the general chronology of events.

1. God, who can do all things, created the universe and life just by giving the word. Despite his complete power, he couldn't seem to create everything in an instant, so it took him several days.

2. The all-knowing God took a few days of work to realize that he was still not fully satisfied with his creation, which ought to have been perfect from the get-go. His creation was not enough, so he needed to make a special creation in his own image. Aside from the notable narcissism, this exposes the all-perfect God as being lonely and in need of companionship (and/or worship; see Isaiah 43:21).

3. God then created a man and attempted to find him a "fitting helper." After bringing all the beasts before the man, God realized that even his own creation wasn't satisfied with it. None of the beasts would do (Genesis 2:20). God recognized this hole in his plan, so he took corrective measures by creating a woman.

4. After completing his creation, the all-powerful God apparently got tired and needed a day off after six days.

5. All seemed good in the world, but for reasons that "God only knows," he decides to tempt his new creations with the possibility of knowledge.

6. Instead of applauding the quest for knowledge, God decides to punish his creations for yearnings he had clearly created in them in the first place. (If one is to take the stance that these temptations were the devil's doing, the obvious question, then, is why an all-powerful God didn't stamp out rebellions against him; indeed, how could conditions for a heavenly rebellion against an all-loving and all-powerful God foment in the first place? But I digress.)

7. The all-merciful God, having been quite easily offended by his own creations, relies on his chief military angel to expel Adam and Eve from the garden. He also decides to inflict chronic pain on them going forward. But it doesn't stop there. The wages of sin would be demanded from their descendants, too, despite them having nothing to do with their ancestors' actions.

8. The all-merciful God then watches for centuries as his creations murder and are murdered to appease his apparent need for blood sacrifice.

9. The all-powerful God is still not happy with his creation, so he takes a divine mulligan and destroys almost all of it via a flood. He hopes that those chosen to survive this do-over will adequately worship him.

10. Even after wiping the slate clean to start over, the all-powerful God remains unhappy with his creation. Turns out that his second attempt has failed, too.

11. God allows ongoing wars between factions of his creation. He actually encourages violence, if not outright demands it (i.e., Numbers 31).

12. Finally, after millennia of bloodshed, God suddenly decides things have gone too far. He will finally forgive the "original sin" of his human creations or at least not hold it against current generations. I'm kidding, of course. He didn't do that.

13. Instead, the all-merciful God decides that he still needs a blood sacrifice, so he sends his only son to be tortured and killed. Not sure why that would have to happen, but God "works in mysterious ways." Apparently, sacrificing his own son was the only way he would allow himself to forgive people who died millennia ago for following a basic curiosity that he instilled in them in the first place. With this being the solution that he came up with, I understand why "the all-creative" is not one of his common monikers.

14. By now, I suspect you're hopeful that this is finally it. Peace at last, right? No. Original sin is alive and kicking. Despite sending his son to be tortured and murdered, the all-merciful God still holds original sin against every newborn baby.

15. Now the game is changed a bit, but the theme of disregarding common sense remains. God only asks that you throw all known laws of physics and biology in the trash. You must believe on faith that a man died, was dead for three days, then rose from the dead, and then floated into heaven. And if you don't believe this, the all-merciful God will send you to eternal torture in hell. If you do believe, you will be rewarded by forever singing praises to that all-merciful God. I suspect it will be like a never-ending Trump rally in the clouds.

I truly hope that you can see this for what it is. It's a story. It's a fairy tale — and not a particularly good one. If you can't see the foolishness that I see, I ask that you replace some of the terms above with the name of known fictional characters.

If I told you that Darth Vader used the force to create humanity several millennia ago, but after humans somehow hurt his feelings, Darth had his henchmen cast them out, you might coax me into a car and then Google the location of the nearest psychiatric hospital.

Truthfully, I see the biblical story as no more objectively believable than this Darth Vader story. It's believed because it has been passed down the generations with limited critical inspection. The story has become so ingrained in our everyday life that it's hard to recognize it as the absurdity it is.

It certainly can be difficult to snap oneself away from this thinking, especially when certain parts of society reward the cognitive dissonance. For many, being a "person of faith" is somehow deemed a good thing, although it flies against all reason. Folks are applauded for following reason when they discover new ways to propel rocket ships or new ways to combat diseases, but reason is to be sidestepped when it comes to theistic belief. When pointing out gaping logical holes in the story, folks suddenly play by different rules. This is telling. A nerve is being hit.

In fact, the whole business of theistic apologetics — arguing that it's logical to believe the fairy tales — tries to bridge this divide. Often, there are nuanced details involved — some claimed hidden knowledge that atheists just can't understand because we remain "closed" to God.

As time goes on, it more and more strikes me as crazy talk. The arguments nearly always seem cosmetic in nature, never adequately addressing the elephant in the room: that the whole basis for the story isn't based on any real evidence, but on wishful thinking.

But Religion Helps People

In seemingly every theism vs. atheism debate of any significant length, theists believe they gain the upper hand by pointing out that certain atheists in history were terrible tyrants. Stalin is one example. Frequently, they argue that the cold and murderous nature of such tyrants arises from a belief in the "survival of the fittest." They misunderstand key points of Charles Darwin and twist this phrase about biological natural selection to infer that atheists believe that anything is permitted in order to get power and survive in society. Meanwhile, they argue that religious teaching is based on helping people, and on being loving and kind to your fellow man.

Unpacking this is quite simple, really. Calling out Stalin or other irreligious tyrants is essentially an ad hominem attack against atheism. Logically, it doesn't hold up. Wonderful people and terrible tyrants throughout history have been theists and atheists. To claim that only atheists act in evil or tyrannical ways flies in the face of direct personal experience and any objective reading of human history.

The argument that religions are based on helping people while secular institutions are not, is simply not true. From my perspective, I see such a statement as simultaneously tragic (because people believe it) and laughable (because it's nonsense).

Although religions frequently have the well-established infrastructure associated with charitable branches, and there certainly are lovely and caring religious people in the world, religions don't have a monopoly on helping people. And several religious groups have directly been involved in wars and/or programs of torture and genocide throughout human history, specifically related to religion. The Crusades and the Spanish Inquisition are frequently cited examples.

On the flip side, countless secular institutions have advanced human betterment via scientific research, the arts, and the development of life-saving infrastructure, such as city-wide sewer systems and water-treatment. Various non-religious charities also work for the betterment of humanity without the requirement for (or deference to) magical thinking.

The most important point to make in this section, though, is something that hopefully is obvious: even if a religion seems to help some people, this still would have no bearing on the truth-claims of the religion.

If I claim that I'm a better basketball player than Michael Jordan and then I give you soup in a soup kitchen when you are hungry, I'd suspect that you could separate my kindness in giving you the soup from my ridiculous claim of basketball prowess. Now, if I told you that my kindness in giving you the soup was a direct result of me being a better basketball player than Michael Jordan, and, but for my basketball skills, I wouldn't have had that kindness to give you the soup, I'd hope you would see that as nonsense. If I tell you that you *have* to believe this about me or you will be tortured for eternity, I suspect you may start looking elsewhere for a charitable soup line.

No doubt, having a religious belief system can be useful for many people. Believing you are fulfilling God's plan when you make questionable decisions might be useful in relieving the burden of difficult decisions. Believing you will be reunited with loved ones in heaven can certainly be useful when dealing with the tremendous grief felt upon the death of someone close to you. But "useful" does not equal "true."

There are ways to deal with hard decisions and the death of loved ones without forfeiting reason in favor of magical thinking. Succumbing to magical thinking is harmful precisely because it diverts our attention from reality and all the wonderful opportunities we have to make life better without the need for rose-tinted glasses.

Can't Disprove God

Finally, we come to the non-argument that one can't disprove God's existence. This is often argued by theists as if it's proof for God's existence. The same "argument" can be used for the existence of leprechauns, Big Foot, the Loch Ness monster, or trolls. The burden of evidence is always on the one making the claim.

Christopher Hitchens said it best: "What can be asserted without evidence can also be dismissed without evidence."

Timing

The merits of the objective arguments for atheism stand on their own for me, but another factor probably influenced me as much as any. Like many things in life, it came down to "timing." In short, life intervened.

I'll discuss more about timing later, but I recognize now that there was probably a good two decades (largely overlapping with my 20s and 30s) when I allowed myself to be exposed to new ways of thinking, yet I still considered myself a theist. This was not because I was a theistic zealot. I was not. By that time, I was already beyond that. I had simply stopped actively thinking about those meaning-of-life-type questions in any deep way. I didn't trash the answers that were handed to me at birth, but I put them on the shelf, to be picked up again at some point down the road for later inspection. The philosophy stuff would have to wait as I dove into developing my personal life and my career.

It wasn't until my wife and I had to start making decisions about what we were going to teach our children about God that I reached back to my teenage years and the promise I made to myself — to always be honest with myself. The line from Hamlet: *"This above all else; to thine own self be true"* was one of the few Shakespearean lines that stayed with me from my high school literature class, but it sunk in deep. This promise *had* to apply to my children as well. I could not teach them things I did not believe. I knew I needed to dig back into this topic again — and this time, I would dig deep with all the tools of inspection at my disposal.

The Debate Summary

Being intellectually open to arguments for atheism was difficult, but it was not as hard as dealing with the emotions that came with (and after) that process, as I'll discuss next in Part 3.

When I was in my calmer, engineer-mode moments, I could separate myself from much of the emotion and could more easily see how convincing atheistic arguments were. It simply made so much more sense.

1. Seeing how small we are in the cosmos seemed to clearly contradict with wishful thinking that we are the center of it.

2. Seeing how the evolution of different myths has played out over history, influencing religious beliefs of all sorts, clearly contradicted claims that the religious stories I was told were somehow immune from that influence.

3. Seeing how religion had so effectively attached itself to our basic human needs for love and acceptance allowed me to understand its enormous influence on people today and why it can be so difficult for folks to break away.

4. Recognizing that many of the common arguments for theism were hardly arguments at all, but distractions from the debate, had me clamoring for a theistic perspective that I would find convincing. The more I explored theistic arguments, the weaker they became.

5. Finally, time and life circumstance forced my hand. Raising children, I could no longer hide from my denial and pretend that I was just experiencing healthy doubt. Practically speaking, I believe this played as much a part in my

conversion as any of the other realizations. If not for that sense of urgency regarding how I would teach our children, I might not have put in the work. If not for that urgency, perhaps I would still be a nominal believer and those questions I had would have stayed safe on the shelf.

In the end, my pathway to conversion was unique to me. Although I've heard similar stories from others, the nuances are always different. I recommend readers do their own research and seek information from experts in relevant fields, whether it be astronomy, history, psychology, or some other field. I expended significant effort to thoroughly research this book, but if you're like me, I expect you might want to confirm much of this for yourself.

Part 3: Emotional Nuance

An Internal Civil War

The idea of God has become such a useful force for so many people. It provides comfort where none is found, it provides answers when answers escape us, and it provides a promise that life has a purpose and death can be overcome. For many, it's quite literally a godsend. It's the solution to every problem.

This said, the enormous gravitational pull towards the God idea is completely understandable. Even after starting to mentally accept that I was no longer a theist, there was more work to do to reach escape velocity in an emotional context. I could see more clearly than ever that religion requires belief in an ultimate explanation of everything that truthfully doesn't really explain much of anything. But it was still hard to pull completely away.

The emotional realm doesn't always play by rules of reason and logic, and there are times that we love it for that. Emotions help us feel alive, as opposed to just being some carbon water machine that sits and subconsciously calculates probabilities all day.

Emotions can also be nuanced and complicated, frequently blinding us from seeing things that we may not want to see. Consider a person who is emotionally attached to the hope that an abusive spouse might suddenly turn things around despite years of abuse. This person would benefit from mentally snapping out of that abusive relationship — to take a step back to consider it rationally and see it for what it is. Despite emotional attachments, we sometimes recognize when it is best to pull away.

I don't know if I'd compare my former beliefs to an abusive relationship, per se, but I do recognize that those beliefs were holding me back, perhaps like a drug addiction might do. They were limiting my freedom and boxing me in, preventing me from exploring the world with clarity and integrity.

I had reached the point where I no longer found theism to be convincing. For my own sake and for the sake of my children, I knew that I could not run from that. I had to be true to myself, come down from the overlook, and walk onto the emotional battlefield.

I would be entering an internal civil war — my childish hopes vs. my integrity, and many of the people I most cared about were allied with those hopes I had once held. I expected emotional difficulties in the process, and I found them. My great and sustaining comfort, however, was the knowledge that I was not lying to myself. This also was my ammunition. Ultimately, that knowledge freed me.

This emotional and internal civil war had many battles on many fronts. Let's walk through some of the different battlefields.

Concern for Reaction of Others

One of the hardest parts of coming to grips with the realization that I was an atheist was knowing that for me to maintain personal integrity, I would not be able to hide it. My atheism was a freeing and life-changing realization and if I acted like nothing had changed, I would be living for other people and not for myself. I would be living a lie, and I'd already promised myself I wouldn't go down that road. I had no plans to flaunt it, but I wouldn't run from it, either. I was learning that it was part of who I was.

If you recall from Part 1, theistic infrastructure can help bind a person to her religious beliefs. It supports an "immaculate conflation" that makes it difficult for people to separate their hopes and fears from religious teachings and dogma. Couple this with the many negative connotations associated with atheism, and I knew that coming out of the atheist's closet might change how people I loved and cared about saw me. Would their view of the world change, or would their view of me change?

In other words, one of the biggest challenges for me emotionally was dealing with how people I cared about would react to finding out about my new understanding of the world. I feared that such news would hurt them; in many cases, I was justified in that concern.

I should first say that there were many people close to me who simply accepted my atheism, and I appreciate them very much for it. They recognized that I was the same person as before, but I was challenging myself and growing.

Others reacted quite differently. For the sake of respecting their privacy, I will not name names and I may purposely mix up the pronouns when recounting interactions with them. Just know that some of these individuals were — and in most cases still are — people close to me. As I suspected, my atheism was not welcome news to them and they responded with sadness and anger.

But the first reaction was shock. Religious family members and friends had a hard time realizing I was no longer a Catholic/Christian, especially because, to many of them, I had seemingly lived a model Catholic/Christian life. I had seriously considered the priesthood in my youth, and some of them knew this about me. For them, this initial shock was significant. I remember one person grappling with the idea that I did not believe in hell. She was convinced that this opened the door for Satan to mess with my mind. I wrote down the interaction the day it happened, so the conversation snippet below is pretty close to verbatim.

> *Person: "Let me ask you something Steven, do you believe in hell?"*
> *Me: "No."*
> *Person (shocked): "So you don't believe in hell?!"*
> *Me: "Correct."*
> *Person: "Well, see Steven, that's the type of thing that will change the way you think about everything."*
> *Me: "Yes. It is."*
>
> *(End of conversation.)*

Sadness

I had several talks with this person after this one, and religion frequently came up. In one conversation, she asked that, as my Christmas gift to her, I would take my family to church. I told her I would go and that I'd invite my family, but I would not force them to go. She was not too keen on the idea of me "asking" my family. In her view, I was the male head of the household and I should not need to *ask* anything. I should put my foot down and demand it. This highlighted yet one more difference between us. (For the record, half of my family went to church. I found it interesting to be back.)

I also recall a phone call with this person that ended with her essentially pleading, even demanding, that I say a Hail Mary with her. There was a sense of desperation in her voice that surprised me, although perhaps it should not have. She was having a hard time with my atheism, and I could tell that I truly was concerned for me. She was worried for my immortal soul, and the souls of my wife and children. I joined in towards the end of the prayer and I could tell that this comforted her. I realized that, with some people, I needed to take baby steps.

In this person's case, I think her sadness stemmed from her concern over my eternity. But I think others were saddened by the idea that I would no longer have this big "thing" in common with them anymore.

One person whom I never personally considered to be deeply religious gave me some interesting feedback. He always struck me more as the Catholic who made sure to check all the required religious boxes — the guy who would go to 6 a.m. mass because it might be 10 (dare I say, 15) minutes shorter than the average mass. It seemed to be a matter of obligation for him, so the feedback he provided really ought to have been something I should have seen coming. After discussing my atheism for a bit, he offered something along the lines of, "Besides, to be Catholic, there are really only a few things that you *have* to believe."

He went on to say that he was fairly sure the dogma that was "officially required belief" was actually pretty limited, and that there were many things that could be up for debate, all while staying under the Catholic umbrella. It sounded like an argument for the big tent that political parties often strive for. I'm quite sure he was referring to things like whether priests should be able to get married, or whether women should be allowed to be priests.

I politely responded that since I didn't believe in God, I most certainly did not believe in even the minimal dogma items that he had in mind. I was quite far from the umbrella. This clearly disappointed and saddened him, but I could see that he was highlighting a side door that he was trying to leave open for me. He was trying to build a bridge as we were separating from each other on this topic. Religion can be divisive, and he did not want it to divide us.

Another person asked where I planned to be buried. When I told him that I planned to change my will to specifically not be buried in a Catholic cemetery, this shook him. He was not expecting that I would have already thought through one of the most final of earthly decisions. I could tell he was still absorbing my response as he continued talking as if he were angling to find some loophole to get an atheist buried in a sanctified Catholic cemetery.

I saw this as another person trying to leave me an opening to sneak back into the church. I recognized, again, that this was to prevent us from drifting apart in this life, though clearly his question about where I'd be buried was also about the next life as well. When I told him I did not think it right for me to seek cemetery space set aside for Catholics under false pretenses, I could feel the last of the air go out. He was trying to keep me in the club, and I turned it down.

My atheism would not just require me to deal with certain emotional adjustments alone. People I loved (and who loved me) would be challenged to do the same. It was not just me fearing that I would lose them; they feared that they would lose me. This put some of them in an uncomfortable position, and it became clear that some took offense.

Defensiveness and Anger

I rarely bring up my atheism in everyday conversations. That said, when it does come up, it can trigger some religious people. Their defenses go up and, at times, their underlying anger is obvious. It forces people to consider that they might be wrong, and many don't want to be in that situation. They are quite comfortable where they are.

At times, it seems as if they find me to be somehow disrespectful for simply being open about who I am. Comedian Ricky Gervais once said something that's worth repeating: "Why is saying 'there is no God' considered disrespectful to believers, but saying 'there is a God' not considered disrespectful to atheists?"

I think the answer is because one threatens a belief system that guards its most prized beliefs from full inquiry, while the other is a belief system that often arises from dogged questioning of sacrosanct beliefs.

Nonetheless, some of the reactions I've experienced felt angry and offended. In one instance, I was attempting to explain how I saw things to someone close to me when I was told to go to confession immediately and then hung up on. One person angrily told me that someday I would "come crawling back to God." In another case, sharing a video showing the immensity of the known universe drew the ire of a childhood friend who lambasted my post as an attempt to "take God out of the equation."

Some people have been more restrained, expressing what felt to me like irritation or annoyance. One person I'd known a while and with whom I had shared several "Catholic" moments seemed to feel somehow responsible for me keeping up with religious obligations. When I did not, I sensed annoyance from him. I may have put him in a position where he felt embarrassed among his believer friends because he wasn't able to keep me in the fold.

Another person close to me accepted my atheism but commented that I should not be one of those atheists who "pushes his views" on others. Fair enough. On a certain level, that's essentially how I feel about many theists. It did strike me as him saying he would not be talking about these issues with me. This person was still a nominally religious person and it seemed clear he did not want to be confronted with this topic. It felt like a warning.

One reaction that I expected was references to my mother, who had died when I was 14. I heard the following from people I love and respect:

- *Your mom would be disappointed.*

- *How do you think your mom would feel with you just walking away from the religion she gave you?*

- *Your mom must be spinning in her grave.*

I could not help but feel these responses were cruel. The people making these comments largely knew that I loved and missed my mother, and I felt they had to know that these comments would be hurtful.

I suspect that my openness put them on the defensive. It must have felt like a direct attack on their most cherished beliefs, so they hit back where they thought it would hurt most. But despite this, I also sensed a sadness. All these emotions intermix and interplay. It's hard to figure out where one ends and another begins. Although cruel, I also felt the references to my mother were an attempt to guilt me into returning to the Church. I think this came from a place of fear and love.

Believers can get defensive at the mere presentation of atheism in a fair light, one stripped of all the terrible connotations. In this light, the arguments in favor of atheism can be pretty darn convincing. I remember fearing some of the arguments being made by atheists as I watched debates about theism. There was a feeling of dread, I'd even say terror. I was terrified to find that several arguments for atheism made perfect sense. (Having now gone through this process, I also know the flip side of that terror was an incredible sense of excitement that I was coming closer to truth. I don't know that I could distinguish it at the time, though.)

Emotional, defensive reactions are understandable. In Part 2, we made the gentleperson's agreement to use logic as a basis, but we know in truth that emotions — especially fear — can tend to overpower logic.

There is a scene early on in Bill Maher's movie, *Religulous*, that I alluded to earlier which seems to capture this fear. Maher is talking to attendees at a trucker's chapel on the side of a highway in middle America. When Maher asks some blunt questions about these truckers' Christian faith, one responds defensively, "I don't like where you're going. You start disputing my God" — he clenches his fist — "and you got a problem." He then leaves the chapel and Maher says, "I'm just asking questions."

In my teenage years, I was involved with Protestant missionary groups and I learned well the call to "put on the armor of God" as directed by Ephesians 6. I recall pamphlets depicting a "Crusader for Christ," all decked out in the "Breastplate of Righteousness," the "Shield of Faith," and holding the "Sword of the Spirit." There is a general distrust of the secular world and an eagerness to defend a religious worldview.

I have even heard people talk about "defending God." This always strikes me as quite bizarre. After all, why would an all-powerful entity need a lowly human to come to his defense? These folks might later clarify that they are "defending the faith." This makes more sense. They are defending *their belief* in God. They are defending the idea of God. They are defending the *hope* that an all-powerful entity is looking out for them.

The God idea has protected them from having to honestly face some of the more unpleasant realities of life and death. There is a desire, therefore, to "defend the defender." Given the comfort such an idea can provide, this desire to defend it — and the fear that it might be threatened — is understandable. Atheism left to its own devices, they believe, may undermine so much they consider dear. Indeed, it might.

The Reaction I Could Not Get

So, yes, some people reacted defensively, and some reacted with sadness and even cruelty. I would be lying if I said I did not expect many of these reactions. One reaction I did frequently think about, though, was one I knew I could never get. *What would my mother have thought?* Yes, people had brought this up, but they didn't need to. It was already on my mind.

My mother deserves a book unto herself. Perhaps one day I will write it. She was a wonderful and loving mother, and I greatly regret that we did not get the chance to develop our relationship as I entered adulthood, got married, and had children of my own.

The following is a short biography of my mom because I think it may be helpful for the reader to get a sense of my attachment to her, as it might better explain the difficulties of thinking about her now in this context.

**

Josephine Ann Gaffney was born in 1939 in Roselle, New Jersey. As a young child, she played with her brothers, drew pictures, and sent letters in crayon to her Uncle Joe, who was off fighting in the Pacific theater during World War II. As a teenager, she apparently was the head of her local Perry Como fan club. She met my father on a ski trip and married him in South Orange, New Jersey, in 1964. Over the next decade, she became a wonderful mother of five children.

She was also a much-loved elementary, middle, and high school teacher until grounded somewhat by several illnesses. She developed a friendship with one of her students, Annie, who went on to become the wife and muse of the singer, John Denver, who wrote "Annie's Song."

My mom became sick when she was pregnant with me. There are stories of my father (and I believe my older siblings as well) going door to door in our neighborhood asking for donations of blood to assist with keeping her (and me) alive. Our neighborhood was a 1970s working middle class New Jersey neighborhood with a mixture of ethnicities. It's incredibly powerful and inspirational for me to think that the blood of Italians, African Americans, Jewish, Irish, Hispanic, and Asian people all likely helped to save my mother's life, and mine by extension.

Thanks to exceptional medical support in Hahnemann hospital in Philadelphia, my mother and I both survived my birth in 1973, something that was not wholly expected. I recall learning that she had several medical issues when I was very young, and I believe some of the medications she took affected her metabolism. I can recall her being both very heavy and almost rail thin at different times. I have nightmarish and dreamlike memories of the night of her first stroke when I was seven. This stroke paralyzed her left side, and she could no longer walk unassisted, let alone play guitar like she used to.

I have a mixed bag of memories of my mother during the seven years between this first stroke and the second stroke that killed her when I was 14. I remember that she would sit almost all day in a chair at home while the kids were at school and dad was at work. Thankfully, she had a wonderful nurse who would come to help her during the day, but that only lasted one year as our family didn't have enough money to pay for more than that. My mother was alone for much of this time.

I remember that she eventually got a motorized chair, and she could press a button and it would help her stand. I remember the sound of her four-legged cane clicking as she walked slowly past the piano, which had all of her pills lined up for the day on the top edge, and into the kitchen, where she would use her good arm to make a stew, the ingredients for which she and my dad would prepare together the night before.

There was a record player and a tape recorder within 10 feet of her chair, but I don't recall it being easy for her to change the records or tapes herself. I remember frequently being recruited for the task. By this time, perhaps partly because of her friendship with his wife, my mom had become an avid John Denver fan. I remember a Joan Rivers comedy record being in the mix as well. Now, when I think of my mom's predicament, I can better imagine how difficult and lonely a time that must have been for her. I suspect any music or comedy would have been welcomed to take her mind elsewhere.

I have some really beautiful memories with my mother during these years and I find it emotional to even attempt to write about some of them. I cannot adequately encapsulate these feelings and I am convinced that even the best poet would struggle.

I remember being 10 or 11 and coming home on the last day of the school year, ecstatic. I ran through the door, threw my bookbag on the floor, and screamed some word of utter joy, all while simultaneously turning to look over at my mother in her chair. I remember her asking me for a hug because she said she needed one. She must have had a hard day. I wish I could remember her face, because it's my hope that my unbridled joy somehow helped to lift her as it left me. I went to her, hugged her in her chair, and, in some ways, I haven't stopped. This memory remains so strongly ingrained in me. It was weird to think at that age that an adult, let alone my own mother, might need this type of support from me.

I remember going to church with her and my dad every weekend. I'm sure my siblings came as well, but some of them were already off to college by this time, so I remember my dad and mom most. After a while, I had gotten strong enough to push her up the ramp in front of St. James Church in Red Bank, New Jersey, and this was a small matter of pride for the growing boy that I was. St. Leo's Church in Lincroft had recently built-out and there was now a side entry with an elevator and a special section for those in wheelchairs. I felt like we had VIP seating.

Not having known my mother as an adult, I have to rely on memories of others to fill in more of the picture. After her death, conversations with my family and my mom's friends reinforced that she was kind, fun, a tad mischievous, and she very much loved being a mom. I knew most of this already, but their stories were helpful in adding color.

My mom was also religious. I knew that, but perhaps not the extent to which she was perceived to be religious. I didn't know, for example, that she purposefully continued teaching at a Catholic school despite meager pay when she had opportunities to earn significantly more money in a public school. I knew she would frequently say the rosary. I didn't know that she apparently would say seven full rosaries each day (one for each child, her husband, and herself), as my sister recently told me. She also made close friends with a Catholic priest and she would periodically invite him with us on family outings when I was young. I only have hazy memories of that, but I know the photos well.

**

In short, my mother was wonderful, I love her and miss her dearly, and she apparently was quite a religious Catholic. So how would she react to me recognizing my atheism?

The truth, of course, is that I don't know. Despite the "your mom would be horrified" comments, I'm not so sure this would really be the case. Of all her traits, I remember her being kind and loving the most. Truthfully, if she were alive today, I think she would have listened to me, she would have understood that I was being honest with myself and, given time to absorb the information, I think she might have come to be proud of me for that integrity.

And in the unlikeliest of chances that she would have been so upset as to disown me, so be it. In the words of the Protestant revolutionary Martin Luther, "Here I stand. I can do no other."

Fear of Losing the Greater Tribe

It makes sense that I faced emotional challenges in navigating the reactions to my atheism from people closest to me (and the memory of my mother). It must be even more difficult for those who have left theism, while their spouse has not.

I know there are many families with a parent who has stopped going to religious services with the family. Others may want to stop, but they stay in the atheist's closet because they think it could damage the harmony of the family if they even crack open the door. I'm fortunate to not have had that issue in my marriage. Although my wife was raised Catholic as well, she's also no longer religious, her outrage concerning the Church's blind eye toward pedophile priests having cemented that for her.

As parents, we constantly think about the well-being of our children, so the quest for familial harmony is understandable. We know, though, that one reason humanity has been able to survive to date is because many of our ancestors evolved to put faith in parental authority. Children with the "excessively reckless" gene millennia ago may have paid no mind to parental authority when they were told to stay away from moving grass in the high brush, ending up as dinner because of it. Teaching children the best you can about the world in an honest manner is essential. This is why I couldn't go along with teaching theism to my own children when I didn't believe it myself.

That unquestioning reliance and trust of parental figures when we are young can be lifesaving, but only when parents are trustworthy. Trusting parents who then sell you into slavery, for example, would of course be a tragic miscalculation. Fortunately for our species, enough of our ancestors sufficiently cared about their children to do what they could to protect them. That trust of parents eventually broadened to include other community elders. There was a belief that the elders of a tribe would see the next generation through safely to adulthood, but this may have frequently required that an almost unquestionable trust in the tribal authority be burned onto the soul.

This strong trust in tribal leadership over millennia ultimately led to sets of rules that should be followed and rituals that should be implemented. One can see how religious belief was the perfect spouse for these tribal leanings, as it, too, could help define the guidebook for life. These different guidebooks evolved over the years and unique cultures were developed in the process. The initial trust of parental authority eventually gave way to rules that kept you in the confines of the culture. If you are a Christian, you must not celebrate Hindu rituals. If you are Muslim, you must not celebrate the resurrection of Jesus.

And, of course, culture is not just religious in nature. It is also political. If you follow King X, you must certainly not follow King Z. It's social as well. With our globally connected world, there are so many different "digital" cultures that confront each other. Some find common cause and overlap. Some do not. Social media provides seemingly infinite opportunities to investigate examples of cultures interacting.

Some folks fear pressure on the outside walls of their culture, and since that culture is what they've trusted for their whole lives, they feel it necessary to push back and defend it. As an example, maybe you're in a culture that's politically conservative, religiously evangelical Christian, and socially skeptical of anyone different. Whereas some people might just respond in kind to a wish of "Happy Holidays," you might forcefully respond with "Merry Christmas" in an attempt to assert your culture on someone you perceive as trying to stomp it out. Although this defensiveness can annoy some people, it's understandable. You love your culture and want to protect it.

What's at Stake

Perhaps, like me, you have fond childhood memories of prayer groups before a Christmas service. You remember the hot chocolate mixed with peppermint on your tongue as you walked the neighborhood singing Christmas carols with other teenagers from your school. Everyone who opened their door to you had a smile on their face as they sang with you. There was a community there. There was a connection there, even with people you had never met before. There was a kinship with that tribe. You were safe, loved, and supported. You were home.

But if you realized you were an atheist, you might feel that revealing this openly would put your connection to your community at risk. The honest truth is that it likely will.

As a former Catholic, I still remember the silent warmth I felt during a Catholic mass and the joy I felt during the sign of peace. (For non-Catholics, the sign of peace is a break in the ceremony when parishioners pause to greet fellow church members, usually with a smile, a handshake, and a "peace be with you" wish). I can't say that I'm particularly nostalgic for those moments, but I do recall that I appreciated them, and there was a time when I thought I might miss all of this as I was stepping away.

**

As I write this, I just realized that today is the day I planned to be at my 25th college reunion for the Catholic university I attended. Due to the Covid-19 outbreak, these plans were cancelled, or at least postponed. I was pretty heavily involved in campus ministry as a lector and also a Eucharistic minister at one point, so I was looking forward to catching up with many of my college friends whom I knew from this group. In the back of my mind, though, was the knowledge that I probably have much less in common with many of them now.

If I were to be invited back into a campus ministry prayer group now, I either would go and remain silent or simply not go. I expect that this would raise eyebrows and eventually lead to a conversation with somebody that might be uncomfortable. Truthfully, this is not a big issue for me, but it goes to show how being honest and open about my atheism can affect parts of my life beyond the relationships with my closest friends and family.

Certainly, for other people, being open about atheism may affect their very livelihood. I've watched documentaries that interviewed anonymous pastors or priests who had lost the faith but continued in their positions because it provided a living for them (and their families if they are married pastors). I often wonder how many of these folks are out there. I suspect it's not negligible. There are also folks who work at companies with religious bosses and there is a justifiable concern that an openness about being an atheist will not win the boss' favor.

**

Due to so many cultural overlaps in our society, as you lose connections to one culture, you may risk losing connections with other cultures as well. If you are politically conservative or even if you are simply a big fan of country music, for example, coming out as an atheist might impact your association with these other groups that, on the surface, might have nothing to do with religious belief whatsoever. Likewise, if you're a Black American at a NAACP conference and you voice concerns about its focus on its "Faith Forward Initiative," you may lose friends in the process (even though there is no mention of religious faith in the NAACP mission statement).

I also believe that many of these overlaps are strategically implemented and tended to. The "God and guns" cultural overlap in the U.S. is an example of this. Type "God and guns" into an online shopping platform and you will see what I mean. I believe many religious folks, like marketing experts, are actively looking for ways to expand their cultural reach by trying to overlap with other cultures. I've been a fan of several Christian rock bands during my life, and they represent some of that overlap. I recently listened to a national Catholic radio broadcast that claimed Batman was likely a Catholic, in a clear attempt to connect with the Comic-Con crowd. I see some of these tactics to win over followers to be quite a stretch — and, dare I say, a bit pathetic.

Simply put, atheists coming out of the closet may fear not just losing ties to the religious community; they may also fear losing ties to many other groups that have a cultural overlap with the religious community.

Dismissing the Ancestors

I'm not sure if this would be a common concern for most folks who are attempting to accept their atheism, but it was not lost on me that I could be ending the long line of theistic ancestry on the "Steve Dow" genealogy chart. I love history and I have enjoyed researching what I can about my ancestors. After learning several stories, I found myself harmonizing with some of their thoughts and actions, while being horrified by others. They, like me, were all flawed human beings, and I connect with them as such, wondering what it would be like to meet them had we lived at the same time. There are similarities between my feelings towards my ancestors in general and my feelings towards my deceased mother. Of course, the feelings are not nearly as strong, but the blood ties are felt, nonetheless.

My family and I travelled to Ireland in 2016 and visited a church in the village of Carrigallen where some of my ancestors were apparently married 150 years or so earlier. It was a nice moment to stand on that same land and imagine the joys of two people that day that partly led to my existence today. I also walked the church cemetery and recognized some last names from my ancestry chart on the tombstones. But I didn't have the religious connection with the place that I might have had a few years earlier.

I also recall as a child being told by my grandmother that her Uncle Philemon had accepted last rights from the Church on his death bed and died a Catholic. I was young and must have asked a broad question about ancestry. It was quite telling that this story of Phil's acceptance of Catholicism needed to be so urgently passed on to the next generation for the ancestral memory banks.

OK, great-granduncle Phil definitely, definitely was a Catholic. OK, got it. No matter what he'd said or done beforehand, he absolutely was a Catholic at the end. Duly noted. Yep, no ifs, ands, or buts about it, good old great-granduncle Phil was good old Catholic great-granduncle Phil, and don't let anyone tell you differently. It will be written down as such for the ages. Forever and ever. Amen.

Something tells me I might have really enjoyed getting to know great-granduncle Phil. Maybe Phil really was a Catholic at the end, but the panicked urgency in my grandmother's telling of the story raised doubts for me even way back then. Why such resolve in the story telling? Perhaps atheism doesn't start with me in the ancestral chain after all.

But who can truthfully know the personal thoughts of anyone back along the line? Unless one kept a detailed journal on these topics, grading the religiosity of long-dead people is going to be a lost cause. I've learned already that ancestral stories are not always told without bias.

For example, growing up Catholic, I learned early on that most of my ancestry is Irish Catholic. I found out years later that one of our ancestors even fought in the famous 1690 Battle of the Boyne north of Dublin between Catholics and Protestants, but — shock of shocks — he fought for the Protestants, even being rewarded by the English king for his efforts in battle. This was definitely *not* information that my grandmother had seen fit to pass down the line, but "Phil died a Catholic" was.

So, when someone tells me that being an atheist is an insult to my Catholic ancestors, I wonder what all my ancestors really believed in their private moments. Even more so, though, I recognize that it's irrelevant anyway. The response ultimately is the same for me as it was concerning my mother. Once more, "Here I stand. I can do no other."

Lastly, I must also say that my thoughts about offending my ancestors are mitigated by my thoughts about setting an example for my descendants. You can think for yourself. You can break away from previous ways of thinking. Doing so in fact may be essential in some cases.

Atheism and Religious Holidays

When thinking about the theistic heritage given to me, I remember old family videos of long-passed relatives celebrating Christmas eve, and I can envision my grandmother as a young girl with her Easter bonnet, coming out of the church door looking for sweets during the spring. St. Patrick's Day had been one of my favorite holidays for years, in part because I could almost feel my Irish ancestors sitting next to me in the pub as I would drink a beer or cider in celebration of that day. But all of these remembrances and thoughts are wrapped around holidays that are theistic in nature. So how am I to deal with this as an atheist?

This, of course, is a question that every former theist will need to consider. For me, I simply take the magic-component out of it. Christmas day stemmed from a pagan holiday that stemmed from a scientific recognition of the placement of the sun in relation to the horizon. The same is true of Easter. On those specific days, I simply celebrate life in general and how amazing it is that we have all survived together on our planetary journey through spacetime. On St. Patrick's Day, I simply celebrate the many things that I love about Irish culture, independent of the religious belief that has attached itself to much of Irish history.

Still, some might say: *"How dry? How absent of feeling? What about the greater lessons of these holidays that come from the religious stories in particular?"*

Well, first I must state the obvious. The religious "lessons" of these holidays have already been lost on many, independent of any theism vs. atheism debate. Commercialism has seen to that. Christmas to many has come to mean an obligation to buy presents for co-workers they don't particularly like; and Santa Claus, though based loosely on St. Nicholas, is essentially an invention of the Coca Cola company. Easter is now almost as much about buying sugared candy as Halloween is (another holiday with religious roots that has been taken over by commercialism). And, let's face it, for many, St. Patrick's Day is just an excuse to get drunk.

Secondly, the "lessons that come from the religious stories in particular" can just as easily be presented without relying on the suspension of reality. Christianity teaches that Christmas is about God's willingness to humble himself to become human. But would we truly not learn humility, but for this example of a newborn who was worshiped and brought gold and other regal gifts? Do we not see humility in the everyday? Do we not see it in the person who sacrifices her own dreams and wakes up early to go to work for people who do not appreciate her because she needs to support her family? She is her family's real-life savior, yet her employers may simply see her as the smallest of cogs in the machine.

And Easter is supposed to teach us of the power of resurrection and renewal, but don't we already see renewal in nature each spring? Is that not a good enough example? The name "Easter," after all, is said to come from the German goddess *Eostre*, who was tied to the concepts of dawn and renewal. Why must I believe that all rules of science and nature were sidestepped so that a man could bring himself back from the dead? I don't need Easter to understand the power in the idea of being beaten down and then rising again. I just need to watch *Rocky*.

So, for me, I don't celebrate these holidays in a religious sense, but I do use them as a reminder to love others and to be kind. This is ultimately what I find most important anyway. Perhaps, for that reason, I don't miss the religious components and rituals like I thought I might. We are still speeding through space and our time is short. Appreciating life under these circumstances is enough for me.

Tree Branches, "Star Stuff," and Giving Cover

There is a fine line between acknowledging the beauty in some religious expression versus tacitly being a proponent of that expression. I'll start with myself as an example.

A few years after college, I moved thousands of miles away from friends and family to the beautiful city of San Diego in California. I've been out here for over two decades and the realization of my atheism only occurred in the last five years or so. When I have Catholic family or friends visit, I (so far at least) have typically accompanied them to a Catholic mass. I know that this is stuff they still believe, and out of respect for them, I've helped them find mass schedules, taken them to the church, sat in the pew with them for an hour, and then taken them home.

As an atheist, I now very much feel like an observer in these situations and not a participant. I see it as similar to when Jewish friends invite us to Passover Seder meals. My wife and I are grateful to have wonderful friends and we get a glimpse of their culture as we enjoy our time with them. Even back when I considered myself a Catholic, I would still accept these invitations out of respect for them. I enjoyed learning more about customs and cultures that were not my own.

I've already written about the risk of losing ties to community when we leave our religion of choice (or upbringing), but I think it's important to realize that, as atheists, we can still appreciate the cultural experiences that unite people. I remember listening to a mariachi band with one of my in-laws when he told me that he gets chills listening to the music of his Mexican heritage. I thought immediately of my own similar chills while listening to an Irish dirge in an otherwise silent pub years ago, and I felt closer to him for his confession. There is a commonality in human experience that is stunningly beautiful.

We are each a leaf on a branch of the human tree. We all share the same roots. It's a joy to explore this tree, our own branch, yes, but beyond as well. We can marvel at the differences of some of the branches and we can likewise admire the interwoven branches that twist upon themselves. There is so much to love and respect from different cultures. Finding the commonalities are especially energizing for me.

But, as an atheist, how am I to view the theistic components to some of the tree? I've already stated how I've observed and appreciated other cultural events and many of these have been religious in nature. How can I say this as an atheist? This, I must say, is a challenging question. I am, to some degree, still working through this question as I write this book.

Ultimately, though, I believe we can gaze at the beautiful architecture of a cathedral, for example, while also viewing that structure as a human attempt to capture something bigger. To me, such buildings symbolize the effort to encapsulate what it means to be alive, or what it means to be such a small thing in such a huge and unknown universe. Simply put, I see religion as one of humanity's attempts to explain our existence. It's a paintbrush stroke by the struggling painter who can't fully capture all that is just beyond. It is an expression of things hoped for.

In this light, the atheist can look upon religions as she might look upon a sculpture or a beautiful painting of a landscape. It's humanity capturing a portion of itself at a specific period in our evolution. One could similarly look at Greek mythology and appreciate it as a past version of this same expression (although, as an atheist, I feel that prominent religions today are not too many steps away from Mount Olympus).

There is an inescapable reality when seeing religion in his light; you will be deemed elitist. Based on what I've just written, I suspect some theists will think atheists believe themselves to be superior: "*Look at me, I have evolved beyond all this. I am enlightened and I see the error and folly of theism. I simply see theism as 'lesser minds' struggling with their place in the universe, making their rudimentary artistic expressions via stories of modern mythology.*"

Truthfully, I don't see a way around this. There are plenty who default to the assumption that atheists are arrogant specifically for this reason. As uncomfortable as it may be, though, pushback is necessary. Were Copernicus or Galileo elitists to argue for the heliocentric theory of the solar system? Are people who recognize the reality of global warming elitists because they draw logical conclusions from extensive data? Since when is education a bad thing anyway? I've already discussed the perceived arrogance of atheists and the distrust of science, so I won't dwell on it further, except to say that fear of being considered an elitist can factor into relationships with people who won't readily welcome your atheism.

At some point, though, you simply can't worry about whether people's feelings might get hurt because you think they're not seeing something that you see. They need not be considered "lesser minds," per se, and I don't see them as such. I see them as people with the same blind spots that I had. The difference is that I came to recognize and acknowledge these blind spots. I don't see myself as better than any other person, just more fortunate, perhaps, that I've had this realization. I hope to help others to recognize this as well. This does not make me superior to others. We are all still the same general mixture of common chemicals — the same "star stuff." Nothing changes that. I still appreciate others as my equals in humanity.

OK, so I'm an atheist who recognizes that artistic beauty may exist in some religious expressions, yet I still see such expressions as subpar and even ultimately harmful because they don't address reality head on. Here we come back to the line I mentioned earlier. Where is the line crossed between appreciating religions as artistic expression and essentially condemning religions for the propping up of magical thinking? Is it right to appreciate the religious components on the branches of the human tree, or should I recognize that some of these are leaving the tree unbalanced and threatening to topple it over? Just where is that line?

For some, the line is easy. Anything remotely religious is condemned. These folks might acknowledge that there could be some beauty in religion, but this is far down the list for them of what is important. They are focused on the danger of propping up magical thinking and how doing so can damage our ability to survive long term as a species. These folks might consider themselves not just atheists, but anti-theists as discussed in Part 1 of this book. They would likely take a harsher approach in a discussion with theists and justify that approach as an expression of tough love. As I said earlier, if it wasn't for the people who forced me to face uncomfortable questions by taking this tougher approach, I might still be a nominal theist.

This said, others will have a softer attitude, and the reason for this is justifiable as well. Some people simply will not react well to tough love and will put up defenses immediately. The softer approach might first focus on finding the commonalities with theists, understanding that some will be more open to listening to your perspective when you've first addressed them on common ground. These "softer approach" people have little issue with recognizing the beauty in different cultures, even their religious aspects.

But once again, that line. We are back to that line. At what point is going along with religious rituals and holidays actually propping up those rituals and holidays as worthy? When does it become tacit approval of them? Most importantly, when does it give cover for more extreme theists to push dogma and propaganda? When more people go along to get along (even when they don't believe it), there are fewer folks who are forced to really question what they believe and why. Those pushing the dogma also feel that they have strength in numbers. It seems as though the general thought is: *"Did you see how many people showed up for Christmas mass? Wow — we still got it. People are still with us."*

If I end up at a religious event and I'm asked my beliefs on the matter, I will make it quite clear that I'm an atheist. So, if I go along, people should know that I'm going along out of respect for them and where they are on their journey — not because I believe what they might want me to believe. They should know that I consider much of what they believe to be nonsense. But truth be told, I still struggle with even doing this as an atheist, and I'm finding myself leaning more towards anti-theism of late. I'm less and less inclined to go along.

But this might be an even greater issue for those who still consider themselves religious, even only nominally so. These folks might not have given the dogma much thought, but they go along for cultural reasons. I consider some of these folks "stage 1 atheists," because they may indeed be atheists but haven't yet forced themselves to acknowledge it. It's comfortable for them to just not rock the boat. So they don't, and religions continue to thrive in large part because of it.

The Deepest Fears

You may have noticed that I'm not writing about the emotional nuances involved in becoming an atheist. Instead, I'm writing about the emotional nuances involved with the realization that *I am* an atheist. The "becoming an atheist" part happened already for me once I was honest with myself about the realities of life. Coming to grips emotionally with these realities has been the greater challenge, as they are so vastly different from what I had absorbed for decades.

As I've discussed so far, it's been emotionally difficult to bridge my atheism with several close personal relationships, as well as with the memories of others close to me. It's also been a challenge to find my way as an atheist in the greater culture that I've marinated in for over 40 years. But there's a deeper issue that underlies it all, and it really is *the* issue.

Leaving the God Idea

Even though I knew I had become an atheist and I knew I couldn't hide from that fact, saying goodbye to the God idea was still quite difficult. Thinking of it now, I'm reminded of kissing my mother's forehead in her casket just before it was shut forever. I was starting to accept the reality of her death, but letting go was still so hard. It was hard letting go of God as well. God, after all, had filled so many huge roles in my life for so long.

God was my protector, my safety provider.

I didn't see him as an "always looking out for me"-type God like some might. I didn't expect him, for example, to make my favorite basketball team win, or to make me only get softball questions in a job interview, but there was a significant portion of my life when I had a real sense that no serious harm would come to me. I had someone powerful in my corner. God, or at least a guardian angel who had been delegated the task, was watching over me.

This difficulty in letting go makes sense, as the desire for a parental figure who protects us is embedded in our DNA. It can especially be hard to let go of the idea once the image of a cosmic, all-powerful, all-protective parent takes hold. There is a temptation to remain the child, and Jesus even tells us to remain like children. St. Paul, however, breaks up the party for us in 1 Corinthians 13:11: "When I was a child, I spoke and thought and reasoned as a child. But when I grew up, I put away childish things." When I first read this verse, I couldn't have imagined that the "childish thing" I'd be putting away was God Himself.

God was my awe-inspirer, the promiser of life in the here and now.

He was ever-present in nature and was the smile on my friends' faces. He was behind everything good and wonderful, and I was the smitten bride, swept off her feet. I specifically remember a handful of moments that inspired awe in me, and I attributed these to God.

One instance happened in the cold night rain at a Catholic retreat during college. It had been more than five years since my mother had passed, but I was still grieving her. I was soaked and crying over the strong loss I still felt as I walked alone in the woods. Suddenly I had an image in my head of a cloudy God-like figure floating before me, but there was a void between myself and the figure. Then like a Tetris block falling into place, another figure came down from above and lay down to fill the void. All was cloudy to me, but I knew it was my mother. I didn't physically see these images, mind you, but they were so strongly "seen" in my head that it was difficult to doubt. Besides, it was exactly what I wanted to see, so I had no intention of questioning it. God had sent my mother to help me get back to him. I felt at peace once more, and once more in awe of God.

Another instance may have happened around the same time, but I believe likely a bit earlier. I was home from college and walking the fields of my old elementary school down the street from where I lived. I was well into the existential crisis of my college years, brought on in large part by doubts about my faith and the lingering grief over my mother's death. I was walking but stopped as the wind went through the trees in the distance. The very Buddhist-like words "*Be, Steven, just be*" came to me as if someone had spoken them, just as the wind blew back the hair that was on my head at the time. I didn't physically hear the words with my ears, but they registered clearly in my head. This, too, filled me with awe. I was sure it was God telling me to relax, to take my time. Peace came to me again.

I'm not sure if either of these moments impress you as a reader, but I can assure you that they were both incredibly personal and awe-inspiring experiences for me, and I had tied them both to God. Even though I've since logically disassociated these moments with the God idea, it was still a challenge to let go of God while still holding onto these memories. They'd been so tied together for so long, and the ties were emotional in nature. They were warm and I had wanted to preserve them as they were. If the mystery of God was removed, I worried that these moments would become cold and open to Spock-like logical calculations and psychological analyses that would chip away from their power. I can report as an atheist now, though, that this is not the case. I still find these memories powerful, even with God no longer in that picture.

God was also my promiser of a life hereafter.

He let me believe I would see my mother again. I'm not sure how long I realistically viewed heaven as it's presented in cartoons and movies. I suspect I may have had those thoughts only during my young childhood, but I did still envision some mysterious way, some other dimension perhaps, where God allowed both love and life to continue on. I loved to think of being reunited with my mother and other loved ones as well. Who among us doesn't have these types of wishes? Is it any wonder that letting go of them is difficult?

God was also the pathway.

Not only was God the promiser of life in the here and now and the promiser of life in the hereafter, but he was also my own personal guide between the two. He was the guidebook itself, the very instruction manual.

Back when I was a young teenager, I would attend a Protestant youth group with my two best friends. In a prayer meeting, one of the older members started singing a song with the lyric: "*Jesus Christ is the man. He's the man with the plan.*" Each syllable had its own note, and to say the song came off as campy would be quite the understatement. As an adult, I still find it funny. As the immature kid that I was, I found it absolutely hilarious! I burst out laughing in the middle of the song and wasn't able to pretend to hide it. If I'd been drinking something, I would have spit it clear across the room.

If I recall correctly, I found out later that this was a song that the person singing had written himself, and I clearly offended him. Of the many laugh-at-inappropriate-times moments I've had in my life, this ranks pretty close to the top.

That said, I ultimately agreed with the premise of the lyrics. I did think that Jesus was the *man with the plan*, and I followed his teachings as best I could. It seemed to be the right model for me. It resonated with me. It felt right.

God was also my connection, the receiver of my yearnings.

When I was a theist, I would think about how the awe and wonderment I experienced in life would frequently come with an undeniable sense of yearning for connection. It seemed at times that the mere fact of my yearning was evidence that there was a God to yearn towards. I wanted there to be a greater, big-picture meaning and purpose to life and that fact seemed to support the likelihood that said meaning and purpose existed. There was something specific, almost a magical quality, to the yearning itself.

As an atheist now, I'm surprised and even a bit embarrassed that I found that way of thinking to be even remotely convincing. Wishful thinking had simply gotten a hold on me. Yes, I still do feel connection, but the desire to connect doesn't mean there's some God to connect with. My yearnings now lean towards connections with others, with nature, and with the majesty of the universe itself.

**

In short, the God idea was hard to walk away from because it had been so central to me for so long. But just as I knew when I was kissing my deceased mother's forehead that she wasn't really there anymore, I knew that the concept of God as a real entity was no longer alive for me. Closing the casket, though, was difficult.

Accepting Mortality

When I wrote that God played a major role in my life as my protector, I was being truthful, but there's a deeper level to that protection that mattered more to me. I relied on God to protect me from a life that didn't have meaning, a life without purpose. I didn't want to consider that I would live and then die and then be forgotten. I relied on God to protect me from death — to protect me from even having to think for a moment that I wouldn't not live forever.

Death is *the* issue. When you walk away from the God idea and its promise of immortality, you walk straight into the arms of death. You raise your chin and your eyes meet the eyes of death. Your mortality is no longer a mere inconvenience to be hurdled on your way to singing endless praise in the heavens. It's the realest of things. It's the most urgent of things.

**

On that happy note, now might be a decent time to mention something that you may be surprised I'd even bring up in a book about atheism. Atheism, by definition, doesn't preclude a belief in some continuance of life after death. It simply means there's no belief in a deity. There's so much we don't know about our consciousness. Presumably, it needs our brain to carry the electrical signals that fire in patterns just so, but could it somehow float in and out of existence as subatomic particles seem to do? Could it be similar to how we've come to understand sunlight, as both energy and matter simultaneously? Can it maybe, just maybe, transform itself and survive without the material home that housed it?

Throw the word "quantum" in front of anything and you suddenly have a vastly different way of thinking about whatever noun the "quantum" adjective describes. "Quantum consciousness" sounds a bit ridiculous, I must admit, but it also seems far more likely than the God idea. After all, consciousness appears to be a real thing. I know some argue that it (along with free will) may, at its deepest level, be an illusion (and I'm intrigued by these arguments), but one can still claim to have evidence of consciousness existing at some level. I don't believe the same can be said about God. Maybe consciousness could survive death in some way that we don't yet understand.

All that said, do I believe there is life after death? No, probably not — not in the conventional sense, at least. I expect I will die, my body will eventually feed microbes, and the circle of life will continue with my atoms, but without me. I suspect my consciousness will simply disappear back into the ether from which it emerged.

Taming the Monster

For those of us who don't hold out too much hope for a continuation of consciousness, facing the idea that we will die can be especially difficult. Most of us have come to love many things about our existence and the idea that we would lose all this can be terrifying.

There is a powerful set of videos that I stumbled upon years ago. Scientists had strategically placed a large mirror in a jungle, hidden a camera in the brush, faced the camera towards the mirror, and then waited. The videos capture the reaction of wild chimpanzees and other apes as they come across the mirror.

Each ape seemed to have its own reaction to its reflection. An initial fear of — or at least a caution towards — the unexpected reflection, however, was ubiquitous. The lead males in particular seemed to default to their instincts in defending the group, reacting as one might expect. Hardwired to go into defense mode upon seeing an unknown ape of equal size and strength, they beat their chests, grunted loudly, and shook branches. Some even ran into the mirror in an attempt to attack.

Other apes were clearly fearful, but also curious. They walked the length of the mirror slowly and tested the reflection. Eventually, most of them seemed to accept it. They might not have understood it completely, but they were able to live with it. In fact, many sat in front of it for long periods of time. They seemed amazed by it and may have even finally come to recognize themselves in the glass.

The philosopher Friedrich Nietzsche famously said, "If you stare into the abyss, the abyss stares back at you." As I understand it, this quote didn't directly address mortality, but rather the darker side of our personalities that we may or may not choose to accept. Nonetheless, I thought of this quote while watching these videos of our evolutionary cousins interacting with the mirror. It made me think of us facing our mortality honestly, and eventually coming to accept it.

The monster many of us see in the reflection is the creature stomping its feet, pounding its chest, and readying for an attack. The monster represents an atheistic worldview that doesn't ascribe to the comforting promise of a fictional deity that everything will be alright — that life will continue forever. A believer may not initially recognize herself in the image, it being stripped of preconceived notions of what we think we look like. After all, *we're immortal beings, glowing with our own immortality. Right?*

The reflected image, however, represents who we are at our root. It removes the cosmetics and shows us our very mortal faces. Many of us are terrified of our death, so we see a horrid and horrifying creature when we look. It's a deep and uncomfortable abyss from which many of us simply turn away, averting our eyes downward. Others may still look, but as they see the monster spiral upwards in aggressive actions and stance, they push more vehemently against it. Our grunts and howls grow more panicked and louder until finally exhaustion sets in.

Just as many of the apes in the video may not have completely understood their reflection but still came to eventually accept it, we likewise may not fully understand all aspects of our mortality, yet we can still accept it as well. We can stop our screams and put down the branch we'd been shaking, and we can inspect ourselves and the mirror with curiosity. We can learn from it. We can tame the monster within and use it to our advantage.

Lessons We Learn from Facing Mortality

That we, as a species, have been good at looking the other way.

One of the first things we learn from confronting our mortality honestly is that the very fear of mortality is what has led us to create so many ways to pretend it away. Mythologies and religions are paths away from mortality. They allow us to look away and run.

We can recognize ourselves in the man behind the curtain in Oz. We have been so automatic in our vigorous pulling of strings to operate the image on the wall that we've come to see ourselves as separate from it. We have become so engrossed with the power of the image we created that we have forgotten that we created it in the first place. The Wizard of Oz is not real, and God also is not likely real. They both were created to serve a purpose. The Wizard may have been created to control a population, and the same could be argued for God's creation as well. But I think the bigger purpose God serves for most of us today is to help us pretend away our mortality.

That mortality can help us truly live.

The image of a devil and angel on one's shoulders is commonplace. I don't know how long such an idea has been around, but I can certainly attest to it being there as long as I can remember. Typically, they sat on the shoulder of a person to get him or her to be naughty or nice. The devil was, of course, the darker personality — deathlike, cunning and focused.

Facing mortality honestly, though, does indeed put death on your shoulder, but this isn't a bad thing. It's a good thing — a very good thing. When you have death on your shoulder, you are constantly reminded of your mortality. You are reminded of the specialness of your time on this planet. Death is not the enemy. Death is the friend whispering in your ear, reminding you to live.

That there is no need to panic.

Just as many of the apes in the videos eventually calmed down after being faced with their reflections, we can do the same when facing our mortality. No doubt there is a sadness that comes with the realization that our lives will end, but there are things we can do with our lives now that can greatly stem that; I'll discuss this more later.

There is no need to panic though. Death need not be a scary thing. Mark Twain said it better than I've ever heard it said before: *"I do not fear death. I had been dead for billions and billions of years before I was born, and had not suffered the slightest inconvenience from it."*

Tricks to Keep You in the Fold

I've discussed several reasons why it was emotionally difficult for me to break away from what I now see as an unwarranted faith. I was concerned about personal relationships. I was concerned with my place in my greater community. I was concerned with facing the realities of what walking away from my faith meant in relation to my mortality. But there were still more hurdles to recognize and clear on my path.

Whether intentional or not, I noticed several of what I'll call "tricks of the trade" used by many in the faith community to attempt to keep people questioning their faith in the fold. It may be helpful to be aware of these if you indeed are on a journey away from theism.

Celebration of Faith

First is the seemingly endless praise of people of faith. Faith in God's existence, even among people who are not particularly religious, is frequently respected as if it's a worthwhile endeavor. Even in cases where it gets some pushback, it's typically still treated with kid gloves. The conflation of religious faith with goodness is on display in so many places around the world. The confirmation bias is stunning, and it expands beyond the borders of the faith community. Priests and preachers, for example, are frequently treated as a step up on the pedestal, even by nonreligious people. Yes, respect them equally as people, but there's no need to afford them an added special respect because they applaud the suspension of reason in favor of magical thinking.

This celebration of faith sometimes pops up in unexpected ways. My cell phone number must have at one time been the number for a local branch of the Veterans Administration. Once a month on average, I'd have to tell folks that they'd called a wrong number. This morning, in fact, an older man called asking about an appointment. I explained the situation and thanked him for his service. The call went something like this:

> Me: "...So that's why I think I keep getting these calls."
>
> Him: "OK, I understand. Thank you.
>
> Me: "Well, thank you for your service."
>
> Him: "Thank the Lord Jesus Christ, Hallelujah. Follow his ways. Have faith — faith in Jesus my Savior."
>
> Me: "You have a good day sir. Take care."

Clearly, this was a religious person who called me this morning and clearly, he believes things I do not. He is of course free to spread what he considers to be the "good news." I made a point not to agree with him, but I also held back from responding as I might have liked. I thought to respond with, *"Yeah, I don't believe all that, and I think it's dangerous to spread a manner of thinking that dismisses one's own reasoning capabilities in favor of things wished for."*

So why didn't I say this? There are two reasons that come to mind. First, it was a wrong number and I really just wanted to get off the phone. Second, this was an older gentleman, and I didn't want to unnecessarily upset him.

But this also highlights my point. This man assumed that I would be receptive to his preaching. At the very least, he likely assumed I would be polite in my response, which I was. Even if he knew he might be talking to a non-Christian, I believe he thought it was unlikely that he could be talking to someone who might be anti-religious. Just as he felt comfortable, perhaps even compelled, to say what he did, I perhaps should have felt equally as comfortable and compelled to respond as I thought to. We're back to the Ricky

Gervais question posed earlier: "Why is saying 'there is no God' considered disrespectful to believers, but saying 'there is a God' not considered disrespectful to atheists?"

The answer is in large part because there is a deeply embedded acceptance of, if not outright celebration of, religious faith. I believe this is true in many parts of the world, but certainly so in the United States where I live. This is seen in many other ways as well, and social media certainly provides many examples. *"I'm praying for you," "thoughts and prayers,"* and *"Thank God I know Jesus, because otherwise I would have done x, y, or z"* posts are common, and they are typically applauded. (Thankfully, the "thoughts and prayers" posts have gotten some much-needed pushback lately, as that phrase is more and more being interpreted to mean, "I wish that didn't happen, but I won't do any real work to minimize the chances of it happening again.")

This confirmation bias towards the validity of religious faith is strong. It acts as a subconscious reminder of just how weird some may find you if you disagree that faith without real evidence is a good thing. It's comfortable to go with this flow. It requires work to stand against it.

Celebration of "Doubt"

As dangerous as I think the celebration of faith is, I think the *claimed* celebration of doubt by the faithful is perhaps even more dangerous.

I can't tell you how many times I've heard the importance of doubt discussed in Catholic mass, or how many times I spoke with a religious person about this. Faith, they will argue, isn't "real" faith if there is no doubt to test it. Yes, there are many who will tell you to never doubt and to just believe, but the number of believers who stress the importance of doubt may be even larger in my estimation.

I want to reemphasize that I'm not saying all of these tactics by believers are done intentionally. This selective emphasis on accepting doubt in faith, though, does at times seem an intentional reaction to the fact that people do indeed doubt their faith. If fewer people had these doubts in the first place, there would be less of a reflexive push to work in the apparent importance of doubt to the narrative.

In other words, if you were to tell folks they can't have doubts, yet they still had doubts, it's more likely that you will lose them as believers. But, on the other hand, if you tell them that having doubts is normal and part of the whole "faith process," you may keep them in the fold longer — potentially much longer. The faith-doubt spiderweb can be sticky indeed. Many will not only fail to find a way out; they will find comfort in the web. They can believe that their faith is being tested while still feeling safe in the home that religion provides.

The inference made by believers when they discuss having no fears of doubt is that they ultimately *know* their faith would be able to take the hits and keep standing — and that their faith will ultimately be strengthened by it in the long run.

I must now ask the obvious question. What type of doubt is it that starts out with the *knowledge* and understanding that it (the doubt) will ultimately be squashed in one way or another? I'd argue that it's not true doubt at all, but rather fake doubt, or at least a controlled doubt. It's a doubt within the boundaries, a doubt with limits on it.

I've expressed doubts about the existence of God and have been told multiple times in response that I should pray to God about it. The response is made with no recognition of the paradox. How can one truly pray to a God that he doubts the existence of in the first place? This is clearly circular and faulty logic, yet there seems to be no acknowledgement of this fact.

I've also been directed to pray as stated in Mark 9:24: "I believe; help my unbelief." Again, if the first part is in doubt, why would I continue with the second part?

The funny thing about all this, though, is that it worked! Not forever, mind you. After all, I'm writing a book about my atheism, but it did hold me over for years. As I said before, the faith-doubt spiderweb is sticky.

Eventually, I came back to this and realized what I'd fallen for and why I let myself fall for it. Rocking the boat, after all, is difficult, but it eventually became clear to me that I couldn't pretend that these doubts had been addressed.

I finally realized that the much-lauded "road of doubt" claimed to be so heavily prized by many of faith *must* have an offramp for denial. Without that, it's not a road of doubt at all, but a circular driveway meandering around the church parking lot. You have mentally left the church building and you've gotten in your car feeling that you're pushing at the edges, but — from the very beginning — there was no real question that you wouldn't end up right back where you started.

Without the real possibility of denial, it doesn't matter how much effort you think you've expended on your doubts. It doesn't matter how many miles you've driven around the looped church driveway. It will still lead you right back to the church door. This is not an honest treatment of doubt.

Once more and for good measure: If a pathway of doubt can't lead to denial, it's not a pathway of doubt at all.

Deflections and Distractions

I also recommend being on guard against simple deflection techniques.

Deflection, of course, has been around for ages, but it's certainly noticeable now as I write during the Trump era. A journalist will ask a politician a question and be given an answer that doesn't answer the question. Good journalists will typically restate the question. The politician will frequently deflect once more providing a response that doesn't answer the question. I've noticed that usually after two attempts, most journalists stop pushing the point. Very few journalists keep at it.

So why is the deflection permitted? Why are politicians let off the hook? I think it's primarily because such a scenario sets up a tense, uncomfortable situation. Clearly, the politician is not comfortable directly and honestly answering the question. Perhaps out of an unconscious and/or tentative politeness, the journalist defaults to letting the politician save face. Maybe the journalist is fearful of coming off as bullying or being rude. I think it's simply rude that the politician won't answer the question.

I can relate, though, to why some journalists may act the way they do in these situations. In September 2016, I called into a live national Catholic radio show and surprisingly felt a sense of fear in preparing to ask two simple questions. I expected they might lead to a tense discussion. Below is a paraphrase of what I asked on air:

"Hello. I'm not a religious person, but I do have many believer friends. It's common that I feel the need to beat around the bush with these friends whenever religion comes up as a topic because I know they have a loving community in their churches and I don't want to hurt that for them, but I will be blunt with my questions here. Why do you believe in God? Doesn't it all seem like a fairy tale?"

I had listened to this station for months, if not years, before calling in, and I knew I had just asked fundamental questions that I had never heard asked on the station before. Most questions addressed the paint color or window covering:

> *What do you do if you accidentally drop the eucharist in the communion line?*

> *Which prayer do you say for someone who is suffering from an opioid addiction?*

My questions were different. They went straight for the foundation.

The speech of the Catholic expert taking questions had a noticeably increased pace when responding to mine. I felt that he was suddenly in a rush to get to the next caller. He rattled stuff off very quickly. Some of his rapid-fire responses included the following:

1. *We have a Catholic apologetics hotline you can call for questions like these.*

2. *I recommend you go talk to a priest.*

3. *I recommend you pray to God for him to reveal himself to you.*

4. *Take a look at this Catholic philosopher from the 1980s who used to be a pagan. He didn't believe before, but he came to believe.*

5. *Christians believe God has revealed himself throughout human history.*

6. *Fairy tales don't hold the intellectual heft that belief in God has.*

Aside from responses #5 and #6, the majority didn't truthfully address my questions. I suppose one might argue that response #5 did somewhat answer the question, but the underlying premise that an invisible God exists in the first place to be revealed throughout history really just reasserts the need for my initial question. Response #6 is a declarative statement that would need some serious supporting information to be convincing.

And, for the record, I did research the philosopher mentioned in response #4, and his thinking made no sense to me whatsoever. He seemed to argue that his draw toward Christianity was due to the mysteries of Christianity *not* being comprehensible. Somehow, he was arguing that this made them more likely to be true. I don't know what to do with that.

In fairness to the radio station and the gentleman responding to my questions, one might expect that attempts to answer these questions directly could take longer than they had between commercial breaks, although, truthfully, I see no reason for that to be the case. If one is so certain of his beliefs that he has made a career out of telling people about them, I would hope that he would have a relatively convincing answer he could provide in short order. Instead, the overwhelming sense remained that my questions weren't honestly answered.

I had an opportunity to ask a follow up question before hanging up, and perhaps for reasons similar to why journalists might not continue to press a politician, I let it be. I could have pushed back against responses #5 and #6, but I had images of vulnerable people listening at home to fundamental questioning of their entire worldview. I felt I might be considered rude for pushing further. In hindsight, I regret not doing so.

**

My ability to recognize deflection has also been honed via similar discussions on social media platforms. I believe discussions about religion and politics should not only be *not* avoided; they should actively be sought out. These topics are incredibly important in determining how we decide to live together on this planet, so I do frequently attempt respectful discourse when possible.

I will happily admit that there have been instances when online discussion has resulted in my thinking differently, or at least in me softening a position that I had held strongly. I welcome these instances and frequently look for them. Unfortunately, my willingness to have my mind changed isn't a trait shared by many that I come across online.

Many of the discussions about touchy topics tend to follow a general pattern. I might make a specific point about something a person claims to believe, and the response is *"Oh yeah, what about x, y, or z?"* The "whataboutism" is designed to call me out as a hypocrite in one way or another, but my initial point remains unchanged whether I'm a hypocrite or not.

Responses also frequently deflect with some other ad hominem attack, or one of my favorites: "Well, that's what I choose to believe." Here we are once more back to the claim that someone can really "choose" to believe anything. For reasons previously discussed, such claims have always rung hollow to me. Not only are the logical reasons for the supposed beliefs typically absent; the accompanying argument will frequently demand that I respect these unsupported beliefs. My typical response in such cases is that I'm only obliged to respect that you have a right to your own beliefs, and I have no obligation to respect the beliefs themselves. The beliefs will stand on their own merit, or they will fall under their own weight.

Word Games and Magic Mantras

In questioning people about religious faith, I've also experienced deflections that weren't obvious to me at the time. One instance I particularly remember was during my early college years.

I was dealing with an existential crisis of sorts and still trying to process the grief of my mother's death years earlier. I recall questioning some pretty fundamental things about my life at that time, one of them being whether arguments for morality were justified. I had recently read an Albert Camus novel and it had a real impact on me. (I embarrassingly can't recall if it was *The Stranger* or *The Plague*.)

I remember having terrible dreams and would awaken in a sweat. My college roommate woke me up at least once because he said I was screaming in my sleep. Dark and disturbing thoughts would pop in my head. They were most unwelcome. I don't know that I could say I was suicidal, exactly, but the fact that the thought didn't seem as crazy to me as it always had scared the hell out of me. I needed to talk with someone.

At the time, I was heavily involved with the Catholic religious community on campus, so I went to talk with one of the adult Catholic counselors. If I recall correctly, it was pretty late at night, so she must have lived on campus and I think we met in her office. I remember this woman as being an exceedingly kind and caring person. When I started to talk, it felt like a confession — and indeed it was. She knew me as one of the lectors who read from the Bible in front of hundreds at mass, yet I was telling her now that I didn't know if I even believed in God.

Her answer was a pithy phrase popular in prayer groups: "Let go and let God." It was akin to telling Jesus to "take the wheel," a term popularized via at least one country song. Essentially, it meant just let go of your burdens and let God handle it. I remember leaving there that night more frustrated than when I came. The fact that I just told her I wasn't sure if I believed in God didn't seem to have any impact on the advice she gave me. This didn't help in the least. She simply didn't understand what I was going through.

At the time, I didn't see her response as a deflection, exactly. It was a poetic turn of words after all, and I could see how some might be comforted by it. It just wasn't going to work on me. Not then at least. In hindsight, I see it for the deflection that it was. It didn't answer my concerns. It essentially told me to ignore them. It was a kinder and gentler deflection than someone attacking me in all caps on Facebook, but the end result was the same. It deflected away from my questions. It didn't address them.

My college years also provided some other phrases for me that essentially acted as mantras for my life at that time, although I do now see them as deflections as well. While "Let go and let God" didn't do the trick, these other phrases worked for me back then.

I now realize one of them was a deflection because it was seemingly given as a response to shore up my faltering belief in God. At least I interpreted it that way at the time, as it came from a priest. I had confessed my difficulties believing in God, and the response was to "put my faith in love." I could ask "love to prove itself to me." I see this as a deflection now because it implied the God-love conflation that I discussed earlier. It didn't independently address whether or not a belief in a supernatural entity was justified — and that's what I was struggling with. I simply didn't recognize the conflation back then.

As an atheist now, "put your faith in love" is certainly not the worst advice I've ever heard. In fact, I consider it quite valuable and I frequently find that it has a place on my shoulder during hard times.

The other word game that I recognize now was the following:

> *I used to think Christianity was confining me; now I realize I was confining Christianity.*

This was a direct hit on my apparent inability to understand just how big Christianity was. Christianity, after all, was more than just the dogma and the rituals. It was life itself, love itself. I simply wasn't letting myself see that — or so I thought at the time, at least. This was a new insight that let me hang on to my religion for years longer than I might have done otherwise.

So, who was the originator of this wonderful word game? Which priest or counselor sprang it on me? Nope. This one was all me. We can't always blame others for deflecting away our doubts. Sometimes, we pull the tricks of the trade on ourselves. Ultimately, if we accept the deflection, we're responsible for its impact on our lives, regardless of where it originates. In this case, I just happened to be the one who came up with the turn of phrase.

Now, of course, I recognize the mantra as a tool I used to avoid the doubt I had been getting so much better at burying. It once more conflated love and God and I didn't realize it. And if on some level I really did see it, I was comfortable at the time turning away. The phrase struck me as poetic and I tricked myself into thinking that was enough. Time would change that for me.

Timing and the Status Quo

I've discussed already that one of the biggest factors for me in honestly confronting theism was that I had come to a point in my life when I needed to determine what I was going to teach my children. Timing was clearly a big reason that I became an atheist when I did.

Timing, however, can also be used as a trick of the trade against you.

Part of my professional career has included detailed scheduling for construction projects and programs. In any schedule, there is a grouping of chronological activities that's determined to be most critical to the timely completion of the project. In fact, the very term for this group of activities is called the "critical path" of the project for this reason.

As an example, when one starts a construction project and considers the thousands of individual tasks that will be needed to complete it, two likely tasks would be to pour the concrete foundation and select the style of shower curtain for the interior bathroom. Clearly, though, pouring the concrete foundation is much more likely to be on the critical path than selecting a style of curtain. Many more follow-on activities necessary to complete the building are contingent on the foundational footings being complete, while only a handful of items would likely come after the decision on curtain style.

All this said, it's still possible that the choice of curtain could eventually become a critical-path item. It would just be much farther down the path than the foundational work. The term for the period of time between the day that an activity can start and the day that the activity *needs* to start in order to minimize the duration of the construction schedule is called the "schedule float." During that period, it may be that the work could be done, but it's not absolutely essential for schedule optimization to start the item until it becomes critical to the schedule.

For me, my life activity of honestly confronting atheism spent a good 20 years as schedule float. I could have kept at it after college, but other things were going on in my life that I deemed more critical at the time (i.e., getting married, developing a career, raising young children). It simply slipped down my priority list — plus, it was some exhausting work to dig into those issues, and I needed a break from it. Once my wife and I needed to make decisions about what to teach our boys about God, though, confronting my theism became critical.

Again, just because I'm listing timing as a trick of the trade, I'm not saying that it's being actively used in a conscious manner. I think many religious people who would prefer you to remain religious are simply content with helping you maintain the status quo in your life, which includes religious components from which religion benefits. These often include ceremonies to tick off key moments of the religious life. Some religious folks may be eager to see their children baptized and confirmed as they were. Among other things, it is an excuse for a party and a whole bunch of pictures for that social media post.

It's a rare circumstance when religious leaders actively invite open challenges to their beliefs, as it might rush a consideration of doubt in their flock that had been successfully kicked down the road for years in schedule float. The preference seems to be for "real doubt" (i.e., doubt that can lead to denial) to remain in schedule float indefinitely, even on the deathbed. Yes, I understand that some churches will hold debates with atheists or similar events, but these are few and far between, and they typically come pre-loaded with many of the defensive tools and embedded anti-atheistic infrastructure that make an honest listen to new ideas difficult.

"But you promised..."

Maintaining the status quo helps religious leaders keep an atheistic worldview away from their followers. It is a passive technique. Some attempts to keep you religious are much less subtle. Below is a nearly verbatim discussion I had with a religious person to whom I am close.

> Me: "... so no, we have no plans to put the boys through the First Communion process."
>
> (First Communion is a Catholic sacrament typically given to children usually around seven or eight years old.)

Person: "But you promised to raise your kids Catholic!"

(This "promise" was in reference to what I believe is a Catholic requirement in order to get married in the church and/or be *allowed* to marry a non-Catholic.)

Me: "How can you be shocked by this? We already had this conversation. Why would you expect me to raise the boys Catholic when I am not a Catholic?"

Person: "I thought you were deciding that for yourself. I didn't know that you were going to prevent your children from receiving the sacraments."

Me: "Why would I raise my children in a belief system that I do not believe? When they are adults, they are free to receive the sacraments if they decide to do so. I have even told them that I will take them to church anytime they want me to take them."

(As I think about this conversation now, I do find myself being more hesitant with what I'd let our children do with religious organizations. It's one thing to expose children to different ideas, so they know they exist and generally what is meant by them. It's quite another to feed your children into an indoctrination that you consider harmful. I think I'm more skeptical about the line between exposure and indoctrination than I was when I had this conversation a few years ago.)

Person: "You gave a promise that you would raise them as Catholic!"

Me: "Well, I changed my mind apparently. I suppose I am reneging on that promise. I care more about being honest with my boys now than I do about maintaining a promise to a belief system that I no longer believe in. So, this will not keep me in good standing with the Catholic Church. Given that I have already left the Catholic Church, this is not something that moves the needle for me."

When I apparently promised to raise my children Catholic years ago, I didn't also promise to lie to my children. Pretending that I thought Catholicism was the way to go would be lying to them. This was an example of a bullying approach in attempting to keep me in the fold. It very much played on the Catholic guilt that seems to be effective in controlling the lives of many people.

The Double Down

There are many other examples of bullying to try to keep someone in the faith. Thankfully, these tactics hold little sway with me at this point, but this is not the case for many who are just starting to dip their toes in atheistic waters.

We've talked about how celebrating faith can be an effective tool in tricking people to stay attached to their religious organization. But the flip side of that coin is the demonization of nonfaith. Earlier, I discussed the anti-atheistic infrastructure prevalent among many religious teachings. It's no wonder that tapping into that vein is a common tactic in trying to bully people back into the church, temple, or mosque.

I recently finished a back-and-forth with a former co-worker and religious friend about evolution and whether the remnants of Noah's Ark are on Mount Arafat in Turkey. This discussion took place over a messaging app, and as is common with these types of discussions, it got more heated than it would have if it had happened in person. In truth, this person and I had just recently reconnected and he was not initially aware of how much my thinking had changed since I'd last spoken with him. I suspect this surprised him and put him on guard.

Although he was definitely not the worst offender I've come across, much of what he wrote was snarky and ad hominem in nature. He exuded a sense of superiority, even after I pulled the rug from under one of his claims. It was an error that would have embarrassed me endlessly had I made it. Nonetheless, some of his comments were forceful double downs on viewpoints that I believed I had already sufficiently dismantled. Apparently, he didn't see it that way, although he couldn't effectively explain his reasoning for not being swayed. It seemed clear that he simply was going to stick to the script regardless.

He also attacked my sources — another common deflection tactic — even though the sources themselves were simply reporting data that had been gathered independently. In fact, a good portion of the data I referenced to refute part of his claims was compiled by a creationist publication. I don't believe he recognized this, as it did not appear he dug too far into the information I provided him. The general distrust of people with different opinions is common, and not just in relation to religion.

**

I've shared articles from sources that are deemed "non-conservative" on conservative social media pages, and I've seen the reaction. Even if the post is only a transcript of an interview, the assumption will frequently be that it has been altered. If it's a video of a conservative politician giving a speech, the assumption is that the video has somehow been clipped and altered. This distrust ultimately becomes part and parcel of the double down. There is a refusal to take in information that could conflict with someone's chosen narrative.

President Trump recently made comments regarding the possibility of injecting disinfectants into the human body as a means to fight Covid-19. I have long seen parallels between the mentalities of avid Trump supporters and cult members. Upon hearing these comments, I immediately thought of the tragedy of the Jonestown massacre/mass-suicide in 1978.

There is harrowing audio of cult leader Jim Jones telling his followers that the government would be coming for them (again, the distrust of outsiders), and that everyone should commit suicide by ingesting lethal chemicals with a flavored powered drink. The term "drink the Kool-Aid" comes from this horrible event (although Kool-Aid says a different powdered drink was used in the suicidal cocktail).

Listening to this tape is simply gut wrenching. You can hear people screaming and children crying in the background, all while Jones uses his megaphone to bully the doubters, telling them to just get on with it and drink the poison. Equally disturbing was the handful of cult members who would take the microphone to thank Jones and, presumably, drink the poison in front of the group (there would be applause afterward), then walk steps away to die.

Jonestown is, of course, an extreme example, but it goes to show that some people can indeed be bullied into place, doubling down on ridiculous beliefs, even when it means their own death, or the death of their children.

Side Doors and Sudden Excuses

Another trick of the trade to keep people in the fold is the rule bending when all else has failed. I've already written of my personal experience with this tactic — being told, for example, that after all was said and done, I only *really* needed to believe a small number of things to stay part of the church team. This is simply the good cop approach after the bad cop bullying failed miserably. It's a softer technique used in hope that it will be effective on certain types of people.

It reminds me of the team of salespeople who rushed my wife and I once we got to our hotel on our honeymoon. Out of curiosity alone, we accepted $200 of hotel credit in exchange for agreeing to sit through a marketing presentation about buying a timeshare at the hotel. These few hours were an education on sales tactics, and I was struck by the similarities with what I'd expect from a stereotypical used car sales office.

We were assessed immediately by a nice person who attempted to give a rational explanation of the benefits of timeshare ownership. We noted some reasons why a timeshare was not in our plans, thanked her for her time, and politely declined. Minutes later, the "manager" came to sit with us. He was much gruffer in tone and was all but yelling at us that we would be stupid to pass on this opportunity. Still, no thank you. Lastly, we were invited to lunch with the softer-sell person. He was closer to our age with a cool-guy feel and a much nicer demeanor. During lunch, we learned that there were ways we could still be part of the program without fully committing to everything we'd been told. The side door, once again, presented itself. (And, no, we didn't get the timeshare.)

Extrication

When I first started to get the idea for this book, I recognized that many arguments for atheism already out there were made by thinkers and authors who were not going to be rivalled by me in way of wit or intellectual background. Although I do attempt to systematically address many arguments for atheism in Part 2, my main reason for writing this book went beyond these intellectual arguments.

I understood very well the personal toll that leaving a lifelong faith took on me, and I recognized the emotional drain that theists are likely to fear when considering atheism honestly. This is where I felt I could say things that I had not heard said elsewhere, at least not in the way that I could say it. I had my own story to tell about how I maneuvered my way out of theism, understanding fully the emotional landmines involved in the process.

In fact, my initial plan for the title and subtitle of this book was "Breaking Up With Jesus: The Emotional Nuances of Extricating Oneself from an Unwarranted Faith." The word "extricating" was important to me because it implied a difficult and convoluted process. It wasn't just a walking away. One had to free oneself first. Ultimately, I changed the subtitle because I felt "extricating" might come off as too scholarly and "unwarranted" as too offensive. I figured if I wanted people to read what I had to say, it was perhaps best to minimize the chances that prospective readers would have a first impression of me as conceited and rude.

It should also be noted that in my would-be subtitle, I refer to the "emotional nuances" of the extrication. I don't mention the "mental nuances" or the "intellectual nuances" involved, and this is for good reason.

In this section of the book, I've been discussing the emotional aspects of leaving theism, but I portray myself as doing so *as an atheist*, not as a theist still considering leaving the flock. I made the initial recognition that I no longer believed certain things, and then I addressed the emotion. I didn't even say that I *mentally* am an atheist but *emotionally* a theist. I said that I'm an atheist dealing with the emotional aspects of leaving theism.

Why did I look at it this way? Because it was true! I realized that I was already an atheist. This made the extrication easier for me because I wasn't pretending to be something I no longer was. It was honest. The ever-so-difficult "first step" for me was the realization that I had already taken it. I knew what I now believed, and I knew it was not compatible with theism. I also came to recognize how my previous thinking had been so tied to emotion. That is where the extrication work was still necessary.

**

For many others, though, it may be different. It can be a real challenge to even get to the point where they can apply the word "atheist" to themselves. As we discussed in Part 1, that word comes with so much baggage in the form of undeserved negative connotations.

I had a good talk with someone close to me about atheism not that long ago. I was making the point that I still cared about many of the same things I did when I was a theist. I still cared about social justice issues. I still cared about family and friends. I certainly still cared about love. I just stopped equating love with God. I stopped crediting that feeling of connection with others to a deity who most likely was fictional.

After the talk, this person said he essentially agreed with everything I had just said, but yet it was still too hard for him to call himself an atheist and too hard to let the term "God" go. Maybe that would have been a great time to introduce my retort to the ubiquitous phrase I heard multiple times while struggling with these issues. Instead of "Let go and let God," I recommend "Let go of God." Of course, I didn't have the wit to think of this on the spot, and it might not have been received well, anyway. I suspect it may have felt good to get off my chest, though, as "Let go and let God" had become more and more annoying to me over the years.

All this said, I understand the difficulty in coming to the realization that one might be an atheist. Again, finding myself agreeing with the atheists while watching theism vs. atheism debates online absolutely horrified me. Those videos touched a nerve, and I felt they were threatening something in me that I held dear.

So much of my worldview had been held up by religious scaffolding. So many of my emotions had marinated for decades in religious belief. It was like being asked to pull apart wet cotton. It seemed nearly impossible to pull myself from parts of my life that I had been so emotionally attached to without causing real damage to myself in the process.

I came later to see it differently, and a different analogy seems more appropriate to me now. I had been swimming in a flood caused by a hurricane for much of my life. I had now waited out the storm and I could salvage my true self from the wreckage.

**

Another emotional component of my fight to free myself from theism was facing my embarrassment. I will not write much about this as there is simply not too much to write. As a new atheist, it seemed clear to me that I had fallen for a feel-good fairy tale. That I had accepted it for so many years, and well into my adulthood, embarrassed me.

Perhaps for some this might spur them to double back through the church doors — to hide from that embarrassment. To me, I felt the exact opposite. The only way to properly deal with that embarrassment was to face it, own up to it, and then move on. Those years of unwarranted belief were a sunk cost. I could not go back and change that, but I could use that experience to help define who I am today and to better connect with people going through this same extrication process.

The Breakup

Embarrassment might be a decent segue into this next topic. The analogy of a breakup was also one of the first things I considered when formulating the idea of this book. Clearly, its influence is seen in the title. Embarrassment is certainly one of the many emotions involved in a typical breakup, especially when you are on the receiving end.

I thought of a relationship I had with a college friend and how it didn't turn out as I had hoped. Dealing with this fact was incredibly difficult for me at the time, and I was later able to draw upon that experience as I saw parallels between it and the end of my relationship with the concept of God. In fairness to my college friend and for sake of clarity, my relationship with her was never a romantic one. I only wished that it could be.

As I mentioned earlier, the first few years of college were difficult for me emotionally. I had good friends and I enjoyed school, but at the same time I was dealing with a bunch of emotional stuff that I had not really dealt with properly beforehand. Into this mix came one of my first female friends with whom I felt particularly close. She was in several of my classes and she was cute, funny, smart, and kind — a dangerous combination for anyone trying to avoid a freshman year crush.

As our friendship got stronger, I started to realize that I was getting quite emotionally attached to her. In an odd way, I think I started to believe that she was going to help me through my religious doubts and my persistent grief over my mother's death. It was certainly naïve of me to put her on that pedestal.

A crush is one thing. Mix in the idea that she was also going to somehow be my personal savior and I had created a pretty unhealthy situation. Ultimately, I ended up telling her how I felt, she let me down easy, and I was left to pick up the pieces of a broken heart. It's a life experience that I think most of us go through at least once, and as hard as it was at the time, I would not trade that experience now.

**

So back to how I drew upon this experience when pulling away from my faith decades later. I had survived this emotional hit in college, moved on with my life, and thrived in the process. I felt that this experience helped provide a model to do the same as I broke up with Jesus.

While I saw the situations as similar, I also knew there were significant differences. I was the one, after all, initiating the breakup with Jesus. And not only was this Jesus thing a mutual relationship, it was one that was promised to never end as long as I was good with it. This was quite different from a love that was rejected, albeit kindly, by a young woman in college. Nonetheless, the pulling apart and being able to stand on my own afterward — those aspects felt the same. Getting to the point where I could move on with my life felt the same.

So what are the similarities between a romantic relationship and a relationship with a faith tradition? And more specifically, why is walking away from faith like a breakup?

First, it's emotionally difficult.

I suspect many atheists might not relate to this at all. They might see theism as a set of beliefs that they always considered ridiculous. I have had at least one person make comments to me to this effect.

I have stated already that there is some embarrassment on my part for coming to this conclusion about theism so late in the game, but in truth, I really ought not be that embarrassed. After all, why would someone be expected to learn something if they were never taught it? As I write this, there are more than 770 million adults in the world who are still illiterate. One might argue that they should be ashamed or embarrassed for this status, but in reality, many of them are likely illiterate because they were never put in an environment where literacy was the norm among their peers. They simply may never have had the good fortune to be influenced by folks who would push them to learn to read.

Likewise, many theists are born and raised in environments that do not favor critical inspection of their beliefs. There is no mystical awakening that automatically occurs upon one's having arrived at adulthood. It's especially difficult to leave a faith when so much is attached to your theistic worldview. The emotional difficulty is completely understandable.

So, yeah, perhaps life-long atheists might not understand the difficulties in leaving feelings for theism behind, but this may be no different than a friend who never understood what you saw in your college crush. That didn't make it any less of a crush.

The relationship was going to be the "silver bullet" for all my problems.

Although I didn't wear my emotional difficulties on my sleeve for all to see, I was going through a lot during my early college years. At the time, I certainly felt that my longed-for relationship with this young woman would have somehow magically helped to make those difficulties just disappear. Of course, that is an immature view of any relationship, but I cut myself some slack in this regard as there is no shortage of grown adults who still view relationships this way.

Similarly, Jesus was going to help me make my problems go away — but in his case, he was the answer to *every* problem. He answered every question. How am I to live my life? How am I to treat others? How can I be forgiven for doing bad things? How do I go about surviving my mortality? Christianity, by definition, holds Jesus up as the silver bullet of all silver bullets. He solves everything — and if you don't see how he solves everything, it's only because you haven't tried hard enough to see how he solves everything.

The relationship turns out to not quite be what you had thought or hoped for.

In the case of my relationship with this young woman, it was pretty clear that once I was honest with myself about it, it had never been what I wanted it to be. Although she cared for me as a friend, my romantic feelings were never reciprocated. It was certainly difficult to deal with back then, but once she made it quite clear, I slowly worked towards absorbing that reality going forward. The fact that she was so decisive likely made it easier in the long run to move on.

In my relationship with Jesus, however, there was no decisive rejection. In fact, the exact opposite scenario existed. Jesus was promising that he would always be there for me no matter what. I could even walk away, and the perpetual promise remained that he would accept me back. He would never turn away from me. That promise to many is quite comforting, whether it be celebrated in the open, or kept in the back pocket.

The letdown in this case came from my end. I began to realize that this relationship with Jesus was not what I thought it had been. In fact, it was fictional. Jesus was simply a stand-in for my projections of what I wanted to be true in the world. I wanted kindness to matter. I wanted self-sacrifice to matter. I wanted my life to be "resurrectable" after death and for life and love to be never ending. This had not been a relationship with Jesus. It was an internal relationship between my fears and my hopes.

Moving on was difficult, but the process made me learn more about myself and I grew stronger from it.

It took a little time, but after a while, I came to recognize what I had done in conflating so many of my own emotions with this young woman. I took time to inspect my broken heart, and I realized that it had indeed survived intact. Truthfully, I think a big part of my getting over this woman had to do with finally being fed up with the endless thinking about the topic. It began to bore me, and it had drained me enough as it was. I still had feelings of affection for this woman, but the transition from romantic to platonic affection came without significant fanfare. A day came when I realized I simply didn't feel the same way that I once had. Even with the depth of the feelings I had felt so strongly only a few years earlier, I had come out the other side.

In moving on with my life, I recognized that it was naïve to expect anyone else to solve my problems for me. Ultimately, that is my job alone, and I learned to be patient with myself in working towards that goal. (This should not be confused with seeking help from others when you are in despair. Getting help from friends, or even mental health professionals, when dealing with an emotional difficulty is something I highly recommend. None of us needs be alone in this world, and others can indeed help. My only point is to say that you can't expect others to do the hard work for you in confronting whatever issues you may have — the "up and down lifting" is yours alone to do. And you can do it.)

I also realized that many of the traits that I loved about my college friend could be found in myself and in others. She had no monopoly on these traits.

I was able to apply all these same lessons to my breakup with Jesus. As discussed earlier, there is scholarly debate regarding whether Jesus of Nazareth truly existed, but if he did, it seems quite clear to me now that the character of Jesus was drenched in mythology. Nonetheless, I still find much of the teachings attributed to Jesus as being worthy of respect; they still have influence in my life. I don't need to put Jesus on some divine pedestal for this to be true, and I no longer do so. No, I do not still worship you Jesus, but it's OK. We can still be friends.

Kindness, truth-seeking, and wisdom are not traits solely owned by the character of Jesus. These traits can be found and developed in yourself and in others.

**

I understand that even after all I have written so far, walking away from the God idea might still be difficult for some readers. I am reminded of my high school yearbook quote back in 1991. Graduating from a Catholic high school, it made sense that my quote was religious in nature. My chosen quote was from C. Day Lewis and it reads as follows:

> *Perhaps it is roughly saying what God alone could perfectly show — how selfhood begins with a walking away, and love is proved in the letting go.*

I selected this quote back then to acknowledge the gradual stepping away from childhood into adulthood, and the love parents need to have for their children in order to nurture those steps. As you might imagine, I see it differently now. The first line about God I simply dismiss. The second line now has additional meaning for me.

Selfhood does indeed begin with a walking away. We may be fortunate to share much of our walk with loved ones and we may cross paths with many in our lifetime, but ultimately, we each have our own road to take. The love proved in the letting go also now refers to a love of self for me. We need to love ourselves enough to be able to walk away from anyone or anything that would hold us back from our true path.

The Emotions Summary

The purpose of Part 3 was to walk the reader through many of the emotions I confronted in dealing with my newfound atheism. I had concerns about its impact on personal relationships, I was worried about losing my place in my community, and I also recognized that it exposed some of my deepest fears.

One fear that I've not explored yet in detail relates to a fear of the unknown. I'm not referring to a fear of the unknown after death. I feel I've already discussed that. I refer now to a fear of the unknown *after* theism.

Theism, regardless of the version, is a set of beliefs that typically comes with rituals and a playbook built in. Atheism is simply an acknowledgement that one doesn't subscribe to theistic beliefs. There is no atheistic playbook, no official atheistic ritual. A common concern, then, among some new atheists is to determine what replaces these things. What fills that gap? In other words, so now what? What does the world look like now?

In the final part of this book, I attempt to paint a vision of a future that may be. It's in many ways what I hope for my own personal future, but I also aim to depict a world beyond me in which the merits of atheism are understood and respected, and where all people, atheist or not, can work together to find common cause.

For those of you who may be relatively new atheists like me, we have finally let go from the edge of the pool and we float in waters of depths unknown. Now we swim.

Part 4: Building the Newer World

Coexistence

When I was still in high school, I came across Arthur M. Schlesinger Jr,'s book *Robert F. Kennedy and His Times*. I was (and still am) enormously impressed that someone could write such a long, detailed, and effective book. Even though Robert Kennedy died five years before I was born, I felt a connection with him. We were both Irish-American Catholics and I suppose some of my fondness for him as a historical figure was due to that similar background, but I also felt like I related to him more personally, as we both had lost loved ones close to us. There was an empathy with others that he seemed to have that I was drawn to.

I don't recall if I ever finished RFK's book *To Seek a Newer World*, but the concept alone left an impact. It attempted to systematically address the issues of his day in a reasoned and thoughtful manner, and to provide goals for what a better world might look like. One of my many backburner projects is to attempt an updated version of that book. Perhaps such an attempt may come later, but I hope to at least outline a vision for such a world in the last part of this book.

First, I feel the need to address the "newer world" reference in the title of Part 4. As this is a book addressing religion, there's a chance that some readers may believe in a fundamentalist and literal interpretation of "end-time" writings, notably the Book of Revelations in the Bible. The topic of the "antichrist" pops up in these circles and tends to dovetail into "new world order" conspiracies. Such conspiracies speak to a fear of a totalitarian world government. Truth be told, I don't expect there would be significant overlap between those who believe these theories and those who would have made it this far in my book, but you never know. Suffice it to say, the newer world I get glimpses of in my best daydreams is hardly totalitarian.

Would I prefer that this newer world be a completely irreligious world? I suppose the honest answer to that is yes, but this doesn't mean that I'd ever want to force such a world.

I simply want truth to stand and be seen for what it is, away from the many shadows cast upon it and mirrors attempting to deflect the glance. My hope is that more and more theists will go through a similar experience to what I went through, and their perspectives will change accordingly. After all, theists can't be forced into atheism any more than atheists can be forced into theism. An honest discussion needs to continue with a focus on truth-seeking. I feel that under such a scenario, theism will lose more footing, and the atheistic ground will seem less scary to stand upon.

When I wrote in Part 3 that I had no plans to "flaunt" my atheism, I could hear the voices of prospective readers as I typed. *"You don't want to flaunt your atheism?! Here you are writing a whole book about it! How is this not flaunting your atheism?"* Once again, the importance of words and their connotations becomes evident.

To "flaunt" is to "display brazenly, especially to provoke envy, admiration, or to show defiance." Yes, writing a book about the eventual recognition and acceptance of my atheism does, I concede, openly display it, so perhaps those making such an argument may get a technical win. But like with so many things in life, the nuances are important.

I'm certainly not writing this book to "provoke envy." I suspect the book may, in fact, draw the opposite response — shame and ridicule — from some in the religious community. Am I writing it for "admiration"? Most of us would love to be admired, so acting like part of me wouldn't welcome admiration would be dishonest. But seeking admiration is not my main reason for writing this. In truth, I'm writing this because (a) I think my experience of leaving theism may be helpful to others having similar thoughts, and (b) I ultimately think reliance on magical thinking is dangerous. Lastly, my book is only "showing defiance" to those who refuse to consider challenges to their belief in an invisible entity.

For these reasons, "flaunt" seems to me a poor word choice for what I'm doing with this book. I simply want to tell my story and educate people about it. Some religious people will argue that atheism is just its own religion, and I hope I have dispelled that notion. But there is indeed a similarity between me wanting to spread my message and religious folks who feel compelled to spread what they consider to be the "good news" of the Gospels. This newer world I envision would very much continue the discussions regarding the truth claims of each perspective. William Cullen Bryant wrote, "Truth crushed to earth shall rise again." As I'm committed to truth-seeking, I don't fear these discussions in this vision for a newer world.

Although I would love my "evangelistic atheism" to be considered convincing enough to sway folks away from theistic beliefs, I recognize that many will not be swayed. Perhaps this will be due to the many defenses and tricks of the trade already mentioned that are used by theists who feel threatened, or perhaps it will be due to some fatal flaw in my logic that no one to date has been able to point out to me. I don't expect that everyone will suddenly become atheists in my lifetime. Although I believe such a scenario could be quite a good thing, I simply don't think it's in the cards. I expect atheists and theists will need to live with each other for years to come.

Embracing Theists, if Not Theism

So how then does this newer world deal with theists? It deals with them with the respect all people deserve.

Everyone is on their own journey and each one is different. Although I might be convinced that I've ended up at the right place, I can't hold it against other people for not reaching this same destination at the same time. Some folks have been put on a path that leads them miles away, while others may have arrived at this destination years before I did. Some may be on a path that meandered back and forth, all around this destination, but perhaps they now find themselves high up on a cliff. They can see the destination below them, and they fear the drop.

As a former Catholic, I'm well-versed in the concept of "hating the sin, while loving the sinner." The same general logic can apply in this case. One might "hate theism, while loving the theist." I'm not even sure that I'd argue that I personally hate theism. Hate is such a strong word. As I mentioned earlier, I see modern theism as one of humanity's attempts to find meaning in existence. I don't know if I could say that I hate it any more than I hate other, older mythologies. I can say that I very much dislike the outcome of much of theistic thinking, though.

As a former theist, I also understand the need to have compassion for theists. Sure, some might interpret this as a condescending pity. Ideally, atheists ought to do what we can to assure against this interpretation, and the best way to do that is to make sure that it indeed is not the case.

There are seemingly endless memes online nowadays attacking theists for being ignorant, weak, or even evil. But, as I wrote in the first part of this book, atheists have been attacked with these same claims for years. There is no need to sink to that level. It's a morally weak position, and also likely ineffective. Instead, attacking theistic philosophy and exposing holes in theistic thinking seems to be the best way to go. This can be done while maintaining a respect for the believer.

I recently watched part of a documentary called *Losing Our Religion* that highlights the struggle to leave theism, especially for people who were (or are) viewed as theistic leaders in their communities. There was one couple in particular that struck me. The husband was a closeted atheist living as a Christian preacher, while his wife was still a believer. The backstory of the wife was heart-breaking, and one could easily understand why she had taken refuge in the church for so many years of her life. As her husband spoke about his newfound atheism, you could see on her face just how much of a torture this was for her. The conflict between the changed perspective of the man she loved dearly and her own reliance on theistic hopes clearly was tearing her apart. I couldn't feel anything but compassion for her.

An internal civil war was going on inside this woman, as was the case for me, and for many atheists who've left theism. We can try to help them understand what they believe or don't believe and why, and we can help them escape entrapment. Whether this entrapment results from a confined way of thinking or from a social situation that makes leaving theism difficult; we can help them. We can show them markers on the path. We can acknowledge the pain they've been through and we can let them know that we will be with them fighting for the truth and a better way. We first need to connect with them on a human level. Philosophical discussions can come afterwards.

Connecting and "Real Magic"

As I've written earlier, part of the concern I had while leaving theism was that I would somehow lose the amazement and awe I felt for life. I know now that this concern was completely unfounded. Life and its fragility remain humbling and awe-inspiring beyond words for me. This fascination with life in general leads me to want to learn about, and connect with, all types of life.

This aim to connect seems to be primordial. If the earliest cells didn't have this "instinct" to come together, none of us would be here for this conversation. I realized that so many of my seemingly varied interests are driven by this desire to connect.

1. My love of science fiction and "space science" in large part hinges on my fascination with the likelihood that other sentient life exists on millions of other worlds in the universe. I want to find them and *connect* with them.

2. My fascination with the commonalities between species leads me to learn more and want to *connect* with these

other species. I'm fascinated by nature documentaries and I'm a dog-lover as a result. (I love learning about all life forms, but dogs just might be the best ever.)

3. I care deeply about social justice issues, partly because I recognize that but for circumstance or a minor flap of the proverbial butterfly's wings, I could have been born in a poorer country, with a different melanin level, and with limited access to education. I feel *connected* to people in these circumstances and I know I have not done nearly enough to right the wrongs that they face.

4. My fascination with history stems from the understanding that but for wrinkles in time and space, I may have known well the loves and desires of those before me. I seek a *connection* with the lives in the past.

5. This likewise applies to my fascination with the future. I write to lay down a string that may *connect* with some future soul, that it will one day be picked up and plucked like a guitar string, echoing life vibrations over time.

6. I also recognize that even non-life is made of the same building blocks that make life, and I'm drawn to *connect* with it. We are quite literally the universe discovering itself. What could possibly be more awe-inspiring than that?

When we cut ourselves off from each other and the world (indeed, universe), we not only limit opportunities to learn about each other, we limit opportunities to learn about ourselves. This is one of the many reasons why I don't simply write off theists as some atheists unfortunately seem to do.

The above explains why I'm still amazed by life, and it hopefully gets anyone reading this to think about these topics similarly, but it doesn't necessarily bridge the gap between theists and atheists in my vision for this new world. Yes, I hope these words about connection will resonate with theists and atheists alike, but some people simply see things differently.

Among many of my personal interests are novice guitar playing and songwriting. A few years ago, I wrote a song called "Real Magic" that attempted to bridge the gap between how I envisioned the world as an atheist and how I understood a friend of mine envisioned the world as a particularly spiritual person. The song imagined a conversation between these two perspectives. The gist of the lyrics is that one believes in magic and one does not, but they both believe in themselves and in each other.

It may be important to focus on the first part (belief/disbelief in magic) where perspectives are not aligned so that those conversations can continue, but I think it is wrong to do so in a manner that forfeits our ability to work together on the second part (belief in each other and ourselves), those areas where we do agree. In other words, instead of only focusing on points of disagreement, we need to focus on areas of agreement as well. Yes, diving into the details of disagreements may eventually lead to new agreements, but we cannot squander the agreements we already have in the process. These represent common ground, on which we can fight for common cause.

Common Cause

An example of this is a recent discussion I had with a religious person regarding climate change. I believe the evidence that it's driven by human activity is quite clear, but he doesn't agree. Do I think he's irresponsible for ignoring science? Yes, I absolutely do, but my strong disagreement with his viewpoint doesn't magically change it. We've had many conversations about scientific consensus and the urgency of the situation, but he remains unconvinced. At some point, you can't keep bashing your head against the wall and you need to move on to plan b.

Plan b was a discussion about how in the Bible, God calls for humanity to be stewards of creation. This seemed to strike a chord with him in a way that scientific data did not. He appeared to recognize that changes to our environment might indeed impact things like the biodiversity of coral reefs. I argued that being a true steward of life on earth required that one understand why that life is being so adversely impacted — and he agreed. This ultimately had the effect of him implying that we should be mindful of how much carbon is in the atmosphere, and it eventually led to a discussion about the many valuable aspects of solar energy.

So here we are, two people with nearly polar opposite perspectives on climate change and the likely causes of it, yet we both came to an understanding that solar energy is an important technology to pursue. We also talked about the likely long-term financial (and other) benefits of building a solar energy infrastructure and this seemed to strengthen his interest in the technology. We came at the problem from vastly different perspectives, but in this case, we came to an answer upon which we both agreed. The need for renewable energy infrastructure is now a cause this deeply religious man and I have in common despite his unwillingness to acknowledge that there's a scientific consensus about the causes of climate change.

Yes, in an ideal world, everyone would acknowledge the science. For the newer world vision to play out, acknowledging scientific expertise is indeed important. As we're not at that place yet, we need to find intermediate steps we can take towards our goals.

Finding common cause is one way to do this. An acknowledgement of common cause can lead to work towards common goals. Once you start reaching some of these goals together, the other side is viewed as less of a threat. The walls come down and communities can be built.

Common Morality

But to find common cause and common goals in a broad sense, we need to at least agree on what is meant by morality — and especially "good morality." Goals and causes, after all, assume an underlying morality of sorts that drives them. While many religious people will claim that they find their morality —

frequently an absolute, fully correct, and uncompromising morality — in their religious text of choice, I've argued that far fewer people actually do this than the number of people who claim they do. If every moral dictate in religious texts was taken seriously, far more people would be hurling stones at their neighbors when they cut their lawns on a Sunday afternoon — stoning their neighbors as required by their religious dictate because they were doing work on the sabbath. Clearly, a moral analysis is going on independent of the text in order to decide how best to interpret that text.

I'd argue that there may be hope in finding a common morality with many of these theists. Unfortunately, there are still plenty of folks who go by the letter of the text, and the result can be terribly dark, such as religious beheadings of "apostates." Finding common ground with these people will be much more difficult. For those who don't take things that far, though, it's likely that the so-called "golden rule" could be effective as a general starting point in discussions of a basic morality. The golden rule is to "treat others as you'd like to be treated" (not to be confused with "he who has the gold makes the rules"). Anytime one discusses the ever sought-for implementation of the golden rule in the world, accusations of naivety inevitably follow. It's important that those accusations be addressed directly, as they're too often the response to anything that seems hopeful.

Fleshing out the golden rule would require additional work, but the rule itself provides an adequate skeletal frame. To simplify it even further, the golden rule can be summed up with two words: "Be kind." When you're kind, you have a willingness to show empathy (or at least sympathy) for the plight of others. You care to listen to what they have to say, and pathways of respectful communication open up as a result. As communication increases, people learn from the experience of others, and a new focus on problem-solving emerges.

Thinking Outside the Theism Box

It's easier to solve problems when we see ourselves as being on the same team, and when we work together. This brings me back once more to 2 Corinthians 6:14 and the advice to "*not be yoked together with unbelievers.*" The yoke, once more, is a reference to a tool that pairs oxen together to pull a plow. If one ox is weak and the other strong, or one is large and the other small, the plowing may not be successful.

This, to me, is one of the most dangerous analogies in the Bible, and that is saying a lot coming from an atheist who has read the Bible cover to cover. It purposefully looks to keep people in their own circles and their own tribes. It undercuts the idea that believers and nonbelievers could work together on common goals.

Most religious people I know preach kindness and compassion towards others, and this is something I'm fully on board with as an atheist. I don't agree with the inference that believers and nonbelievers would have little in common. Do believers not care to comfort the mourning? Do believers not want there to be social justice? Do believers not want to take care of our environment? Do they not want to treat the sick, feed the hungry, or make peace in the world? If these believers consider themselves Christians and they don't share these values, perhaps they should just strike out some of the most frequently quoted verses in their Bible (most notably, the Beatitudes in Matthew 5:3-12, which essentially lays out the heart of Jesus' social teaching).

I've reached out to two interfaith groups in my community to ask if there would be an interest in opening up their groups to people of no religious faith. Just as members of those groups are able to find commonalities, I want them to know that they have much in common with atheists, too. To date, I have not heard back from either group.

This greatly disappoints me. Interfaith groups, after all, are people looking outside of their small boxes, considering other perspectives, and finding common ground and common cause.

Unfortunately, cracking one's head out of the larger "theism box" (which holds the individual "religion boxes") remains difficult for many. In some cases, I think an unwillingness to team with atheists is purposeful, and in others, I think it is simply the result of a blind spot.

**

A few years ago, one of our Jewish friends was lobbying us to let our youngest son join the Boys Scouts. Their son had joined a troop and he loved it. I had been a Boy Scout for part of my childhood, and I had mixed memories, but some were good. The Scouts had recently become more open to the gay community and that was a plus for us. And, of course, the group got the kids away from video games, outside in the fresh air, and it taught them things that could be useful in their lives. Our son also really wanted to join so he could spend more time with this friend, and we were considering it seriously.

I had a few talks with the mom of my son's friend about the Boy Scouts and she frequently reiterated that scouting was open to people of all beliefs. She told me how they had assumed it would be a Christian group, but it turned out that several non-Christians were part of the troop, including children of Jewish and Hindu parents. When I told her I was an atheist, she seemed a bit surprised, but she responded rather quickly that she was quite sure the troop leader was an atheist as well. I took the leader's phone number and planned to call him, but I figured I'd do some more research first.

It did not take long for me to realize that this was not going to be something I could support. Despite the many claims regarding openness, it was right there in the registration guidebook, which said a person needed to believe in God in order to "grow into the best kind of citizen." Not only did you need to believe in God for this to happen, but you also needed to recognize "an obligation to God." I ended up not even calling the troop leader. If he was an atheist, he was either unaware of this text, or he didn't care that much about it. My wife and I did.

Unfortunately, the friendship between my son and this woman's son weakened over time. They were no longer going to the same school and not having Scouts as a means to stay in touch, the strength of the friendship simply faded. I felt badly about that, especially because we liked the friend and the family, but I ultimately feel that we did the right thing. I couldn't help but think how our friend would react if someone told her son that he couldn't "grow into the best kind of citizen" unless he refuted the Jewish beliefs of his family. I think she would be rightly outraged. It never seemed to me that she understood the parallel.

The Workaround

Even as I write this, I'm dealing with people close to me who continue to make it clear that they are unwilling to discuss certain topics. How can one convince people that we would benefit from working together on problems that need solving when they shut you down the second you start to discuss certain issues?

Recently, one of these people said he didn't think he was even capable of thinking differently. It was a startling confession. He was so emotionally attached to his beliefs that it was nearly impossible for him to even consider anything else. It was obvious that this terrified him.

So, what to do with these folks in the newer world? The people I speak of aren't even theists necessarily; they're just generally closed off to other points of view. What do you do with people who are so closed off to other perspectives? I have no magic wand to wave here. It's a real problem.

In 1996, the author Carl Sagan wrote of his fear that the America he knew was moving towards a "celebration of ignorance." I thought of this during a recent conversation. This person had just finished telling me that history meant little to him; he also displayed ignorance regarding science. He reveled in repeating talking points that sowed distrust of expertise and he seemed to celebrate his own ignorance. He had not received much of an education and this reaction seemed to come from a place of exceptionally low self-esteem. I imagine it might hurt him or anger him if he knew that I thought this, but it did seem nakedly obvious.

So, what do you do with these folks? I think the answer is to respect them as people, don't give up on trying to get them to consider new perspectives, try to find, and then focus on, mutual objectives, and when all else fails, work around them.

Find those people who will find common ground with you. Work with them to start solving the problems we need to solve. By making progress towards these goals, we are not only addressing the problems at hand, we are also making it more likely that more folks will become open to working together in the future. Nothing draws people in like success.

As more theists and atheists mix together to work towards common goals, it seems likely that more theists will start to recognize that atheists are not the crazy evil people they may have been taught about since their youth. If this happens, we have a better chance of working together to build this new world envisioned herein.

The Importance of Reason

The vision is that, over time, there will be fewer people with whom workarounds will be necessary. There is no guarantee this will be the case, but if we stay focused and vigilant, this should eventually be within our reach. Until reason is respected by all as the irreplaceably powerful tool that it is, building this greater world will be a challenge. The gardens of the new world must be grown with clean water, not water laced with the toxin of magical thinking.

Honest truth-seeking must be paramount. It must be the very basis of our educational system. Healthy skepticism and criticism regarding how we educate each other, and even the educational curriculum itself, is fair game. The system always needs to be open to challenge and self-improvement. That said, the excessive level of distrust in expertise nowadays needs to end. People need to understand that the scientific method is, by its very definition, a self-correcting tool. This point needs to be driven home in our schools. Formal logic classes need to be ubiquitous in schools as well. We must stop the celebration of ignorance.

If we can nurture this way of thinking, we will start building an infrastructure based on curiosity, teamwork, and problem solving. Unlike the theistic infrastructure discussed in Part 1, it will be an infrastructure that is not undercut by baseless claims of magic and miracles, wishful thinking, or gaping holes in logic. It will be an infrastructure that can say "we don't know" without immediately fabricating an answer in order to make some of us feel good.

As this infrastructure continues to lead to real solutions that we can experience directly, its roadways will become more attractive to people, and more heavily trafficked. These roads will provide for self-driving and sustainable cars and self-flying transportation drones on the safest and most modern of travelways. Meanwhile, the theistic highways will start to wear down. Soon they will be the old highway roads in parts of the western U.S., potholed and gravelly, a mere ghost of what they once were as they now stop and start sporadically in the modern desert.

Avoiding the Symbols Trap

In order for us to live in a more reasonable world, we need to be able to detach ourselves from our emotional ties to symbols. I've written about the kneeling protests during the national anthem prior to NFL football games. The associated controversy is just one example of this.

The newer world must be able to recognize in a practical sense the difference between a symbol and what it is said to symbolize. A symbol loses its value the moment it becomes the value. An American flag, for example, may represent freedom, but the *flag itself* is not freedom. If there is no freedom to destroy the symbol of the flag, then what is it really symbolizing? I'd argue that at that point, it represents something quite far from freedom.

We must recognize this with religious symbols as well. Throwing a menorah, star and crescent, or cross on a building does not, by default, make the people inside the building more moral than anyone else. The same can be said for the symbol of the priest's collar. Instead, we ought to focus on upholding the values that we claim are important and not get hung up on imperfect symbology of those values. The newer world as imagined will recognize this and stand guard.

We also need to be on guard against the "takeover" of symbols by others. For example, the Black Lives Matter (BLM) movement started in 2013 as a means to draw attention to how Black Americans frequently are treated differently in America. We put a BLM sign up on our property in 2015, only to have someone remove it a few weeks later. I was so angry that I immediately put up two BLM signs in its place. These also disappeared, compelling me to consider buying an army of BLM signs to cover our entire property.

But by this point, two things had changed.

First, I read our homeowner's association (HOA) agreement and realized that signs, regardless of the message, might be interpreted by some as a violation of HOA rules. I question such restrictions, but I understand their intent. More importantly, by the time I was looking to replace the signs for the second time, their meaning had changed for many people.

I'm not saying it was fair that this happened (it was not), but a shift was clear to me by that time. Several people — no doubt many of them did so purposely — were relatively successful in portraying BLM's message as different than the original one. Fox News and others played certain video clips on loop that showed a handful of people at a BLM protest march chanting in a manner that implied they wanted police officers to be killed. Indeed, some police officers were victims of what appeared to be assassination-type killings. This was horrible, of course, and it didn't help BLM's message.

Given that BLM signs now seemed to be perceived by some as a tacit approval of murdering police officers, I did not replace the signs a second time. I'm torn on this. Part of me regrets not standing my ground, but I felt it was important to understand what that sign now symbolized to different people. Just like the American flag means respect for military for some people and broken promises for others, the BLM sign represented multiple things now. It represented the original message for me and many, but for a good portion of folks, it became a symbol of domestic terrorism.

Like I say, I have regrets about not doing more about that incident. I don't like that people were so easily able to pervert and deflect away from the initial message. But this is one more reason why we need to be wary of symbols. When we can't even agree on what they mean, the discussion will stall. The message (or value) must be the object of focus. Focusing too much on the symbol allows us to easily get knocked off course. We must guard against this in the newer world.

Practical Steps to the New World

The Parable of the Shipwrecked

A precursor to any step along the pragmatist's path to this newer world is understanding the big picture. It's a big world, with lots of countries and lots of cultures. These cultures both conflict and intertwine. When they intertwine, they do so in both expected and unexpected ways. When we drill down, though, many of our actions as human beings are driven by a perceived limitation of resources and our insecurity related to obtaining a share of those resources.

This insecurity can frequently distract us from addressing our real needs. I wrote "The Parable of the Shipwrecked" to highlight this situation.

Three sailors, A, B, and C, rode harsh waves in the darkness. They had lost their captain months ago to a storm and that storm had damaged the ship's navigational instruments to the point where they couldn't be trusted. After burying their captain at sea, the three didn't encounter severe weather for months. They had fishing gear and tools to desalinate the ocean water, and this was enough to keep them alive during this period.

As a new storm came upon them, the dim moonlight that pushed through the clouds allowed the three to make out the outline of what appeared to be an island not too far away. It was a small island — perhaps several acres in size — but it offered possible respite from the storm and maybe even a source for food. Hope against hope, it might even be populated with people who could help.

A immediately took the ship's wheel. Confident that years of study under the captain would guide his hand, he turned the bow towards the island as the waves swayed the boat side to side. Within seconds, B came to protest. After all, he also had studied for years under the captain. Why wouldn't he be the one better suited to guide them to safety? For a time, they worked together, even took turns at the wheel, but when C called from the bow to report that he could see rocks between the ship and the island, tension mounted.

A attempted to plow straight ahead, faster than before. The faster they went, he thought, the less time they'd be exposed to the risk of hitting a rock. This course of action might seem counterintuitive he admitted to himself, but the waves were strong and would impede their movement the slower they went, potentially slamming them into rocks they might have avoided if they built up enough speed.

B disagreed and was no longer OK with just taking turns at the controls. This had become too urgent of a situation, and this was crazy. He urged A to slow down. Speeding ahead in the darkness was reckless.

C kept on eye on the front but visibility was even worse than a few minutes earlier. Rocks could be anywhere. He started to scream back through the rain that they should go slowly, and he would tell them to turn port or starboard and gun the engine at certain intervals to avoid the rocks. He considered suggesting they turn the boat back completely, but they had already passed several rocks and there could very well be more rocks behind them than in front of them.

C yelled his plan to the others multiple times with no response. The roar of the waves and wind were significant, and he was worried that they couldn't hear him. More concerning, though, was that he could hear A and B arguing over the sounds of the storm. Within seconds, he saw their silhouettes locked in a struggle for control of the ship. Before C could intervene, the ship jolted forward and knocked C off his feet. His hands broke his fall, but as he tried to stand after a few seconds, he heard a loud crunch and felt himself fly backward and off the ship.

Panic, water, struggle. C found himself fighting for his life. He raised his head just as a wave lifted him and he could see the island not much more than a hundred yards away. He turned and called out for the others. He couldn't see them or the boat. Exhausted, he focused his remaining energy on swimming to shore. He reached the land, walked several feet, and collapsed in the sand.

At some point later, he was woken by a shake on his back. Both A and B were checking to see if he was still alive. Neither of them had been thrown from the boat, but they both had crashed hard into the ship's wall when the boat hit a rock, leaving A with a broken nose and B with a huge gash on the side of his head. Before the ship sunk, they were able to gather themselves and each grabbed onto floating remnants in their attempts to reach the shore.

A mentioned that he had already walked the small island. There were a handful of trees, but only one might have coconuts. There were no people on the island and there did not appear to be any significant animal life. As C gathered himself, it dawned on him that the desalination equipment was in a locked cabinet in the now sunken ship. The fishing equipment also was lost.

As they each began to recognize the gravity of their situation, their anxiety surpassed their exhaustion. B started hard into A. He had played with their lives, he said. Sprinting into the darkness had nearly killed them all, and now they would probably all die anyway. He was an arrogant idiot to do what he did. C joined in with his own criticism. A told them they didn't know what they were talking about. Yes, they crashed, but it was the better of two choices and B and C were just too stupid to see it. B would have nothing of it, lashing back at A. A responded with a push. B returned a punch. The two ended up on the ground until C was able to separate them. A and B each walked to opposite sides of the island to cool down.

B lurched forward on the sand and punched it with a fury, releasing an existential scream. After exhausting himself, he sat down and allowed the severity of the situation to sink in. He thought of his wife who he would never see again and his baby girl who he had known for only a month before starting this failed voyage. He was inconsolable. With his face buried in his arms, he sat crouched on the wet sand. As he raised his eyes, he noticed that the tide was rising. He recognized then that he hated A. Despite their history, he truly hated this man for what he had done to him.

On the other side of the island, A paced the sand, continuing his argument with B in his head. "You don't know. You are too naïve to think that your way would have worked any better. My decision was still the better decision. You are just too stupid to know any better. The captain would have done what I did. He would have been ashamed of your inability to assess the bigger picture." C walked towards A and could hear him talking to himself. C told A that the tide was rising, but A only responded that he had done the right thing. C repeated that the tide was rising. A once again repeated that he had done the right thing.

C walked towards the center of the island, into a small area where there were some trees. He noticed it was a good five to ten feet higher than the current tide. One tree did appear to have coconuts. He discovered several crabs hidden underneath rocks. He realized that the palm leaves could act as makeshift string. He found sharp rocks that could cut. He would find a way to survive and get off the island, hopefully with the others in tow.

This parable is intended as a commentary on the current political climate in the United States. A and B are political parties. The captain represents the founding fathers. The waves, storms, and rocks represent significant problems we need to address as a country. The damaged navigational instruments represent the likelihood that we're using outdated metrics to determine what comprises a healthy society. The fights between A and B represent the endless arguments between pundits on things that are not essential to the well-being of the nation. C represents those who may feel strongly about the current situation, but they do not let this get in the way of staying focused on solving problems.

We need more Cs.

The success of this vision for this newer world depends in large part on people of differing beliefs becoming more like C. The C people need to get together, research our problems, build consensus, and then act. Real work needs to occur. Thoughts and prayers won't cut it, either. A reading of the Parable of the Three Servants (Matthew 25:14-30) suggests that even God agrees.

A Global "Government"

Given that many of our problems are global in nature, it makes sense that the solutions will require global brainpower and cooperation.

For example, even if you've eradicated a virus within your national borders, it's still a problem until it is eradicated globally. Likewise, a country needs to do more than address climate change within its borders; there must also be agreements with other countries to take similar steps. It makes sense therefore that there be some agency or body that can help act as a conduit for the needed information exchange. Such a body could also be an avenue to share potential solutions to local problems that may at times be globally applicable.

Uh oh — watch out! This is starting to sound a lot like a "one world government." Cue the Q Anon and illuminati conspiracy theories! I honestly don't know how to respond to folks who believe that Satan is looking to plant an antichrist in charge of a totalitarian world government.

There are a handful of people I know who, if given the chance, will talk endlessly about the evils of government. It has become clear to me over time that most of these folks tend to conflate corruption in government with government itself. I also want corruption out of government — in fact, I want it out of everything. The focus on government itself as if it's inherently corrupt is damaging. These folks would do well to remember that anarchy and chaos have a history of rushing towards the vacuum left when government leaves.

In the case of a global entity, I might still at times hesitate to call it a "government," per se. My hesitation is not based on end-times conspiracy theories, but rather on the realization that we haven't yet figured out just how powerful of an entity we might want that to be. Would it be a body that solely provides guidance and helps negotiate treaties, or would it be a more powerful government that can make binding dictates and demands on citizens? These details are important, and I don't have the answers. I suppose trial and error would be in order. Several multi-national/global organizations already exist (e.g., the United Nations), so there is already a pool of experience from which to draw lessons.

**

I was born in Philadelphia in early July, and perhaps, as a result, I remember loving the spectacle of July 4th. I was generally a patriotic child and I assumed, along with all my peers, that we were part of the best country in the world, no questions asked. As I grew, however, I started to become a bit skeptical of the spectacle. I began to see imperfections. No need to go through them all here, but I recognize that we frequently do not live up to the grand vision of ourselves that we often proclaim to the world.

I do believe, however, that the United States remains a special country and that its founding documents are prized global possessions. While I believe these documents could use updating, they were history-changing when written and still remain useful as a general model for a governmental framework in a newer world going forward. (Of course, I am aware of authoritarian dictatorships that would never abide by such documents or rules. Recall here that I am laying out a vision. This is a necessary first step.)

Some of the important concepts set forth in the United States' founding documents include:

Democracy: The United States is a democracy. Or, at least it's a democratic republic. Or, at the very least, it claims to be a democratic republic. If I were to dig into the details of this last sentence alone and started writing about who many of our elected leaders actually represent, I might need to write a separate book altogether. It's not difficult to argue that many representatives tend to most represent those who put them in office. Yes, technically the voters are responsible, but wealthy donors frequently have an inordinate influence.

Nonetheless, the idea that people ought to have a say in their governance is absolutely essential. I would like to think that any governing body that would take control by force and rule by force would be setting its own countdown clock, ticking for an eventual overthrow. World history, however, does not always show this to be the case. Certainly, previous kingdoms and empires dominated the planet for centuries. Yes, most of them have fallen over time, but some lasted far longer than our current democracies.

Democracy in the mold of the U.S. is still an experiment and a work in progress. It is a worthwhile experiment, though, and it ought to continue as the base clay, as we work improvements into the art we create. It will be tested by the furnace for sure, but if we construct it well enough, it has a good chance of surviving much longer.

Transparency*:* The United States has laws that allow access to government documents. Such transparency is important in any government in our proposed newer world. Yes, there may be justifiable exceptions, but the exceptions can never be allowed to overtake the rule.

The Trump era in the United States has highlighted the need for transparency. Despite his ridiculous claim of being "the most transparent president, probably in the history of this country," Trump has blocked important documents from seeing the light of day and has explicitly blocked subordinates from testifying under oath. I wrote a separate book related to Trump already, so I will not go much further here. Suffice it to say, I believe U.S. leadership has failed significantly under Trump with regards to honesty and transparency.

The U.S. Constitution protects the rights of the free press, and it is no accident that those rights are laid out in the very first amendment to the Constitution. A free press is indeed essential as a check against corruption in government. The press' ability to access facts about how we are governed and then present those facts effectively to citizens is something the newer world will do well to protect.

Unfortunately, the newer world will need to be on guard against corruption, not just in government, but in the press itself. Some "news" outlets today are less experts in how to transparently present facts as they are in how to obscure them. The way certain "facts" are highlighted, while lacking essential context, is frequently done on purpose to mislead. It's rarely the clear lie that's the problem. But when several lies are bundled together with small truths, this seems to confuse. Many will focus solely on the small truths while they swallow the largely untrue bundle whole.

I write this at a time when the term "fake news" is brandished by anyone who does not like the news as reported. My experience is that those most fond of hurling "fake news" claims frequently believe news reports that are untrue and/or misleading. Independent fact-checking will need to be front-and-center in the newer world to guard against this. This effort will only get harder as we enter the world of high-tech manipulation, such as "deep fake" videos.

Educated Citizenry: In order to recognize corruption in the free press (and in government), we need to be informed enough to know when something does not make sense. The flip side of the media reporting facts is the populace that draws conclusions from them. Education in the newer world must be grounded in logic. As I've mentioned in other parts of this book, I am not referring to logic as some active anti-emotion element that seeks to have some cold, Spock-like world. It's simply a necessity for critical thought. "Logic" is not just a term you throw out in a debate to attempt to bolster your standing. The study of formal logic gives us tools to address the biggest of philosophical questions.

Studying logic also helps us recognize key tactics that many people use in attempts to persuade that should not be found persuasive. Understanding concepts such as ad hominem attacks, strawman arguments, causal fallacies, appeals to authority, equivocation, and others are incredibly important for us to discern the truth. I am not saying that most people purposely use these tactics to steer a conversation away from the truth; I believe many folks simply are not educated in logical thinking. There are, of course, exceptions. Some people manipulate while seeming to know exactly what they are doing.

Institutions: The fundamental framework of the United States Constitution is the establishment of the three branches of government — the executive, judicial, and legislative branches. The checks and balances built into each are the product of philosophical thinking on both sides of the Atlantic at the time. The U.S. today remains a good example of this system in action, although — especially with the current Trump presidency — it is significantly strained.

I will not dive too much into this topic as it relates to Trump. Again, I have already written a separate book about him. It is important to note, though, that Trump seems to be intent on dismantling, or at least weakening, multiple government institutions. I am a believer that all institutions should be reviewed critically and be open to change, or even disbandment, when it makes sense, but Trump seems to be well beyond reason in this regard.

You never know when certain institutions (and government agencies) will rise to the forefront. The current Covid-19 pandemic has made that clear. Had Trump not weakened (and/or ignored) the institutions created to handle things like pandemics, the United States would likely have been significantly better prepared. And it's not just the United States that needs to learn from this mistake. The newer world needs to have such mistakes high on the lessons-learned list.

"God *Less* the USA" (a lesser focus on the God idea and more focus on claimed values): I believe that the newer world needs to be one less deferential to religious belief. Clearly, this will be the crux of disagreement with some religious readers, but many of our country's founders seemed to specifically have this in mind. Yes, the newer world I envision is indeed more secularly focused. For example, I do not think it is appropriate to imply that "In God We Trust" on our money represents the country as a whole. Not only is the statement — from my perspective at least — putting trust in a fictional character and likely influencing some among us to abdicate our responsibilities to the larger community, the statement also is likely a lie. Many people in the U.S. don't believe in God. "In God We Trust" implies a consensus that, if it still exists, is likely on shaky ground.

This newer world will strive to differentiate the values that we agree are important from the reasons we consider them important. If, for example, we believe that everyone deserves to be treated with respect, does it matter that I strive for that based on a connection with others while someone else may strive for it based on some divine dictate? My honest answer is that it does matter, but it matters less than making sure that respect for every person is upheld.

Again, I don't want this newer world to attempt to autocratically stamp out religiosity. It's my hope that more people will embrace an atheistic worldview simply by engaging in critical discussions about their faith. The focus will hopefully remain on our common goals and be supported by the "be kind" ethic. This will not automatically address every detail of every issue, but it sets our gaze on compassion, listening, and problem solving instead of beliefs that may not relate to the issues at hand.

As much as they can, the institutions of the newer world will protect and foster this "be kind" ethic. If their foundation is an embrace of logic, open communication, and reason, we should be on our way to developing laws and/or guidance than can address many of our problems in a balanced manner that works towards the greatest good. Such a process is wholly independent from the God concept.

Adaptability: Perhaps the most powerful part of the United States' founding documents is the built-in ability to make changes and to adapt over time. The power to amend is paramount. We can't always see around the corner and we don't always know what's coming our way. New challenges come to us all the time, and these frequently have an impact on the context of our laws as they're written.
The often-debated Second Amendment to the U.S. Constitution, for example, lists "the right of the people to keep and bear Arms," but the world has changed significantly since this amendment was drafted. There was no nuclear threat during that period, for example, and the nuclear age changed the context completely. Laws have rightfully been passed to prevent citizens from obtaining these types of armaments.

This openness to changing our laws in reaction to changing world context must be a key trait of the newer world, but this hopefully goes beyond mere reinterpretations of old legal documents, despite how foundational those documents may be. This openness needs to be active in nature. We need to be continually comparing the world around us with the systems we have developed to address our place in it. It's not just that we need to be open to thinking from outside the box. In some cases, we may need to consider a full dismantling of the box that had been passed on to us from previous generations. To be clear, this is not intended as a call *requiring* us to dismantle our previous ways, but to *consider* that, in some cases, it may make sense to do just that.

A Practical Example

Sun Money

This section provides a detailed example of what I mean by considering the dismantling of a box. The box represents the limitations on our thinking today based on previous ways of thinking. In many ways, we are prisoners of the way things have always been done, but the cell door is unlocked. We only need to open it and walk out.

So how do we get to this fantasy newer world where we focus on common ground instead of what separates us, and respect and kindness win the day? How do we prevent the realities of life from squashing any hope that the idea is anything but a pipe dream?

I've talked about the "be kind" rule. No matter how much you dive into it, though, many will still consider it a naïve way of thinking. I've also mentioned earlier the importance of tribalism in our evolution as a species, so it's understandable that many will find it hard to imagine that we could just break the chains of tribal thinking so easily.

What real-life real work has to be done on a practical level to help bring about this newer world? I envision that many steps are required, but the example scenario below may help us towards this end.

This section goes into detail of the potential benefits we may draw from a strong renewable energy infrastructure. This may seem like a pretty sharp veer off topic for a book about leaving theism, but I don't see it that way. It is one example of a practical step towards building a world where people may be less reliant on magical thinking.

**

A 2015 Business Insider article described how a properly maintained array of solar panels the size of Spain could provide enough energy for *all* the world's current energy needs, forever. This represents 0.34 percent of the Earth's land surface area (and significantly less of the Earth's complete surface area). For a species that has figured out how to land on the moon and create machines it would lose to in *Jeopardy*, this seems to me to be easy pickings. The technology to do this already exists and it requires relatively minimal maintenance once installed. Prices for solar energy have plummeted over the last decade and are competitive if not cheaper than some other more traditional sources of energy. One of the bigger solar cost issues relates to energy storage and costs for batteries are expected to fall sharply as well. It's also noteworthy that solar panel efficiency continues to improve and has done so even since the article cited above.

In short, we can do this. It's far from science fiction or fantasy. There is plenty of land (obviously panels would not just be in Spain), source materials appear to be adequate (especially since newer technologies using different materials continue to be developed), the technology is used every day and ready to go, and the cost already is reasonable. We require the political will alone at this point.

So how would this work? Let's assume that enough politicians develop the courage to push for this solution, and the necessary level of investment in renewable energy is made, resulting in the construction of the necessary infrastructure. What then?

Well, photons from the sun are free and endless. Let's start there. There is nothing to mine for and nothing to drill for. Yes, it's true that there will be infrastructure development costs and, given that the sun does not shine for 24-hours a day on each solar panel, energy storage and distribution systems will need to be part of this infrastructure from the beginning. Once this is set, however, there is little to maintain, as the panels have no moving pieces to break down. Operation and maintenance costs will therefore be minimal, and once the capital costs are paid off, the cost to provide and distribute this energy becomes minimal as well and should push towards zero cost.

When energy is essentially free, costs to heat or cool a home are essentially free, drastically reducing fear for some people (often the elderly) of death by freezing or dehydration during extreme weather.

When energy is essentially free, costs for clean water should plummet as well. I live in San Diego, and a desalination plant in a nearby beach town now provides a growing percentage of clean water into our water distribution system. Desalination of ocean water to make it potable requires significant energy to build enough pressure for ocean water to be pushed through filtering membranes. When the energy is abundant and nearly free, however, costs to do this decrease significantly. With essentially free energy, this water can then be pumped throughout the region for minimal cost as well.

Solar-powered pumps can then push water to farmland that might not typically get a reliable water supply. When energy is cheap, power to operate farming equipment — and eventually farming artificial intelligence (AI) systems — will also come down drastically. When you have the proper seed, essentially free water, and eventually near-free AI labor, all you need is sunlight and time, and you have yourself some relatively inexpensive healthy food. As these farming systems are honed, food costs should continue to decrease significantly.

Costs for food distribution and energy distribution (via batteries) will push toward zero as well. Self-driving, low-maintenance electric trucks that can run on the very solar energy stored in the batteries they strategically transport will likely cost little compared to current practices. Such an energy distribution infrastructure would be a welcomed alternative to the current power grid system, which is always vulnerable to attack.

I mentioned artificial intelligence. The clear trajectory is that machine learning will continue to advance in complexity and the types of things machines can do will increase as well. This appears to be written on the wall regardless, whether there is an adequate renewable energy infrastructure or not. As a result, more people will become unemployed or underemployed. This happening in a world where food, water, temperature control, and even energy for entertainment (i.e., virtual video games) are all essentially free (or close to it) is far preferable to a scenario where losing your job could lead to misery and fear of hunger or worse.

When businesses have essentially free power, their operations costs and product prices should also decrease. Power needed to run artificial intelligence that operate manufacturing floors (and/or 3D printers) will not be a problem, and we can theoretically use this "free" power to further drive the upward spiral of AI-development and machine learning. The net impact is that nearly all consumer products should become significantly less expensive.

**

What I just described is a drastic change from how our economy works today. Moving to "sunshine currency" is more than just switching from dollars to yen. It's so fundamentally different that it forces us to reimagine what an economy can be. The capitalism vs. socialism debates may not completely go away, but this shift to sun money will likely make many of those arguments moot. This is a new world being created.

Financial investments are typically made expecting a healthy monetary return on that investment. Investments in the noted infrastructure, however, are effective not when the financial return is high, but when the product being supplied (energy) pushes towards zero cost for customers. That is hardly a strategy most business investors will be eager to chase. This, therefore, may ultimately be better suited for management by a governmental body. Once more, I expect that some anti-government conspiracy theorists might protest such a statement as too "socialistic" of an idea.

Just as roads are maintained by the government and are free to ride, so may be the fate for renewable energy infrastructure (I grew up near the heavily tolled New Jersey Turnpike, so I know the "free to ride" part is not true in every case). President Eisenhower focused on the interstate highway system in the 1950s as a means for military flexibility, but also for the benefit of the average American. I can envision energy infrastructure following a similar road (pun intended). Building the proposed infrastructure helps us become energy independent as a nation, while drastically improving living conditions for our citizens.

Sunshine currency is something new. You set up the infrastructure and the large ball of exploding hydrogen and helium 95 million miles away does nearly all the rest.

The Post-Economy Economy

I recall in my business courses that the fundamental building blocks for modern capitalism are labor and property. Figuring out what land and property rights might look like in this future is a tough nut to crack (I'll have to get back to you on that one), but labor is changing drastically with technological advances in artificial intelligence, and it's not just blue-collar labor being replaced. In general, us organic beings are still being replaced by mechanical and digital ones — and these can run on renewable energy. The industrial revolution has not stopped since it began, and it's now looking to skyrocket upward. This will likely have a drastic impact.

Typically, when more paper currency is printed and floods the market, the value of the currency decreases, and prices increase, resulting in inflation. But what happens when the currency is infinite sunshine? If the standard macro-economic model follows suit, the value of the currency would decrease as more and more photons are received. The difference though is that we aren't talking about paper that's intended to represent value. We are referring to something that *is itself* value (energy). People currently trade paper money (including via plastic credit cards and online transfers) to pay for their local power precisely because it has value itself.

Even if every paper dollar were still backed by a dollar in gold, would that mean what it used to? Our currency is now supported by the good-faith trust and backing of the U.S. government, but I can foresee several scenarios where that trust could be broken.

Truly, if doomsday comes and 95 percent of the population is wiped out in a day, would an IOU piece of paper really be what people would be looking for? Would people even be looking for gold in that situation? I would take clean water and power over a shiny yellowish metal in a heartbeat, and I'd take a fully functioning solar system over blocks of gold just as quickly. (Side note: Scientists appear to be discovering that small amounts of gold may be able to increase solar cell efficiency, but I trust that, despite this, the reader gets the general thrust of my argument).

The End of Tribalism

The title of this section is purposefully provocative, and admittedly a stretch. Given the current state of political affairs in the U.S., it's understandable that tribalism is increasing. As it was likely the major factor in keeping us alive as a species throughout our evolution, I suspect it will be difficult for most of us to rewire our brains to put tribalism in our crosshairs. For an improved future, however, I believe this is urgently needed.

There are some very entrenched tribal systems (e.g., nationalism and religion) that I suspect may never fall but will instead simply change and soften over time. As this new energy infrastructure helps more people feel secure in their own wellbeing and that of their families, the "other" will seem less a threat. There will be more incentive and opportunity for different groups of people to get to know each other and to find common ground. The result should be much less motivation to war with these folks in this world or to damn them to eternal flames in the "next." The cracks in tribalism's armor will be exposed, and the sun will shine through.

I am aiming slightly at poetry as I write this, because I do see this as a potentially transformational idea, but I am also no fool. There is always pushback to change. Anything that seems communal in nature is often misinterpreted as communism, and that's enough for many Americans to hit the brakes. The United States, after all, has been ideologically fighting communism for over a century now.

This section highlights solar energy as a technology that can be leveraged to undermine the root causes of tribalism (namely, fear for survival). I must also acknowledge, however, that it's not reasonable to expect that such a solar infrastructure will be developed evenly throughout the world. Some regions may see the benefits before others, and this could result in neighboring have-nots wanting to infringe upon successful communities or countries. It is my sincere hope that those who fall behind will instead focus on replicating success instead of commandeering someone else's. Ideally, those benefiting from such an infrastructure initially will get to the point where they have plenty to spare and share.

Many of the political debates going on now are important and fully worthy of our efforts. We should have these "tribal" discussions as respectfully as possible and try to bridge the gap between the sides when we can. In some cases, we may succeed in doing this, but because some of those details might never be fully hammered out, we also need to be working on ways that could bypasses the current impasse completely. We need to be imagining ways that could completely change the calculus. Aggressively building a renewable energy infrastructure is potentially this type of an opportunity for us today.

**

Writing about a hopeful vision for the future is always a challenge, not because I don't have hope, but because I know the realities of the headwind against that hope. Many people simply don't want to change. As discussed earlier, this applies to changes in worldview regarding theism, but it applies to political and economic worldviews as well.

I suspect that if we get the political will behind the plan, we will make progress towards the vision put forth. We will need to expect bumps in the road, and we will need to build flexibility into our systems to be able to at least address what we can imagine. Fundamental changes tend to have fundamental impacts.

Sometimes these impacts are wonderful, and sometimes they may run counter to our goals. I have had several discussions with people of all different political stripes about this example of an aggressive solar power infrastructure and the chain of benefits it may provide, and I have yet to hear any reason why such a push for this would not be worth the effort.

Bending the Arc

In describing the "practical example" in the last section, I conceded that plans like that should expect resistance. Many people benefit from the way things are currently, or at least they think they do because they haven't imagined a better alternative. That said, it's no shocker that some will fight hard to prevent changes to the status quo.

I had always loved Martin Luther King, Jr.'s quote, "The arc of the moral universe is long, but it bends toward justice." It was comforting to me in a way similar to how "God is love" comforted me. It helped me to feel that things would eventually just work themselves out — that as hard as it may seem, things would eventually be OK.

I no longer find comfort in such a hands-off approach. I've learned that the arc of the moral universe bends towards justice only when we bend it that way. People are hanging on that arc, putting all their weight on it, giving their lives for it to bend towards justice. It doesn't happen automatically. I remember having that poetic insight and feeling the need to share it, only to find that I was not alone in having that vision. Others had expressed similar sentiments, and that comforted me more than the initial insight. It told me that others were interested in working towards this goal as well.

The newer world cannot be a complacent one. There is no guarantee that things will just get better over time. The newer world must be one striving always for continuous improvement. "Continuous improvement" is a buzz word (OK, buzz phrase) used frequently in the world of business and manufacturing. It's a relentless self-examination to find ways to be better. It's honest and it listens to all critiques, regardless of their origin. After all, the seemingly smallest of things can bring down the ship if they are neglected. The 1986 Space Shuttle disaster is an example of that.

The Past Strikes Back

The relentless needed for improvement is the same relentlessness the newer world will need in order to guard against the faults of our past (and present).

It is the summer of 2020 as I write this, and my wife and I are home with our two teenage sons during the Covid-19 pandemic. Many of the summer activities that the boys would normally be partaking in have been understandably stalled, so we have attempted to find other ways to keep the boys busy, beyond video games. I've recently been watching a half-hour of the *Lord of the Rings* trilogy with them each day. (Of course, it would be better if we read the books together. I also imagine some readers asking how watching a movie is much better than playing video games. All parental advice duly noted.)

There are many lessons in fantasy stories like *Lord of the Rings*, or even the *Harry Potter* series. They both show an "evil" that was thought to have been vanquished. In the case of *Lord of the Rings*, it's Sauron. In *Harry Potter,* it's Voldemort. Both Sauron and Voldemort were evils that were vanquished but not eradicated completely. They simply went underground. They reformed themselves and hid, constantly looking for opportunities to regain lost power, finding allies where they could. Ultimately, both stories build towards a battle for the fate of the world.

These stories warn us of the threats of the past. Recently, the United States has been painfully reminded that racism, for example, still exists. At one point, it was as blatant as a KKK hood, but it's adapted over time and taken different forms. It's attached itself to our very systems of interaction. The KKK garb may have gone away for a period, but laws have been written and interpreted to allow a "softer" version of racism to continue for years. Many Black Americans, for example, were unequivocally refused the chance for key wealth-building opportunities like buying suburban houses in desirable neighborhoods as they were built. The financial effects of this are still seen today in the wealth gap between different racial groups.

Some may have felt that the war against racism in the United States had finally been won by the election of President Obama in 2008, but this, too, was wishful thinking. Although he will claim otherwise, Trump has given new breath for many of the -isms that we had hoped to have banished by now. Sexism, racism, and nationalism (and other phobias as well) all seem to be "reappearing" in ways that have surprised many, but we should not be surprised. Just like Sauron and Voldemort, these were simply looking for their opportunity to rush back into the light, and they found it in this current Trumpian environment.

I had hoped that things like racism would die out with older racists, but I was wrong. There are plenty of young racists out there now. It was handed down the line to them, and enough of them appear to not question it. Do not mistake me here. I'm not calling everyone who doesn't think as I do a racist. Many folks don't feel personal animus against other races, but many also feel no urgency to become educated on the ways that racism has gone underground and attached itself to our systems and procedures. Yes, we make progress, but the progress is made by those out there bending the arc, not those unwilling to recognize the problem.

The newer world will need to learn from this and guard against it. Viruses can come back with a vengeance. This applies to anti-atheism as well. In so far that progress may be made in softening anti-atheistic sentiment in the future, we must stay on guard for the return of that as well.

Procedures and Ethics

Enron, an American energy company, had engaged in accounting fraud activities for years. As this fraud became public in 2001,

Enron's stock price plummeted from approximately $90 per share to essentially $0. The Enron scandal, coupled with similar scandals at the time, led Congress to pass the Sarbanes-Oxley Act of 2002.

This act is important, and I believe it is a model as we develop laws in the future. The act does not (and could not) guarantee that there will be no more ethical violations in corporate settings, but it does make some ethical violations more difficult to get away with. It describes procedures that require corporations to disclose connections to outside entities, and others that forbid someone from being able to write herself a check from a corporate account. These are detailed requirements that can have a real impact. They are concrete rules that address ethical violations, a topic many people see as inherently ambiguous.

A good portion of my day job involves developing processes and procedures. When done well, this work requires an eye for detail, an effort to seek other perspectives, a willingness to accept criticism — and take corrective action when necessary — and an ability to communicate effectively enough to build a consensus. These are all skills that the leaders in the newer world must have. They must balance the desires of many, while maintaining a focus on shared communal goals. These leaders must continually seek to improve ethical norms within the activities of our institutions and government entities, while balancing individual freedoms and collective well-being.

Building the Garden

When I started writing Part 4 of this book, I anticipated spending more time discussing the diminishing role of religion in the world. It strikes me now that much of this vision of a newer world has little to do with religion at all. It is about finding common ground and working together. Religion is a side thought — and that, I now realize, is perhaps the heart of the point I am trying to make.

I assumed that my "atheistic" vision of the future must be preoccupied with discarding religion. Now, I simply see my vision of the future as hopeful. It is not a vision of pending doom, wars, and famines. It is a vision where humanity finally gets serious about working together to end the things that have separated and hurt us. It is a future world in which we create our own garden of Eden. If we can build this garden effectively, the magical thinking found in religions will start to fall away.

Years ago, I took a business class that focused partially on crafting corporate mission statements. In one exercise, we were tasked with coming up with a personal mission statement. I never would have dreamt that a single homework assignment would have had such a significant impact on my life. I don't think we even had to hand it in, so I suspect many did not even do the assignment. I did.

My personal mission statement, written almost 20 years ago, has not changed: "*Live life to the fullest and help others to do the same.*" It is effectively the meaning and purpose that guides my life. I will try to explain what this means to me as I conclude this book.

"Living life to the fullest" means to appreciate it fully. Understand that we are all on borrowed time and that our existence is amazing and to be celebrated. It means to seek new experiences, meet new people, and learn new things. It means to absorb knowledge like a sponge and strive towards wisdom. Yes, it means to stop and smell the roses, but it also means to not shrink from challenges. We will all experience death soon enough. Now is the only time we have to experience life.

Part of living fully is making connections with others. What a joy to be able to share this space and time with other star "stuff" like ourselves. To have lives that overlap with those who have gone before us and those who will stand after us — ships passing in the night through the immensity of the universe. To look into their eyes, laugh, smile, and make that connection. When this mindset takes hold, there will be no need for a weekend church service to feel connected, although I expect we will find many excuses to get together. These connections are central to improving our world, and they need not be limited to human life. All life resonates, and bonding with animals and other forms of nature is a joy as well.

"Helping others" to live fully is simply acting upon these connections. When we connect with others, we see ourselves in them. As we strive to live full lives, we strive for others to do the same. We fight for social justice, understanding, and peace.

In his inspirational poem "Some," about standing up for social causes, my friend and poet Dan Berrigan wrote that *"some stood up once… and sat down… some walked a mile… and walked away… some stood up twice… and then sat down."* Strive to be the one who keeps standing.

In short, "helping others to live fully" means we do the work. We do the work of our hands, we do the work of our brains, and we do the work of our hearts. We build the world we seek.

In the earlier example of a built-out global solar energy infrastructure, a self-sustaining world is created that helps to provide for the necessities of life. People would not need to work as hard to survive. There would be more free time for the arts, entertainment, self-exploration, and exploration of the universe. And that was just one example of action we can take. We can

"Imagine" the world dreamt of by John Lennon, and we can also use our imagination to build the way to get there.

I feel I have done a decent job in this book of hedging against claims of naivety when I discuss my hopes for this better world. I have stressed several times that we have much work ahead of us to build this world and that the resistance we face will be strong while taking steps towards it. I have no illusions that anyone can just snap their fingers and we will be there. I also expect there will be plenty of setbacks along the way. After all, examples of such setbacks can be found throughout history.

But history also gives us real cause for optimism. We have come a long way even from just a century ago, when the average life expectancy was significantly less than what it is today. Education level and other measurements of quality of life have increased as well. It is rarely a straight line or homogenous worldwide, but the trend towards improvements over time is clear. Steven Pinker's book, *Enlightenment Now: The Case for Reason, Science, Humanism, and Progress*, captures this sentiment very well.

In fact, I believe the naïve ones are those who do not acknowledge this trend. It can be hard to see this big picture, especially in the middle of a global pandemic, ongoing wars, and political systems that seem to pander to the fringes; but global progress continues. While some see this newer world as a fantasy beyond our grasp, I see it quite clearly within our reach. No, not within our reach during my lifetime perhaps, maybe not my children's lifetimes, either, but within humanity's reach, nonetheless. This newer world may not quite be a perfect heaven, but it will be ours and it will be real.

**

Lastly, I want to finish this book by addressing the reality that I will see how humanity progresses only for a short while longer. No, to my knowledge, I'm not dying, and I hope to have many years of a full life ahead of me. But the keen awareness of my own mortality has never left me from my childhood years. This does sadden me, but I know that life is short, and as much as I love my life, I have come to accept this.

One day, I will be gone, a memory to some, and then as the generations pass, that, too, will be gone. The question for me now is whether I am going to use the time I have to try to leave the world better for those after me. What will I leave behind?

In the introduction to this book, I discussed a long walk I took across beach cliffs at dawn. The bridges built over ravines and the stairs built into the cliffside allowed me to continue on my journey. As the sun rose, shining light while creating shadow, I came to see my walk that day as similar to the human journey. I could get as far as I could because others had come before me to build these structures. Each step is a passing of the torch to the next generation. It is a responsibility and a pleasure to be part of that journey.

www.ingramcontent.com/pod-product-compliance
Lightning Source LLC
Chambersburg PA
CBHW062158270326
41930CB00009B/1576